Goodbye History,
HELLO HAMBURGER

ADA LOUISE HUXTABLE

Goodbye History,
HELLO HAMBURGER

An Anthology of Architectural Delights and Disasters

Foreword by John B. Oakes

Landmark Reprint Series

THE PRESERVATION PRESS

The Preservation Press
National Trust for Historic Preservation
1785 Massachusetts Avenue, N.W.
Washington, D.C. 20036

Printed in the United States of America.
90 89 88 87 86   5 4 3 2 1

Library of Congress Cataloging in Publication Data

Huxtable, Ada Louise.
    Goodbye history, hello hamburger.
    (Landmark reprint series)
    Includes index.
    1. Architecture — United States — Mutilation, defacement, etc. 2. Architecture — United States — Conservation and restoration. 3. Urban renewal — United States.   I. Title. II. Series.
NA705.H89   1986   720'.973   85-28110
ISBN 0-89133-119-0

Designed by Meadows & Wiser, Washington, D.C.
Edited by Diane Maddex, Editor, The Preservation Press; with Gretchen Smith, Associate Editor
Composed in Galliard and Clearface Gothic by General Typographers, Inc., Washington, D.C.
Printed on 70-pound Astrolite by the John D. Lucas Printing Company, Baltimore, Md.

CONTENTS

FOREWORD

AT THE TIME THE POSTWAR MANHATTAN BUILDING BOOM exploded in the 1950s with all the force — and all the destructiveness — of a volcano, there wasn't a newspaper in New York City (or, so far as I know, anywhere else) that regularly carried a column of architectural criticism. But, as those ticky-tacky boxes along Third Avenue and all around the town proliferated, and as superbly crafted and still viable buildings of an earlier day fell before the wrecker's ball with painful frequency, the need became increasingly apparent for someone to speak out loudly, clearly and rapidly in the mass media on what was happening to our city and to cities everywhere. Here was the picture, as painted by Ada Louise Huxtable:

America the beautiful,
Let me sing of thee;
Burger King and Dairy Queen
From sea to shining sea.

Architectural and urban planning criticism had to be drawn out of the esoteric closets to which it had been largely confined.

One day around this time (in the late 1950s), a member of the *New York Times* editorial staff observed to Arthur Hays Sulzberger, then publisher, that the newspaper's great tradition of artistic criticism was deficient in one area: architecture, and, by extension, urban planning and design. "In fact," he noted, "the *Times* spends time and talent, and valuable space, in criticizing every fourth-rate film or stage show that comes to town and doesn't last a week. But what about the permanent fixtures now going up all over this city that are going to last for decades? Yet the *Times* has never a word to say about them, or what they're doing to the city. We need a critic in this field, too — and we need one badly." Not too long after that conversation, articles by a brilliantly talented analyst of the built environment named Ada Louise Huxtable began increasingly to appear in the *Times*. They were distinguished by elegance, wit and vision — and by a trenchant understanding of what was going wrong and why. By the early 1960s she was writing occasional (unsigned) editorials for the *Times*'s editorial page — one of the very few "outsiders" invited to do so — and in 1963 became a full-fledged member of the *Times* staff as the newspaper's first architecture critic, subsequently (1973) moving up to the editorial board.

All of the essays and editorials from the *New York Times* reprinted in the following pages were written during these years. This was the period when the limited public understanding of the need — and the ethic — of conservation of *natural* resources blossomed into the environmental movement as we know it today. Paralleling this evolution — and forming a significant part of it — was the growth in public appreciation of the relationship between architecture, city planning and

---

New York: the city as magnificent catastrophe. Glamorous from afar, magical at night, its energy and beauty masking chaos and decay, it survives and renews itself with unparalleled drama and apparent immortality. (New York Convention and Visitors Bureau)

development, landmark preservation and basic social values.

In this, the coming to life of the *urban* environmental movement, Ada Louise Huxtable — for all her diminutive size — has been a monumental figure. Her rage against the shoddy and the meretricious (of which she found innumerable examples right at hand in New York's real estate market), her reportorial skill, professional expertise and ethical standards gave to her articles a unique quality that aroused the conscience as well as the consciousness of lay and professional public alike.

In vivid language, never fearing to name the names of the malefactors — whether developers, speculators or architects — Huxtable fought for the kind of living landmark preservation that relates the past to the present and to the future. Only in the rarest cases does she champion preservation *as such*. But she is merciless in her denunciation of the public officials and private operators whose lack of civic responsibility time and time again has permitted the destruction of irreplaceable monuments and viable neighborhoods in the face of "New York's *force majeure*, the divine right of real estate economics."

While she has lost many a battle, she may yet be winning the war. There is little possibility that the kind of wholesale urban devastation that was regularly taking place only a decade or two ago — because it was seen as the natural and inevitable order of things — could occur today. And that's not because all that's worthwhile has already been lost. It's because more people speak now with courage, conviction and sensitivity on behalf of a livable urban environment for the future. They can take considerable satisfaction from the change in public — even political — thinking on these issues.

Ada Louise Huxtable has made a difference. Read what follows and see why.

John B. Oakes

INTRODUCTION

How Do You Like Your McHistory?

TWENTY YEARS AGO, the shattered remains of the travertine, granite and marble columns, coffers, eagles and angels of McKim, Mead and White's Pennsylvania Station in New York were carted off to New Jersey; they turned the Secaucus Meadows into the world's most artistic dump. That famous demolition left indelible images, like the one on the cover of this book. It also led to New York City's landmarks law.

Five years later, in Madison, Wis., a solid sandstone house called Mapleside that had spent its first 116 years in classical tranquility was torn down for a Burger King headquarters after a notable confrontation between past and present cultures, if culture is the right word. That incident is the source of this book's title; it represents a typical and increasingly common sequence of events in the 1960s and 1970s — a controversial loss followed by the recognition of values destroyed and the creation of an effective mechanism of response, in this case, the Madison Trust for Historic Preservation.

During those same decades we were in the midst of the discovery of something called the environment; it had always been there, but no one had really noticed, at least not until it began to get thoroughly fouled up. It was a time of Earth Days, those annual big-city druidic spring festivals that celebrated each emerging blade of grass and resulted in changes in perception and attitude toward air, water and land that ended in an obsession with — and exploitation of — anything that could remotely be called natural. This led to some very real and striking gains in environmental cleanup and controls; witness, for example, waterfronts then and now.

The growing ideal of the conservation of resources was not unrelated to the husbanding of the historic heritage. At the same time that the preservation movement was gaining strength, the built environment was developing its constituency, although the whole earth faction always had a populist base that architects and planners lacked; stones, once shaped by art, run the danger of being considered an elitist concern. But those who were dedicated to the design and construction of a better present and future were beginning to be heard. The quality of the environment was finally beginning to be seen as a whole thing, intimately related to the quality of life.

For slightly more than that length of recent environmental time, I have been pursuing the task of establishing an understanding of this relationship in the public mind and eye. Most of the work was done as architecture critic and member of the editorial board of the *New York Times*, where almost all of these columns originally appeared. It is a cheerful thought that they still read with some relevance, immediacy and even urgency. When I began writing I did not think in long terms; I was usually responding to today's crisis rather than considering tomorrow's perspective. I noted that the newspaper critic's work was of little lasting value, that traditionally today's words were good for wrapping tomorrow's fish. How gratifying to find that these articles make a coherent body of commentary, with a consistent philosophy, through which significant developments in planning and preservation, and even more significant developments in consciousness and judgment, can be traced and understood. It turns out to be, in fact, a kind of history — allying the event with values and attitudes. It can also be read as a nonstop drama, complete with heroes and villains and tragic chorus; there just is never any ending.

What is gathered here is a generous selection of the hopes, fears, illusions, preoccupations and successful and unsuccessful campaigns and battles of those years, with some updating to indicate how things, for the moment, have come out. (This updating is often in the picture captions.) The advantage of putting together such an anthology is the obvious one of hindsight, although even with that help, things are seldom what they seem. Tricky business, the environment, particularly the built world. Its true architects are economics and expediency. There is much more money and politics involved than art, and much of that art is a subtle, subjective and transitory thing.

But I can see now that my two constant concerns — this country's unique, diverse and sometimes problematic heritage, and the architectural and urban quality of the places we build and rebuild at such enormous cost and with such shattering results — have come together in a permanent and conspicuously changed way. Those mutually exclusive, traditionally sworn enemies, real estate and the public realm, are now routinely united in the profitable and exemplary restoration, remodeling and reuse of the distinguished older structures that enrich the quality and character of the present by retaining the spirit and the substance of the past. Strange bedfellows, preservation and development, but with a little nudging from the tax laws and other incentives, the marriage works.

If it turns out that the end of the preservation rainbow looks suspiciously like the shopping mall, a prediction made here with some accuracy but not much joy for New York's South Street Seaport, there are also an increasing number of buildings, like the Hudson County Courthouse in Jersey City, N.J., that have been restored to their original majesty and public functions. It is possible to document, over a quarter of a century, changes in attitudes and laws that can never be completely undone. The circumventions become more skillful, and barbarism and philistinism will always be with us, of course. Backsliding is the correlative of salvation; smugness and self-congratulation are the only truly dangerous sins. But no one can quite know the relief and delight with which I have reread the accounts of issues that seem as pertinent today as when they were fresh on the page, of beauties that have risen from the ashes, of enthusiasms and conclusions that have passed the test of time. I am not happy about being right about so much that was, and still is, wrong, and has not changed at all. Some of these pieces could be reprinted as they were, intact in circumstance and meaning. Others have become rueful exercises in nostalgia, evidence of the infinite human capacity for folly, caprice and greed. A few have surprising later chapters for which I could never have summoned sufficient optimism, although I obviously believe in miracles.

I would never have thought, for example, that the wholesale destruction of St. Louis's historic and urban heritage could be reversed; after massive urban renewal demolition, all signs of life had moved to suburban Clayton, a typical commercial development a typical highway's-length out of town, the ultimate plastic-and-glass strip city of numbing, homogenized mediocrity. Even the flashy was dull. (The view from the cloned hotel was of the expressway; forget the river.) Clayton had all the earmarks of the extruded American future.

Back in the wasteland of St. Louis, Theodore Link's Union Station, one of the country's most elaborately magnificent 19th-century structures in its rich and profligate space and decoration, was a massive set-piece of ghostly abandonment for decades, while Louis Sullivan's seminal skyscraper, the Wainwright Building,

Salem has proved that preservation and physical renewal can be partners, although its economic renewal depends on attracting more young professionals. Sensitively and stylishly updated, as with this bank addition, it still relies on tourism. (© 1978 Joseph Borysthen-Tkacz)

lingered in shabby uncertainty. Both were surrounded by the unique 20th-century desolation of redundant parking lots. Today the station is a restored urban complex of hotel, restaurants and stores, and developers who could not be lured to downtown St. Louis before are vying to put up prestigious new buildings. (It should be mentioned parenthetically that structures as strong as Union Station, or Alexander Parris's Greek Revival Quincy Marketplace, take their shopping centers without loss of their essential integrity. It should also be repeated how important tax credits for historic building renovation have been to all of this revitalization.)

Boston, which has racked up an exemplary record of center-city planning and preservation, is currently facing a critical moment in the balance of old and new construction that will determine the city's future quality and identity. Call it a *crise de succès*. Can a new mayor whom no real estate interests wanted, or supported, and who therefore has no obligations to developers for campaign contributions, keep the city's strengths and consolidate its gains? Can he balance the future against short-term profits and political popularity? Tune in next year. In New York, where the mayor's campaign chest is heavy with developers' dollars, and choice sites such as Columbus Circle are virtually auctioned off, the future has already been lost. Even New York's landmarks law is under pressure.

Small cities, like Salem, Mass., have proved that preservation and urban development can be perfect partners, in a physical renewal of outstanding sensibility. But Salem's sophisticated new style is out of sync with the tastes and needs of its traditional working-class inhabitants, and it has not yet attracted enough young Boston professionals to make its planning assumptions work. Historic Salem survives more on tourism than on revived sales and services.

All in all, the built environment continues to yield fascinating new facets, complexities and contradictions. Not least are the enormous changes taking place in architecture itself. After speculative building had reduced modernism to its lowest and cheapest and most replicable common denominator, a reaction was inevitable. One benign side effect of the many directions being pursued under the soubriquet of postmodernism is a reawakened interest in history, with a renewed appreciation of the monuments and artifacts of the past. The understanding of history is broader than ever before. Its perception has been enlarged by such unorthodox viewpoints as the populist and pluralist architectural vision of Robert Venturi, and Aldo Rossi's enormously influential theories about the city as the receptacle of history, through its buildings, and the autonomous strength with which such buildings establish and retain their particular sense of place. Architects are facing a far larger task than learning how to scribe a cyma molding again.

It takes a lot to keep ahead of the past today. Last November, in one of journalism's more familiar rituals, the *New York Times* noted — one cannot say celebrated — the 25th anniversary of Penn Station's notorious demolition. It was a good newspaper story then and now — from impassioned controversy to nostalgic feature, one of those milestones editors delight in. But there was as much news as nostalgia involved: The consummately ordinary rail facilities that had replaced the old station in the base of a new office building had deteriorated so badly in that quarter of a century, and proved to be so much less than ideal, that reconstruction was being planned. Not a phoenix, exactly. And an even more interesting story followed. In New York's true spirit of expendability, the owners of the new Madison Square Garden built on the Penn Station site (the old-new Madison Square Garden on Eighth Avenue that it replaced was demolished and is to receive a new hotel-office complex, while Stanford White's old Madison Square Garden at Madison Square is a Hispano-Moresque memory) propose to build a new-new-new Madison Square Garden farther west, demolishing the present Garden for another large office tower. Real estate *semper triumphus*, particularly when aided by elastic zoning.

And hamburger stands? They've gone straight — traded in their architectural exuberance for a kind of select-a-style contextualism: McDonald's environmental models come in everything from rustic-suburban to something that looks sus-piciously like incipient postmodernism, served up in uniform brick-walled, mansarded containers.

Meanwhile, preservationists — young ones, of course — enamored of the immediate Pop past and its quaint streamlined diners and porcelain-enamel White Towers, are fighting to save McDonald's original golden arches as a uniquely American architectural and cultural artifact. The romance of the road replaced the romance of the wagon trail. It all depends on how you like your McHistory — rare, medium or well done.

Ada Louise Huxtable

PREFACE

"Huxtable Was Here"

A CRITIC writing for the daily press does not deal in immortality. In the classic putdown of his trade, today's words are for wrapping tomorrow's fish. If he works in the fields of architecture and urbanism, what he deals in is immediacy — the day-to-day pressures and proposals and decisions that can make or maim a city. He fights city hall, vested private interest and popular apathy with an urgency that can easily lose its meaning a few years later when his particular crises have been consigned to oblivion. His words, being newsprint, have yellowed and crumbled. The only thing more ephemeral than newsprint is the shape and condition of the world that is his concern, and which he sees as the environment.

People have been looking at the environment, as environment, for only a very short time. It has always been there, but it has finally been recognized as something that is terribly responsive to acts of will and judgment that have an endless impact on the state of humanity. The way we live, or exist, is the generator of many of the problems called the urban crisis. How we live, or exist, is what urban design and planning are all about. Aesthetics is not some kind of optional extra or paste-on for pretty facades; it is the satisfaction of the needs of the body, the spirit and the senses through the way an environment looks and functions — two inseparable factors. Every social plan has a form, good or bad. The art of design is an unavoidable part of every urban decision. Until this is understood as the planning process, and design is accepted as an inescapable determinant of the result, we will simply produce more environmental failures. And the urban critic will have failed as well.

The critic's role in architecture and urbanism is quite different than in any other field. For one thing, this is a relatively new field in the popular press and a growing one. The function of this broad kind of architectural criticism is educational; it must in many ways fill the gap that our schools have left so conspicuously vacant — the yawning chasm between the "educated" man's perception and understanding of the man-made world around him. Without this, no campaign for better ways of building can succeed. George Kennan, in his *Memoirs,* analyzing the areas of thought and experience opened to him by a Princeton education, noted that the one serious omission was visual instruction of any kind. "No one, to the day of my graduation," he wrote, "ever taught me to look understandingly at a painting, or a tree, or the facade of a building."

The critic in this field, where everything is transient and temporal, hopes that something may testify to his efforts. He hopes that he may have taught someone to see. He would like to feel that there is just a chance that he may have changed some degree of practice, helped effect some shift in philosophical base, revised the climate of thought and feeling to some small extent or influenced public awareness to the point where the world those few years later may be a bit more in the image of the kind of life and environment (again, they cannot be separated) for which he has fought his battles. He expects no miracles but he is an optimist with some fairly tough beliefs. In architecture and urbanism those beliefs must be based on history, art and humanism. They must have strong ties to modern sociology and technology. And they must be grounded in a knowledge of the past for the shifting present and the uncertain future.

The art of design and the contrast of styles — calculated or accidental — determine the texture, quality and continuity of the city. Every urban decision affects the way our world looks, feels and functions. (D. Nels Reese)

What I really want to say in assembling these pieces is that, like Kilroy, Huxtable was here. They are a record of a continuing professional passion, of an occasional mitigating triumph in a job of unending frustration, a testament to involvement and, it is hoped, evidence of a vision. Critics are not by nature existentialists; if they accepted things as they are, they would be in some other business. But only mock philosophers pretend to provide answers for the questions they raise; the purpose is to provoke thought and the possibility of solutions.

Criticism of this sort has an unavoidable messianic sound. Instead of dealing in the pleasant esoterica of aesthetics, one finds oneself at querulous and sometimes tiresome odds with ignorance, bureaucracy, cupidity and political and personal opportunism. One becomes a scold, and that can be deadly. Without redeeming wit, this kind of criticism can also be a bore. With shifting climates and conditions, it can soon seem jejune.

But if the obsessions of the journalistic critic are quickly obsolete, what does not become obsolete are his standards — those philosophical and aesthetic yardsticks by which he measures his subject and his world as acts of art or blasphemy. The architecture critic cannot be enamored of fashionable polemics. It may be tempting to make a small, rarefied splash in the upper intellectual stratosphere but it will not matter. In the long run, what he has to say must matter or he might as well not say it. His reality is compounded of politics, economics and human fallibility. He is essentially a pragmatist, but one with professional principles that become over-familiar to the constant reader, who is hit repeatedly on the head with them.

If his standards are to be relevant, however, they must not be absolute. If they were inflexible or unchanging in these revolutionary times, they would produce judgments of instant obsolescence and supreme fallaciousness. It is no measure of a critic's worth whether or not he has changed his mind. If he has not to some degree, it is more a measure of his lack of growth in a field of stunning transmutation. But I find that I do not feel that I wish or need to take back a word that I have written here; the only revisions have been some updating of tenses and figures, the occasional vanity of a smoother or emphasizing phrase and an expansion of the Pop architecture theme into a more recently developed concern for whatever functional lessons about 20th-century life an otherwise appalling Pop environment can teach us.

"The only way the critic can improve his capacity for making the right kind of choices is by continued exertions," Edouard F. Seckler, the art historian, has said. "He must match his sensuous and mental equipment time and again against new phenomena in a spirit of openness and with a willingness to bring his full being to bear in each case. He may have to revise his criteria in the light of a new creation, for the architect may have established something which is not amenable to treatment in a critic's established terms and the critic forever has to fit into a new context. He remains a concerned observer in search of possibilities for a positive interpretation of the present."

I have written as a concerned observer in search of possibilities for a positive interpretation of the present. I believe in the present, partly because, like Mount Everest, it is here and partly because, as a historian, I see it, in spite of the cataclysmic problems that have resulted from a series of concurrent human and scientific revolutions, as one of the greatest and most challenging periods in history. It is the age in which man has reached first the clouds and then the moon. It is the age of the skyscraper, when new technologies have finally made it possible for him to build as high as he has dreamed of doing since the beginning of time — but it is also the age that has turned the dream of a better world into a fouled environment. When, in the past, we of the critical press have pointed out the price of wasting our natural and technological resources and sabotaging our skills, we have been dismissed as idealists. We are the realists now.

HOW TO KILL A CITY

Death by Development

THEY ARE TERSE headline notices — "Three Town Houses Bought by High-Rise Builder," "Midtown Expansion Forcing Music Street to Sing Swan Song," "Real Estate Deal in Village." On the surface, a factual, newsprint chronicle of urban change; underneath, the death of a city by "development."

There was a time when, Candide-like, New Yorkers bought the arguments of progress that this was all for the best in the best of all possible worlds. As their favorite neighborhoods were pulled out from under their feet to be replaced by the profitable sterility of the standard real estate model, wisdom came, slowly and painfully. It was the grass-roots, or rather cement-roots, wisdom of bitter experience, but it paralleled the more cerebral lessons being taught in planning schools and environmental studies and redundant urban symposia: Without variety of function and humanity of scale, the city becomes monstrous and insupportable.

Take "Three Town Houses Bought by High-Rise Builder." The three houses were in the center of the 79th to 80th Street block on Fifth Avenue, flanked by apartment buildings at either corner. The 79th Street tower is a brand-new skyscraper that makes a pathetic gesture toward the elegance of its older neighbors with somber brick and elementary stone trim. The three town houses were of richly detailed masonry in variations of turn-of-the-century French taste — Gothic, classical and Beaux Arts. The story will end, perfectly predictably, when another new apartment house replaces them. [The apartment house went up in the spring of 1969.]

The story started when the 79th Street skyscraper displaced a landmark building, the Brokaw mansion. The little Gothic town house that stood for a while next to it like some piece of bungled surgery had been built to match the mansion. The Brokaw House went down over the howls of preservationists who were unable to find a way to make that magnificent white elephant useful in today's cut-rate, computer society after the institutional owners had exchanged it for a pocketful of cash. The new apartment house quickly became known as New York's most expensive cooperative. Next to the Gilded Age mansions, it represents a kind of architectural poverty for the affluent.

In addition, it represents irreversible environmental damage. A brutal breaking of the streetscape, both historically and aesthetically, is the developer's most notable achievement. That block was part of one of the city's finest, continuous landmark group of mansions, an irreplaceable row that stretched from the Duke House at 78th Street to the Stuyvesant House at 79th Street, crossing to the Brokaw House and ending at the 80th Street corner. Until the 79th Street tower was built, this magnificent urban complex was tied together by a unified street line and the facing park and an incredible period richness of material and detail. These low buildings against a large sky, tinted gold and lavender at dusk or bathed in an extra measure of sun and light, had a civilized beauty. That beauty has been violated. Nor is there any guarantee that some of the succulent real estate of the remaining 78th Street block is not vulnerable, in spite of current institutional uses.

In New York, neighborhoods fall like dominoes as they become succulent real estate. The Upper East Side Historic District protects the new-and-old mix of Madison Avenue and handsome side streets from overdevelopment. (Stephen L. Senigo, Landmarks Preservation Commission)

A second environmental tragedy illustrated here is the destructive force of the new zoning when it is applied literally and without adjustment to specific urban conditions. A feature of the 79th Street apartment house is a wraparound corner plaza. Open plazas opposite the open space of Central Park are an absurdity. But this awkward, meaningless windswept setback from the street gives the builder a bonus of extra rentable floors in a taller tower. Builders, notoriously, are not urbanists. This trend can destroy the little that New York has of genuine urban elegance or greatness, its few handsome avenues and sophisticated plazas.

In New York, neighborhoods fall like dominoes. Everyone knows about the small electrical supply stores uprooted by the World Trade Center; the thrift and antique shops chased by the apartment builders from Third Avenue; the small businesses, bars and coffee dealers displaced from the Lower Manhattan waterfront by office construction; the artists' lofts eliminated in the Village for more luxury apartments.

What follows demolition is preordained by the divine right of development. There will be the same new buildings out of the same old mold, sleekly commercial or shoddily residential; and in the ground floor store space of all, as if by some holy decree, there will be banks.

Even an expanding Rockefeller Center has repudiated the superior planning principles of organized massing and multilevel circulation that added a superb urban heart to midtown. Its subsequent preoccupation has just been to make the facades blend. Somehow, it fell over Sixth Avenue on the way to 48th Street. [Publicity plus persuasion by the city, using zoning bonuses as incentive, resulted in the addition of a midblock passage behind these new Sixth Avenue buildings to accommodate shops, restaurants and pedestrian uses.] New York, anyone? Come and get it before it is too late. This seems like a death-wish city.

The Architectural Follies

NEW YORK'S LONGEST-RUN SHOW, the Architectural Follies, goes on. Performances as usual.

First, the comedy act. The New York Bank for Savings annnounced that it will build a 27-story apartment house next to its main office on Third Avenue at 72nd Street, utilizing the same "colonial design" as the earlier building. Horace Ginsbern will be the architect.

Since the earlier building is a Williamsburg-type Governor's Palace, and a 27-story apartment building is a high-rise tower that was not only structurally and stylistically impossible but also as remote as a spaceship in colonial times, this will be an amusing design trick. The "colonial" label seems to be no more than a wistful thought, however, because the rendering shows a typical New York 27-story apartment house with familiar curtain wall and projecting balconies that might have made George Washington giddy. Funny? Boffo.

But this kind of joke is something that New York should have outgrown long ago. It is a hangover from the days before modern cities recognized their own magnificence. It doesn't work, as architecture or nostalgia.

Witness the original Bank for Savings building that is to inspire this addition. We banked there, until we were shifted to a newer neighborhood branch that was all "modern," with a wall-length pseudo-Mondrian subsequently painted out so that everything was reduced to safe, washable, plastic-coated middlin' gray and green, including the plants. Call it the Plastic Aesthetic.

A prime piece of Fifth Avenue real estate, the Brokaw House bit the dust in a weekend wrecking of its chateau-style stonework. An apartment house followed. (Philip G. Bartlett, Museum of the City of New York; Carl T. Gossett, *New York Times*)

Saving money — considered a dubious virtue today, anyway — becomes a singularly depressing experience. Dreams die easily at the Bank for Savings. In the main office they die in an inflated, dehydrated, imitation colonial shell, built with all of the handcrafted colonial sincerity of big city commercial construction, housing the unparalleled mechanical impersonality of the modern banking operation. Were banks first to reduce people to numbers? This one has the intimate 18th-century charm of its IBM computers. There is nothing sadder or funnier than this kind of misuse, or abuse, of meaningful architectural style.

It's sad and funny to see it done again by the Franklin National Bank at Madison Avenue and 48th Street. Watching this building being transformed from 20th century to 18th century was one of the top midtown acts of last season's Follies. First, there was the steel frame, strong, severe, handsomely rectilinear (the bones are best in most buildings), suggesting the logical shape and design that its covering surface might take, subject only to the architect's talent, imagination and respect for the inspiration of the structure. Painstakingly, brick by brick, the lie was laid up for anyone to observe.

Eighteenth-century arches were hung on the facade like theatrical scrim. Originally, of course, arches like these were carefully built up to wedge-shaped, locking keystones to make openings in a brick wall without having the wall fall down. They were as natural and beautiful for masonry construction as the thin curtain wall is for the metal-framed building today.

Presto change. The hand is quicker than the eye. The arches aren't arches because the masonry is nonsupporting. It's all backed by steel. Fooled you. What we have here is a kind of large architectural practical joke. It is tiresome, like most practical jokes.

But the undertaking was carried out in consistent comic spirit to the end. The opening luncheon, which featured authentic colonial cooking, was served by waiters in knee breeches. (Authentic Madison Avenue.)

So much for comedy. The tragedy was the razing of the Brokaw mansion. The hoarding went up at the end of the week and major demolition began on a Saturday. Saturday, obviously, is not a normal building trades working day and the wrecking crew got double time for its efforts. The Campagna Construction Corporation, the owners and builders of a new apartment house on the site, were taking no chances. It was a dandy way to do enough massive damage at a time when no normal channels are functioning, to assure the building's doom.

No Marquesa de Cuevas had a chance to step forward with $2 million to save it, as with the Pyne House group on Park Avenue. By Monday it was too late. Perhaps the American Institute of Architects, which produced a nice scroll for the Marquesa, could arrange for a suitable trinket for the Campagna Corporation. Something like profit rampant on the seal of the city, upside down.

There is no denying that this is the most dramatic act in the Architectural Follies in a long time. There's nothing quite like a good house wrecking. Come one, come all. You are cordially invited to a demolition watching. It's a great performance of a kind being given with increasing frequency in Manhattan, one that could replace the "happening" as the most chic of avant-garde anticultural events.

Watch an architectural landmark demolished piece by piece. Be present while a splendid building is reduced to rubble. See the wrecking bars gouge out the fine chateau-style stonework. Hear the gas-powered saws bite into the great beams and rafters. Thrill to destruction. Take home samples. Hurry to the show.

On second thought, don't hurry. There will be many more performances. Good demolitions could outrun *Abie's Irish Rose*. Free demolition watchings will be offered in all of New York's best styles and periods: High Victorian, Early Skyscraper, Cast-Iron Commercial in Lower Manhattan, Greek Revival on the waterfront. If this isn't going to be faced as a public responsibility, it might as well be taken as a public spectacle. Anyone coming from city hall?

Singing the Downtown Blues

HURRY, HURRY, HURRY, as the pitchmen used to say; last call for anyone who wants to see the wonders of old New York, the real, live, genuine, remaining bits of the old city in Lower Manhattan, sitting at the feet of the most famous skyscrapers in the world. Come see the biggest buildings on the smallest streets, the newest next to the oldest, the soaring present and the small-scale past. There is no doubt about it, this jam-packed mass of spectacular stone and steel with its dash of historical seasoning is the most spontaneously romantic and shatteringly magnificent cityscape ever known.

But if you can't get there fast, forget it. In a few short years Lower Manhattan will be just another Third or Sixth avenue.

Good enough, if you fancy the bland, commercial homogenization of postwar Third and Sixth avenues. Their chief fanciers, however, are those builders and investors whose sense of environmental aesthetics is limited to the calculable beauties of rentable square footage by the square block and who do more to plan, construct and seal the fate of this city than any combination of officials and municipal agencies theoretically entrusted with the job. A government man on the highest federal level of urban renewal once remarked to this writer that New York is the only major city in the country that has been planned exclusively for profit and built to that pattern by its businessmen with the city easing the way.

New Yorkers who do not build the city but merely live in it frequently fancy other values. They have a fondness, based on sound instincts of what a great city should be, for the enrichment and contrast of the kind of early buildings and intimate streets that are grist for the speculator's mill.

They esteem the cobbled slips and lanes, the Greek Revival coffee and spice houses just above the Battery that are rapidly disappearing and taking with them the sense of the harbor's historic sailing age; the shabby Georgian-Federal structures redolent of fish in the old Fulton Market; dormered and pitched-roof brick houses against the Gothic stone and spiderweb steel of the Brooklyn Bridge; the granite blocks and Greek lintels that still face ropeworks and casual bars and beaneries in the old city; the 19th-century breaks in the 20th-century skyscraper-lined canyons that let in the sleety New York sky and the ghosts of New York history. It is all going, going, gone.

In Lower Manhattan, historic streets have been demapped and eliminated by the City Planning Commission to make profitable superblock parcels for private builders. Historic districts in the path of powerful business interests have been left undesignated by the Landmarks Preservation Commission. What has not already been destroyed or damaged waits resignedly for the speculative developers, who are known to be assembling more superplots.

Until recently, in every possible fashion, city agencies have aided and abetted the process in the biggest urban giveaway of past and future ever negotiated for cash or taxes. What the city has put its stamp of approval on is one of the largest standard-model commercial developments that New York has yet seen. With few exceptions, the names are chillingly familiar — Uris, Rudin and Rose, Emery Roth — the "stylesetters" of commercial midtown. Downtown, here they come.

It isn't just that New York has had no muscle; it has had no vision. Whatever amateur or archaic attempts it has made to guide redevelopment have been tacitly understood to be totally subservient to commercial prerogatives. Until a very short time ago, it set no standards and made no plans. No other large city can make this statement. Whatever has gone wrong, whatever triumphs or fiascos have resulted,

Fulton Street and others like it have been ruthlessly razed in Lower Manhattan; the city's past has been exorcized by superdevelopment. Only a few remnants and districts — South Street Seaport and Fraunces Tavern — have been designated as landmarks. (National Trust Collection)

cities such as Boston, Philadelphia and many more have had a framework for some kind of coordinated construction and urban design. That same federal official quoted earlier found New York's lack of plans and standards unique even in the roster of mediocre urban renewal efforts across the nation.

The problem, now, with an awakening consciousness of the quality of the environment in municipal circles, is that the old pattern is set. In the financial community the old blinders are still on. The old priorities are considered inviolate.

With a Lower Manhattan plan belatedly on the city's books, its potential is being eaten away by New York's relentless *force majeure,* the divine right of real estate economics. Said one of the architects involved in a major downtown project, "We only wish that there had been a more cohesive city plan from which to work than the bits and pieces left over by the wheeler-dealers."

Examples? They abound. The investment firm of Atlas-McGrath assembled enough prime Lower Manhattan land not only to frustrate the city's urban renewal designation for the area but to make it possible to create, with ease and art and single ownership, a small-scale Rockefeller Center on one of the city's most superb waterfront sites. This would have been compensation for historical destruction. It is not being done.

Instead of coordinated planning and design, the *modus operandi* has been simply to milk the most out of each separate, negotiable parcel independently. The architects of the blockbusters for two of the huge plots have no idea what will be on the third, and their relationship is cordial but not collaborative. Actually, it is quite clear what will be on that third site: the biggest deal possible. Community waterfront uses? Parks and plazas united in open-space planning? Human amenities? Urban aesthetics? Municipal sense? Public good? None of it balances against private profit.

And so the city closed the streets and handed them over to the developers, moved

Jeanette Park and widened Water Street, all in the most pragmatic way possible. There will now be two huge commercial superblocks with oddments of open space that result not from thoughtful urban design but from the bonus provisions of the zoning law, which gives height increases (read rentable floors) for setbacks from the street.

It makes it hard to take the city's talk seriously about using street closings as a negotiating tool with the World Trade Center. As it stands now, the Port Authority is throwing away the remarkable spatial opportunities that this massive project creates, for just another big commercial venture. There will be plazas, yes. But since the Authority seems determined to burrow all circulatory activity underground to concourse level, these plazas promise to be vast, desolate, dull, windswept and empty most of the time. This, where so much could have been done to improve pedestrian functions and pleasures.

It is equally hard to take the Port Authority's gesture of cooperative planning with the city seriously, based on its claim that city officials have sat in on meetings and concurred in decisions from the time of the project's inception. Looking at the record, it is impossible to take past municipal planning efforts seriously at all.

Consider another downtown planning example: Water Street. To provide a broad traffic artery among the narrow, congested streets of the old city, all of the historic brick warehouses on the east side of Water Street were ripped out some years ago, the road enlarged and the gaping wound filled with parking.

Now the entire length of Water Street south from the bridge is a city-made, aesthetic slum. It consists of the raw backs of houses revealed midblock, enhanced by raw parking lots. This is one of New York's best examples of official urban mutilation. The objective now is as obvious as it is insensitive and commercially oriented: Clear out whatever old, interesting structures still remain just beyond on Front Street, and bring on the superblock developers.

They will undoubtedly build banks. Most of the new downtown buildings are banks. They are, let it be said, fine and necessary institutions, but en masse they make streetscapes of suffocating dullness. There is, in fact, a kind of creeping bank disease laying a cold, dead hand on New York wherever the shiny new construction appears. Try counting, for example, the new banks from 47th to 59th streets on Park Avenue; add up the number of banks on ground floors of new buildings everywhere. It is as good as counting sheep. Soigné ennui.

Downtown, the days of small shops for fresh-ground coffee or odd electronic gadgets or conviviality in a not-too-pure circa 1827 bar are past or numbered. (It's not very convivial in the personal credit department of a bank and the place smells of computers, not coffee.) If New Yorkers survive the rape of the city, or just crossing the street or breathing the air, there is one last, lethal urban hazard: boredom.

Side Street Sabotage

NEITHER PLANNING NOR PRESERVATION nor people nor consideration of style, function or livability can stay the profit-motivated speculator's hand. And no wonder. With the "leverage," as it is called in business parlance, of tax advantages and borrowed money peculiar to the real estate world, leading to returns, generally, of 15 to 35 percent on investments requiring little of the operator's own money as opposed to a median return of 11.3 percent for the country's largest corporations where equity runs much higher, real estate is the closest thing to the proverbial pot of gold. (Argue this with *Fortune,* please, not with us, from which these unblushing facts of business come.) And who pays income tax?

Any city that invites destruction at a return of 15 to 35 percent plus a few depreciation benefits and capital gains bonuses and tax shelters can hardly be saved. Interestingly, when real estate men turn to philanthropy, they always do so outside of the building or land-buying fields. That would be *too* philanthropic.

And so those who care about what happens to New York — and its future as a city of civilized amenities balances on a surprisingly thin line — put their hopes in those institutions, corporations, foundations and educational organizations that supposedly support noncommercial standards and will balance them against purely economic factors. Again, in business terms, one looks for the "trade-off" between profit and the urban humanities. These institutions, one assumes, will help keep some kind of desirable urban balance. They will preserve. They will build better buildings. They will consider the city's design, function and aesthetics, if the speculator will not. And on occasion, they do all of this conspicuously well.

This brings us to the depressing fact that one notable case of serious side street sabotage is the work of an educational institution theoretically committed to an understanding of urban and cultural values — Syracuse University. Obviously, a 15 to 35 percent return looks good to a university endowment fund, too.

Since last spring, Syracuse University has purchased 12, 14, 16 and 18 East 62nd Street. It is currently negotiating for the houses at 4 and 6 East 62nd. The school already owned 11 East 61st Street, which is operated as an in-town admissions office and cultural center named for its donor, real estate man and philanthropist Joseph I. Lubin. Lubin, a Syracuse trustee, has been the university's prime mover for the purchases.

Syracuse has now assembled most of the block between Fifth and Madison avenues on both 61st and 62nd streets, from the Fifth Avenue frontage to the Carlton House apartments on Madison. On Fifth Avenue the Knickerbocker Club is at 62nd Street and the Hartley Marcellus Dodge House is at 61st Street. This building, since the death of Dodge closed and shuttered by his elderly widow, Geraldine Rockefeller Dodge, is clearly destined to complete a large, extremely valuable and negotiable parcel of land.

The houses at 4 and 6 East 62nd Street, being negotiated for as part of that parcel, belong to the York Club, one of the city's private women's clubs. Because Syracuse University is known to be involved in the purchase, some club members feel that they should sell for a vaguely altruistic reason suggested by the fact that the buildings are being sought by an educational institution. Others feel that they are simply being subjected to a rather familiar and unpleasant kind of commercial real estate pressure to give up and get out.

The offer for these two houses has gone up from $1.7 million to $2.7 million in a few months, although the five houses purchased earlier were bought for a total of $1,245,000. That, of course, should be the tipoff that nothing else is involved here than the completion of an investment purchase that will be worth a fantastic amount on the real estate market. Yet there has been a strange reluctance on the part of club members who favor selling to entertain open or competitive bids. Ladies, you are being had. Speculation, and only speculation, is what Syracuse University has in mind.

That fact was confirmed to this reporter by Francis A. Wingate, the university's treasurer. Except for the house that Syracuse now operates at 11 East 61st Street, he made it clear that there is no question of using any of this property for educational purposes. Even if such a use were being considered, which it is not, it would be debatable in that area.

What Syracuse intends to do, after having assembled the land by paying no more than it must and, it hopes, not on the open market, is to resell the properties eventually at the highest possible profit for demolition and development. "This is simply an endowment fund investment," Wingate says. "We have no intention of keeping these properties. We will carry them until such time as we get a good offer."

The doomed 62nd Street block is an unusually handsome and characteristic example of a well-preserved row of elegant five-story stone town houses in the French Renaissance or Beaux Arts style popular after the turn of the century. Their landmark quality is enhanced by the completeness of the block. Nothing like them will be built again. Greetings, New York City, from Syracuse University.

Still another case of side street sabotage is taking place on West 78th Street between Columbus and Amsterdam avenues behind the Museum of Natural History. Here a row of brownstones has been patiently and privately restored by their owners. They have been renovated with loving care and architectural sensitivity and not much encouragement from the city or its lending institutions, which tend to consider the individual New Yorker's attempt to stay in the city and maintain its human and architectural character as some kind of deterrent to economic progress.

Now the work of these owner-residents is being destroyed by an owner-investor who has begun remodeling two of the houses, at 120 and 122 West 78th Street, in a manner that will ruin the scrupulously preserved block. He will extend the frontages of his property beyond the present building line, making damaging, out-of-character "improvements." Evidently banks are rather good about giving loans for this kind of thing, called modernization, which is supposed to jack up values, rather than for sympathetic restoration, which retains values not in bankers' books. Ultimately, of course, proper historical restoration sends property values way up.

Advice and help offered by block residents — including an architect — on ways that would do the job and still save the street architecturally and urbanistically have been summarily rejected. Perhaps the city should make the gentleman a gift of an antilandmark plaque, engraved "owner-saboteur." One more way to kill a city.

"Senza Rispetto"

THERE IS A NEW YORK LADY who had a Tuscan father and an English mother and has been married to an American and watching New York architecture for most of 50 years. She has seen the old buildings go down and the new buildings go up. Observing a typical apartment house rising on York Avenue recently she asked a workman, in Italian, "How do you build them so fast?"

"Senza rispetto," he replied, "without respect."

Bad News About Times Square

IT IS NOT THE BEST OF TIMES, and it is not the worst of times, just somewhere discouragingly in between. With the commercial market overbuilt, New York no longer has the look of a city in construction, which means that at least fewer good old buildings are being torn down for bad new ones. The developers are crying all the way to the Caribbean. And the city's planners, theoretically, have time to sit and think.

The Times Square cleanup is really a buildup; the size of the proposed redevelopment will be equalled only by the size of the potential profits. This model shows the alarming bulk and density possible under the city's zoning. (Richard Crawford, Municipal Art Society)

They have plenty to think about. The change in the economy and the change in the municipal administration have left the city's planning offices in a kind of paralysis, or limbo. After establishing a remarkable record for tangible achievements in the guidance of private development through progressive urban design, they have virtually no construction to guide. This means that there must be a radical reordering of programs and priorities if the planners are to continue as an effective force in the city's life. And unless this reassessment is made with vision, speed and skill, there is no place to go but down. As the planning offices go, so goes New York.

Most of the news about Times Square, that symbolic heart of New York and crossroads of the world, is bad. On the plus side, it has what every city needs — tremendous vitality. On the minus side, much of that energy is channeled into high-visibility pornography and other fast-buck operations. The area is encrusted with the dark and gritty sediment of endless seasons of concentrated use and abuse that no rain or garbage removal ever touches. But the crime statistics are down. And the theaters are virtually full.

So much for the surface. Underneath, the district is particularly hard hit by both recession and inflation, in terms of rentals, building health and the future of certain key projects. Because the area is tenuous anyway, these factors are critical. Within months, Times Square and its environs lost a Liggett's, a Woolworth's, at least two restaurants and the Royal Manhattan Hotel. The Franklin National Bank demolished one of the area's few fine buildings to save taxes and maintenance. The real estate base is in serious trouble.

The hotel, stores and restaurants represented the kind of sound, diversified services that the district desperately needs. But when rent and expenses went up, the tenants went out. Whenever rents rise and legitimate commercial activities leave a fringe area, peep shows and massage parlors come in. After the demise of Deli City on 42nd Street, only the withholding of a state liquor license staved off a topless bar at this focal point of Times Square. It was an empty gesture; it became a porn supermarket. The trend in such an economy is inevitably down. And the farther down the ambience slips, the greater the pathologies of the public it attracts, and the more difficult it is for any stabilizing, legitimate activities to remain and compete. (No one is looking to make Times Square genteel or the playground of the effete rich, only reasonably secure and appetizing.)

In fact, the future of Times Square seems to depend on one large, tide-turning project: the $160 million hotel planned by the Atlanta architect-entrepreneur, John Portman, for the west side of Broadway between 45th and 46th streets. In size and scale, in design bravura, in its ability to attract the middle-class tourist and to be an environmental catalyst, it would provide an essential stability for Times Square, in character with its traditional functions and style. But this hotel, in turn, depends on a $200 million convention center proposed for a riverfront site a few blocks west, and this project is hung up on the city's financial crisis and the present state of the economy.

That is the situation, and the future is clearly in the balance. In the Lindsay era, the city's planners would have been in there with a strategy compounded of Machiavelli and Sixtus V. When Fifth Avenue began to change in character and style a few years ago, the Office of Midtown Planning and Development (OMPD) devised the mixed-used Fifth Avenue zoning district to control and upgrade the street's activities. The special theater district was taken over by OMPD from the Urban Design Group that had devised the zoning, and the planners worked with the builders to bring new playhouses to the Times Square area. It initiated plans and negotiations for the convention center and the Portman hotel. Farther east — OMPD's authority extends to both rivers — there was the defeated, but imaginative, Madison Avenue Mall.

OMPD, one of about a dozen special planning offices located throughout the city according to districts, is in uneasy transition. A new director, Dick G. Lam, has replaced the first director of the office, Jaquelin T. Robertson, and the acting director, William Bardel, after months of delay due to changes at city hall. (Robertson has embarked on the redevelopment of Tehran for the Shah of Iran, with the planning firm of Llewelyn-Davies International — a far cry from Times Square.)

None of the planning offices has the high-priority status in the Beame administration that they enjoyed under Lindsay; at that time the top-line authority of the mayor's office was actively behind them. The power of his concentrated interest and backing was no small advantage in getting things done. In the uncertain transition from Lindsay to Beame, some of the best urban planners and directors left. In the midtown office, five of the top planners were lost as a result of insecurity and conflict, and the Robertson team has been reshuffled.

Now that the period of high publicity and dazzling innovation is past, New York has ceased to attract the brightest young professionals in the field. Loss of talent is matched by loss of leadership; the charismatic directors, such as Robertson and Richard Weinstein of the Office of Lower Manhattan Development, who put the public and the private sector together with a blend of political magic and pragmatic idealism, are gone. The days of working with large-scale development are also gone, at least temporarily, and so are the charismatic, large-scale projects. There are limited funds for anything at all in the current budgetary crisis.

If there is neither money nor development, what are OMPD's planners doing? There are some commendable undertakings: a continuing study of zoning controls for signs and street access that could reduce the impact of porn joints around Times Square, coupled with an ongoing collaborative effort with law-enforcement agencies to monitor and clean up illegal and dangerous activities. There is a study of proliferating single-room occupancy hotels with the aim of controlling their conversion. Block by block, surveys are being made for computer digestion and other forms of analysis. There also seems to be an increasing amount of planning busywork, such as "exchange and comparison" of information from other cities from Caracas to Miami, for which grants are usually available. These have, at best, risky and limited input into the New York planning process.

No longer are developers being pulled in by their jacquard silk ties to take a strong

The Times Square Center would feature four huge, fancy-dress towers by Philip Johnson and John Burgee. Portman's Marriott Marquis Hotel went up in 1985; by then both its need and its design were dubious. The convention center was built a few blocks south of the original site. (Park Tower Realty)

dose of higher design standards, often for mutual benefit and stimulation. The Villard Houses–Palace Hotel project in east midtown is not being guided into appropriate as well as profitable design solutions by the midtown office. Nor is the planning being done during this building hiatus that would prepare the city for development when construction resumes. (A "public entertainment district" could be mapped out for Times Square where peddlers and tourist activity could be coordinated. A comprehensive midtown traffic study needs to be pushed while pressures are low.)

What is actually coming out of the office is less than encouraging. A Broadway Mall, a holdover from the Lindsay years, has been shorn of its most important element in its most recent public appearance. Part of its purpose as a pedestrian precinct was to have a tourist information billboard, or building, at one end that would centralize visitor activities attractively and informatively. That is gone, and the mall is reduced to street dressing, rather than something that deals inclusively with the needs and functions of the area. But what is most disturbing is the planning climate: not apathy, but slowdown; not lack of interest so much as lack of vision; a lowering of standards and a lessened conceptualization of the job. What has noticeably slacked off is the passionate pursuit of a better city through the imaginative, far-reaching application of the creative processes of urban design. It was a kind of passion that pulled bureaucrats and businessmen along with it to very real planning achievement. It is not just Times Square that hangs in the balance; it is all of New York.

New York: Dead or Alive

THE CONVENTIONAL WISDOM about investment construction — tear down the old and put up the new for maximum return on the land — is taking a beating. And so are cities, in terms of some of the things that the real estate recession is doing to the urban environment.

In New York, in particular, with tight money, inflation, cost overruns and a decade of commercial overbuilding, the traditional development pattern has bombed out. And so have a dismaying number of big new buildings. In an almost unprecedented situation, paralleled only by the Great Depression, completed skyscrapers stand empty or near-empty, deep in the red. Eerily silent sites attest to the fact that construction has stopped on important buildings. Costs have escalated beyond the possibility of satisfactory returns, and the money — in a business where virtually every penny is borrowed — has run out. Crisis has quietly turned into catastrophe, and not the least effect is the damage being done to the city itself.

The most cautionary tale comes from Chicago, where nothing could illustrate the problem more forcefully than the story of the Old Stock Exchange. In a casebook adherence to investment practice, Adler and Sullivan's landmark structure in Chicago's Loop was demolished for new construction in 1971. Critics and preservationists bled profusely in print before it came down, and even New York's Metropolitan Museum lusted after the 76-year-old Sullivan terra cotta ornament and rusticated ground floor arcades. Arguments about quality, style and the Chicago heritage were to no avail. The fate of the building, which stood on prime commercial land, was sealed with the statement that it was "economically unviable."

And so it was bulldozed, and a 43-story glass and steel replacement, called the Heller International Building, went up at 30 North LaSalle, backed by astute investors undeterred by art or sentimentality or anything but the higher truths of the real estate process. Sound business practice, as defined and revered by the development community, prevailed.

Ready for the big switch? The *new* building has proved to be "economically unviable." According to a report by Rob Warden in the *Chicago Daily News,* the structure is in serious financial trouble. Among the gruesome details listed by Warden: The developers were unable to meet the $400,000 monthly payments on their $41.3 million first mortgage, a deal for a second mortgage fell through, and cost overruns sent the building's price tag soaring beyond the $48.3 million in total financing to $51 million.

Anyone who keeps score on life's large and small architectural ironies has hit the jackpot on this one. What is economically unviable now is a big building barely distinguishable from any of the other $50 million jobs anywhere, and what was economically unviable before was a unique work of art and genius. Rehabilitation might have been considerably better. There is a bitter lesson here in economics and environment. Sound business practice turned out to be both unsound investment and destructive urbanism.

The Chicago tale has a clear application — and warning — for New York. The obvious parallel is Penn Central's determination to build a large new office tower making use of the air rights over Grand Central Terminal, or on the site itself. When the landmark designation of the terminal was overturned in a recent court decision, Penn Central and the developer won the right not only to use the air rights for new construction in this fashion, but even to demolish the existing building. Fortunately, the decision was reversed on appeal.

There is virtually no doubt that such a project, at this time, would run into the same kind of economic unviability in New York that the developers of the Stock Exchange site have suffered in Chicago, if not greater. The prognosis is resounding financial failure, in addition to the architectural impoverishment of the city. But no astute developer would be dumb enough to build under these circumstances, you say? Probably not. But the fact is that some of New York's major new buildings, put up by astute developers in the 1970s, are currently huge money losers; they went right ahead, like the Stock Exchange developers, even with storm signals flying. The more conspicuous New York disasters include 1166 Avenue of the Americas (untenanted), Two New York Plaza (empty until sold recently at a huge loss), 1500 Broadway and 55 Water Street (running in the red). Their astute developers have taken an awful shellacking.

The situation is worse than anyone except real estate insiders realize. In addition to those ghostly, untenanted or partly filled new towers, construction has actually been halted on more than a half dozen major new buildings in New York. There is simply no action on the sites, which may range from gaping excavations to partial structures. Some are luxury apartment buildings. The Citicorp Building, a 46-story tower projected a year ago as one of New York's more eye-catching skyscrapers, luckily has its own bank, Citibank, to fund it.

The disaster is taking still other forms. Sound buildings are being destroyed not for new construction, as has always been the case in New York, but for that particularly blighting form of noninvestment, the empty parking lot. The demolition is a hard-nosed way of saving taxes when the properties cease to be profitable, and no buyers or investment builders are in sight. It is a vicious form of disinvestment.

In New York, the size of such mutilated sites makes bomb damage look puny. The Cities Service Company, which moved from New York to Tulsa, has defaced the Wall Street area by destroying six adjacent buildings that it owns on Wall and Pine

Only the orphaned arch and trading room of Adler and Sullivan's Chicago Stock Exchange were saved from demolition, an empty gesture to art and history. Federal tax credits for rehabilitation now help tip the scale to preservation. (Richard Nickel, Commission on Chicago Historical and Architectural Landmarks; Carleton Knight III, NTHP)

between Pearl and William streets. To pull out the jobs — and then add insult to injury by pulling down the buildings and the tax base — is, by any measure of social responsibility, unconscionable. The Cities Service sabotage has produced a vacant lot of more than an acre and tax savings for the company of $280,000 a year. There are times when sound business practice becomes the business of wrecking cities.

The W.R. Grace Company tore down a fine Renaissance-style structure at Pearl and Water streets, at Hanover Square, for the inevitable parking lot, rather than maintain it and pay taxes on it. The Franklin National Bank further weakened the shaky West 42nd Street area by demolishing a landmark quality building — for parking and taxes. While there is no investors' market, these eyesores will remain and increase in number as old structures become unprofitable due to inflation and recession, with diminishing rental returns and rising fuel and operating costs. The possibility of demolition of Grand Central Terminal for tax savings — even without building a replacement — undoubtedly occurred to the business minds involved. It is a terribly expensive blitz for the city not only in terms of taxes lost, but of sound buildings destroyed and devastating damage to the city's architectural and environmental quality.

The tax structure, of course, rewards unimproved property and demolition, giving benefits in inverse order to the owners' positive contributions to the city. And except for the device of tax relief in landmarks law, it works against preservation. (Under New York's landmarks law, it is impossible to give the only form of relief — tax abatement — to already tax-exempt institutions, which makes all landmarks owned by charitable or nonprofit organizations hopelessly vulnerable.) A belated national study of the effects of assessment and tax policies on a city's planning, growth and preservation has been undertaken by HUD.

And so the ultimate shaper of cities turns out to be, for better or worse, so-called sound business practice, or economic viability. That this often distorts or destroys more than it contributes is becoming perilously clear. If there were no other way than to let sound business take its course, there would be little hope for the urban environment.

The planners have their role, however, which is to deal with these financial and legal realities, turning them into constructive tools in the service of an environmental vision. Among the tools are tax policies, zoning regulations, land use codes, and design and legal controls, tied to the incentives of profit and loss. These devices not only profoundly affect the builders' bottom line; they guide the city's life processes toward desirable or undesirable patterns of growth and development. This is a kind of planning that New York needs more than ever, if it is to survive.

Covent Garden: Omens of Absurdity

ENGLISH PLANS, unlike American plans, which tend to remain in the blue-sky category, have a way of becoming reality. They are assisted by strong government legislation and participation. The Covent Garden plan, with the famous Covent Garden market at its heart, is considered one of the most important and far-reaching of the proposals for London's future. If it goes ahead, Eliza Doolittle would never recognize her old neighborhood.

Fifteen acres of the center-city site are devoted now to London's colorful fruit, vegetable and flower market. It is in what is left of Inigo Jones's celebrated 17th-century design for the city's first great residential square.

Covent Garden as Eliza Doolittle knew it, before the produce dealers moved out in 1974. Local Londoners did not find the redevelopment proposed by the Greater London Council "loverly." (Fox Photos)

The market is scheduled to leave for a South Bank location in 1972, just over 300 years after the Duke of Bedford obtained the first market charter when produce became more profitable than the handsome houses, since demolished, that he had built. St. Paul's Church, Jones's Tuscan masterpiece, still stands amid stacks of Brussels sprouts at the west end of the square.

The redevelopment program is a multiuse, multilevel scheme to reuse the market buildings and add a new convention center, drama and recreation centers, hotels and commercial buildings, change traffic patterns and double the amount of existing housing. Financing would be carried out with public and private funds in a three-phase construction program that would continue over the next 20 years. The project area is bounded by the Strand on the south, Charing Cross Road on the west, Shaftesbury Avenue and High Holborn on the north and a line following Newton, Great Queen, Wild, Kean and Tavistock streets on the east. This is a substantial section of central London.

The proposal is part of a continuing, official replanning and reconstruction program that is changing the face of this city's most famous sites and squares in the name of modern functional needs and urban problems.

New plans and construction in London include the war-damaged environs of St. Paul's Cathedral and the high-rise Barbican district, both already rebuilt. There are schemes in the study stage for Piccadilly Circus and Regent Street, Trafalgar Square, Whitehall and Parliament Square. The South Bank development presents a massive new cultural center. Most of London's historic core is on the boards of the city's planners.

The 93 acres centered on the market form an important "downtown" area where the economic return on old buildings has not kept pace with rising land values. There are almost uniform five-story structures dated from 18th-century Georgian to 19th-century Victorian. The most historic will be preserved.

The land is considered ripe for redevelopment. Prices range from $50 to $100 a square foot, close to London's highest. For comparison, the most superinflated prices anywhere in midtown Manhattan are $200 to $400 a square foot. In the classic pattern of all cities, small enterprises and low-cost housing are threatened. With the removal of the market, speculative opportunities will skyrocket.

Private development has been deliberately held off by the government for the last 10 years, pending the completion of a comprehensive Covent Garden area plan. This can be done under the British Planning Act by not issuing development permits to private builders.

The area under study contains the market, 16 of the 33 West End theaters, the Royal Opera House and an assortment of one-man, small-scale businesses and shops of spectacular variety and interest. It is a literary center, for publishers, printers, engravers and bookstores. The low-rent loft space accommodates art and theater services, and its stores range from take-out Chinese food to dealers in antiques, hardware and stamps. Londoners speak warmly of "bananas and ballerinas cheek to jowl." It is one of the most successful mixed-use neighborhoods in the world.

The Covent Garden plan is a sophisticated proposal, containing much new theory that has been learned by trial, error and catastrophe in the last 20 years. It claims to recognize the special character of the area and to update it to modern city needs. Whether the two objectives are not mutually exclusive is something the planners have not really faced.

It also raises serious questions about the degree and extent of master-planning control that is desirable or necessary for problem solving in a city whose distinctive character and appeal have been created by scattered, organic growth. As the Danish planner Steen Eiler Rasmussen has pointed out, the best thing that ever happened to London was the city's failure to adopt Christopher Wren's master plan after the fire of 1666.

The Covent Garden scheme is for a continued mixed-use neighborhood, with even greater emphasis on entertainment and tourist attractions. The vacated market hall would become a kind of galleria with shops and commercial enterprises.The square, freed of Brussels sprouts, would be an open pedestrian plaza. The Royal Opera would expand to form a new southern boundary. Between Covent Garden and the Strand would be a "spine" of tall new buildings replacing small, old ones. The chief feature would be a 4,000-seat convention center and one or more 2,000-room hotels.

Another "spine" along the northern edge would be the site of new housing. An open green would be created where commercial buildings now stand just north of the market square. New traffic and service roads would be below ground, with pedestrian walkways above to separate people and cars. The walkways would be determined in part by present landmarks and small, paved courts that thread the area.

There are no firm designs yet; the plan is schematic, pending acceptance by the collaborating local and Greater London governments.

There would be massive demolition in the phased stages of construction. Listed landmarks, such as the Royal Opera House, the Theater Royal, Drury Lane and St. Paul's Church, would be kept. So would what is called a "character route" through the center of the site. But the area is dotted with historic buildings that could not be saved; old streets such as Henrietta Street and Maiden Lane would go, and so would Rule's Restaurant, a London landmark since the 18th century.

The "tradeoff," to use a business rather than a planning term, is the picturesque and problematic past for possible solution for the equally problematic present. Much of the new construction already in the area or in rebuilt precincts such as that of St. Paul's Cathedral is so appallingly characterless that one fears for both past and future.

There are questions raised by the plan that its authors have undoubtedly considered carefully but that will haunt any London-lover.

Is this the place for a convention center at all? Should this ever be the site of concentrated, large-scale building? Does it make sense to remove the market and its trucking congestion to replace them with the congestion of conventions and tourist hotels? At what point does urban sensibility bow to the need for foreign exchange?

Are those "spines" of housing, culture and commerce, and particularly the convention center, not totally destructive of indigenous characteristics? What will happen to the rich mixture of small enterprises and the cohesive community of elderly residents on small incomes when this construction, with its inevitable inflation of land values, moves in? Is this plan not certain doom rather than salvation, even if it is of the ordered instead of the speculative variety?

If there is blight here, it is minimal. This is a neighborhood rich in comfortable, historical continuity. It is sociologically and urbanistically sound in spite of the fact that private bath counts make a negative statistic and modern traffic, here as everywhere else in London, has paralyzed old streets. Its character is bound to change some when the market goes, but it need not be willfully mutilated. The incentive seems to be rising land value, not urbanism or sociology.

To all except planners it is blindingly obvious that as little should be done here as possible beyond the appropriate conversion and reuse of the market buildings. Covent Garden's distinctive kind of urbanity and history is an irreplaceable asset, as cities have learned when they have destroyed such qualities for "improvement."

It is both fashionable and necessary in these days of exploding urban problems to think ahead and to think big. The Covent Garden plan is conscientiously, professionally comprehensive, and that is its danger as well as its value. As the vision grows large in planners' eyes, existing values and buildings tend to fade and disappear long before the bulldozer arrives. For that vision, 55 of the 93 acres of the Covent Garden district would be destroyed. Come and get your London while it lasts. Even Christopher Wren could make a mistake.

I N THE TWO AND A HALF YEARS since the announcement of the Covent Garden Draft Plan, opposition to the redevelopment project for central London's famous market and theater district has been increasing.

No, it wouldn't be lovely, is the growing refrain in response to the Greater London Council's master plan for almost a hundred acres of the city's historic heart. As a result of the reaction among the public and in the press, further studies were conducted and a revised proposal has just been released. It seems certain to trigger more protest, although objections were neatly turned at the news conference held to introduce it.

The proposal was unveiled by the Countess of Dartmouth, recently appointed as chairman of the Covent Garden Joint Development Committee of the Greater London Council. She presented arguments for keeping the area's charm while turning it into a hotel and convention center — an exercise in contradictions at which no one turned a hair.

The plan was not actually presented; it was simply there on display, in fine multicolored graphics, for anyone who wanted to look. The essence of it was available in a handsome, super-rational brochure.

The original plan was undertaken because Covent Garden Market will trundle its fruits and flowers across the river to a new location next year. (It is hard to imagine St. Paul's Church, by Inigo Jones, or Henry Fowler's glass-topped market building without a fronting sack of broccoli.)

Because one of the dictums of planning is "think comprehensively," a 100-acre site was selected for redevelopment, including the 15-acre produce market. New roads were drawn, a hotel and convention center "spine" paralleling the Strand and a housing "spine" at the northern edge were suggested, and pedestrian "character routes" were plotted to keep the most historic sites and buildings.

Less historic sites and buildings were doomed, including many from the 18th and 19th centuries, as were the wonderful streetscapes that England is still so casual about and Americans are beginning to wrap in cotton wool.

There were only a few problems in the way: a large colony of elderly low-income people who had lived their lives there; small, low-rent businesses of remarkable cultural and artistic variety; and a passionate sense of community. There is also the fragile social and economic balance of a fluid, lively, mixed-use neighborhood of a specific and valuable nature, combining people, arts, entertainment, shops, business and industry with the spontaneous preservation of the past.

These last factors are valued highly now by American urbanists, who have learned from grievous planning error and who see the Covent Garden district as an exemplary case of healthy self-regeneration. Such matters as toilet facilities can be corrected.

Changes in the revised plan include a reduction to 96 acres, with housing and open space constant, but with present housing doubled. Shopping space would be reduced from the first plan, offices increased marginally and hotels increased considerably.

The convention center, a calculated magnet for tourists and transients, has drawn the most fire. The public seems more aware than the planners that nothing short of a bomb will change neighborhood patterns and character more totally than massive tourism.

The key to the plan is not so much "humanity" or "amenity" — words dropped constantly in discussion — as it is "economic viability." The belief is that "economic," or high commercial rentals and land uses will support more public and humane functions, including housing. In practice, the principle usually sends the best intentions down the drain.

"We cannot carry high holding charges on the land or conjure money," says a "valuer" for the council. "We need developers."

Knowing that, any developer worth his speculative spurs calls the tune. Developer pressures have already raised the original 10 million square feet of floor space contemplated for the area to 30 million.

As a result of the protests, a larger proportion of older buildings will be retained in the new plan. But at the end of the project's three-phase development, in 1985, a third of the area will be new construction. The character of the new, from other London examples, is as predictable as porridge.

The rationale for planned redevelopment is not only the moving of the market but the fact that the Covent Garden area is some of central London's most expensive land. The government has clamped a lid on private development in the last decade, pending a comprehensive plan, in the hope that the wholesale destruction and tenant removal that go with uncontrolled speculation could be avoided.

The damage will be done instead by gentlemen's agreement, based on a set of planning principles that are all wrong. This is a plan resting on the fact that land values have gotten too high to permit a healthy, historic, irreplaceable, spontaneously regenerating neighborhood of proven social uses and attractiveness to exist — because it is "economically undeveloped." That anachronism has not been resolved or even faced by the council.

Through a process of double-think, no attention is paid to the fact that the "contemplated improvements" would either destroy or sterilize exactly what the plan promises to conserve.

Pressures for redevelopment are intense. The planners' intentions are pious. The Greater London Council "hopes" for quality design from developers. It "hopes" for a balance between profitable and unprofitable enterprises. It sees compatibility and compromise. American observers who have been through the same planning wringer see disaster.

The council is still indulging in a kind of paternalistic, centralized planning that has gone violently out of style in other places. It may get its body blow in London through the unpopular Covent Garden proposal. Questions from the press seem politely antagonistic. Council members looked a little grim.

To queries about the role of community participation — there are no community members on the planning team — Lady Dartmouth, who has been in public life since 1954, replied by explaining the democratic process according to council procedures.

When a hirsute young man wearing a "Stuff the GLC Covent Garden Plan" button identified himself as a community spokesman, he was resolutely cut off. To a member of the press who suggested that the young man might be allowed to speak, a determined Lady Dartmouth explained, later, that the protester, James Monahan of the Covent Garden community, was an unrepresentative outsider who had been "unconstructive" in a previous meeting.

"I may have curls here," she said, pointing to one of London's smartest coifs, "but I have steel here," putting a finger to her brow. "I will not be bullied. He thinks we should start all over."

He may be right.

I F EVERYONE WILL HOLD ON for a fast ride on the environmental roller coaster, we will examine some of the cumulative ironies and inconsistencies of which the plans of men and the world they live in are made. The point to remember is that each step seems reasoned and logical, but the ultimate result is absurdity. This might be called the First Planning Law.

A prime example is the relocation of Covent Garden Market in London, a process that was masterminded by professionals in a city of notably rational men. (That means the British sit still for an awful lot.) In a planning decision that goes back to 1957, with a study of all of London's food markets and a recommendation for their coordination, it was decided that Covent Garden Market should be moved. In its crowded, picturesque, traffic-jammed, chaotic setting in London's heart at the portal of St. Paul's and the Opera, it had served Londoners from Inigo Jones to Eliza Doolittle with fruits, vegetables and flowers.

After the appropriate number of feasibility studies and reports, a new market site was selected in 1964 at Nine Elms, a short distance across and along the Thames. The move was full of ineluctable planning logic, even if the first objective of total market

coordination had been lost along the way. London's major produce market was therefore replanned without too much consideration of other London markets' placement and practices. (If you embrace the "kiss of death" theory of large-scale plans, this may even have been a good thing.)

The new and greatly enlarged site would provide plenty of room for the mammoth trailer trucks that were turning Covent Garden's historic streets into a nightmare of congestion. The location included both rail and water facilities, which it was believed would reduce truck traffic. The old market area in the center of London would be released for extremely profitable redevelopment. That redevelopment would then pay for the new market. And, of course, there would be the latest facilities: acres of modern sheds, forklift trucks instead of barrows, color-corrected lighting for the flower hall. A neat set of planning syllogisms.

So what happened? Planning logic — as well as the plan — got stood on its head. The market moved, all right; it was recently installed in its new quarters at Nine Elms. It has parking and 400-yard-long warehouses. It will undoubtedly work as a market because it will have to. But British Rail, beset with economic problems, has refused to date to build the railhead for servicing the market, although the presence of the railroad was one of the prime reasons for site selection, and trains hurtle right through its center without stopping. As a result, the trucks now converge on the populous residential areas of Lambeth and Wandsworth. This is driving the good people of Lambeth and Wandsworth (appropriately) bananas.

The redevelopment plan proposed for the Covent Garden area turned out to be an ambitious casebook of planning horrors. It was recognized as such, not by the planners, but by the people. A rising wave of citizen sophistication and participation aborted the scheme. Enough speculative redevelopment had already taken place in London — often with the planners' conscientiously calculated blessings — to make both the delicate nature of the urban fabric and the destructive results of reordering it ominously clear.

The proposal called for keeping monuments and some historic streets in a really appalling form of tokenism, while the rest was to be bulldozed for a much-argued mix of hotels, convention center, offices and/or what have you. This was all to be serviced by the kind of through roads that planners love to draw on maps. It was a formula guaranteed to eliminate the magic life and quality, human scale and style that had made Covent Garden such a special place for so many centuries.

By pulling out the market, the city of London virtually pulled the plug on the Covent Garden community that had actually been preserved by its messy presence. (Too hard to redevelop.) With the area's less than logical but patently irreplaceable urban values belatedly recognized, and the community protesting, the comprehensive plan was called off. ("Comprehensive" is the key professional word, implying rationally coordinated objectives. Antiplanners react to it with Pavlovian terror.)

This also pulled the plug economically; all the anticipated revenues of land disposition and new building went down the drain. And so did the funds for paying for the new market and the move to Nine Elms. Now the yawning gap left in Covent Garden by the move threatens what was a uniquely creative, colorful and successfully integrated urban entity. The heart is gone. Sterilized museums or artsy-craftsy boutiques are depressing prospects.

Why did each logical step lead to an unexpected and ludicrous result? One

---

In a much scaled-down plan, boutiques have replaced bananas in the market's South Hall, and office workers inhabit warehouses that once held aromatic foods. The upscale renewal took off as a classic case of gentrification. (Greater London Council)

explanation is that there seems to be some vengeful god with a dark sense of humor watching those who attempt to impose intellectualized order on the complex and subtle accretions of urban civilization. Multiple disasters have become the familiar fallout of assiduous tidying up.

Another explanation, supported by an increasingly sensitive and far less sanguine approach to the difficult business of dealing with the urban organism, is that planning has been through the fire and is in a revisionist phase. Experience and empiricism have been the painful teachers, with a notable assist from such critics as Jane Jacobs and the Venturis. Mistakes are bound to be built into the complexities involved, but planners are humbler and more cautious about monkeying with people, places and profits and centuries of urban culture. They have learned a lot.

Still another point of view would have it that planning at best is a kind of necromancy. The omen of absurdity was there in the Covent Garden affair for anyone with an instinct for clairvoyance. Nine Elms had no elms. What clearer sign and signal to all subsequent absurdities? According to *The London Times,* the Central Bureau of Fruit and Vegetable Auctions in the Netherlands has donated nine sapling elms to the completed market. According to observers, they look dead. According to the experts, they are fine. But look what the experts did to Covent Garden.

Skyscraper Asparagus

T HE POSTWAR CROP of highly controversial skyscrapers in London has been almost universally undistinguished — or worse. They stand like lonely stalks of asparagus against the sky.

The reasons that Londoners dislike them have less to do with their conspicuous lack of architectural quality than with their disruption of tradition and the skyline.

London has finally been promised a top-grade skyscraper by one of the world's most celebrated architects, Mies van der Rohe, and the project has become one of the city's most controversial subjects. The proposed building, a distinguished 290-foot office tower, is to be the new headquarters of Lloyds Bank. It will be in the City, the financial district, adjacent to Mansion House, the lord mayor's residence, and close to that fortress of financial and architectural probity, the Bank of England.

The building, to be carried out in collaboration with the English architect Lord Holford, will be one of Mies's characteristically chaste, elegant, meticulously detailed and superbly proportioned sheer shafts, richly finished in bronze and faced with bronze-tinted glass. It is similar to his Seagram Building in New York, done in association with Philip Johnson.

The site, a triangular open plaza to be made by the staged demolition of existing Victorian structures, is bounded by Poultry, Victoria and Queen streets. These structures include the large Mappin and Webb jewelry store and many small shops.

The argument about the Mies building has been entered full tilt by the public, which was invited to comment at an official exhibition of the project, and the press, which does not lack for architecture critics. The debate focuses on the height and style of the tower and the creation of the proposed plaza.

As is not the case in New York, no new office building can go up in any part of London without permission of the appropriate planning body. This is a requirement of an extremely strong set of town and country planning acts that have controlled national development since 1947. The public exhibition is a recent addition to this

Developer Peter Palumbo's 25-year dream of giving London a Mies van der Rohe building (shown in photomontage) died in 1985. Permission to build the tower was denied on grounds of incompatibility with the site and its historic neighbors. (Greater London Council)

planning process meant to ensure public knowledge of and participation in the planning procedure.

Incredibly, 26,000 Londoners attended the exhibition of this project put on by the Corporation of the City of London.

The city's architects and intellectuals have made the point that London's 18th- and 19th-century building achievements are matched by nothing of comparable quality in the 20th century, and they have voted heavily in favor of the Mies tower. The more visceral and traditional public clings to its fear of heights, new materials and change. Lloyds and the architects have submitted their official application to build and are waiting for the city's decision.

The Corporation of the City of London's planners and architects have worked out the project with the bank — the customary procedure for any astute developer intent on getting the city's permission to build. They clearly hope to avoid Royal Fine Art Commission involvement; the commission has been quite consistent in lopping off the tops of buildings too tall for its taste.

Height must be understood as a relative thing in London. Even the word "skyscraper" is a comparative term. Twenty stories seems high in this solid, horizontal city, and tall buildings range from 250 to 400 feet. The popular idea of a tall building is eight stories. Until the end of World War II, no London building had gone higher than 150 feet. That had been the limit since Queen Victoria was displeased by the intrusion on her view of a rapidly rising development called Queen Anne's Mansions and the height lid was clamped on by the first London Building Act of 1894.

As postwar buildings have grown bigger, their architecture has gotten meaner. In this stronghold of tradition, architectural excellence is one tradition that seems to have been forgotten. The new large-scale London construction, with few exceptions, can be listed in two categories.

One is the apogee of the nadir — an implausible but necessary term — of the most completely ordinary and disruptive kind of routine speculative building. It could be called, kindly, international commercial, and it sits with particularly bad grace in London. The other is a British commercial mutant best described as Miami mod, or Pop architecture with an English accent.

Some of London's most conspicuous big buildings are the following:

The British Petroleum Building, 1967, 35 stories and 395 feet high, bordering the Barbican area, near a row of nondescript little Lever Houses along London Wall and three soaring, close-to-400-foot apartment towers in the Barbican area developments; Joseph and F. Milton Cashmore and Partners, architects. An overly familiar, uninspired exercise in the glass curtain wall.

The Shell Building, constructed in the late 1950s, 26 stories and about 350 feet high; Easton and Robertson, Cusdin, Preston and Smith, architects. Lumpen-skyscraper style, this one looms squarely, in every sense of the word, on the horizon, dwarfing the South Bank Arts Center beside it.

The London Hilton, 1963, 28 stories and 328 feet high; Sidney Kaye, architect. This slick commercial tower not only broke Mayfair's uniformly scaled domestic and discreet business gentility but also peered into Buckingham Palace's yard. That was a double affront, to propriety and to urban sensibility.

Centre Point, 1964, 35 stories and 383 feet high, at St. Giles Circus; built by London's mysterious millionaire-developer, Harry Hyams, and R. Seifert and Partners, the city's leading commercial architects. London planners got a road under this building, now useless because of changed traffic patterns. The developer got an immensely valuable site and London got the architectural Jazz Age.

The National Provincial Bank headquarters, 1967, 30 stories and 335 feet high, at Drapers Gardens, near the Stock Exchange. An outstanding Hyams-Seifert speculative, if not architectural, triumph, its flashy commercialism is singularly unsuited to the financial area's substantial, classical style.

The 20-story, 322-foot high Stock Exchange on Throgmorton Street; Llewelyn Davies, Weeks and Partners, architects. This promises to be an overdesigned, precast facade in Concrete Wishful Think, meant to offer a dubious bulky blend with its stone neighbors.

The 23-story speculative building at 20 and 24 Fenchurch Street, also in the financial district. A blatantly average commercial building.

The Commercial Union Assurance Building, 23 stories and 389 feet high, near Leadenhall Street, in the same area; Gollins, Melvin Ward, Architects and Partners. A clearly Mies-inspired tower of considerable, cool style, by far the best of the lot. It belatedly demonstrates the kind of contemporary dignity and presence that London requires and rarely gets in its new construction.

London needs its new Mies building badly. It is going to get the 20th century whether it wants it or not, and the question is how much architectural quality will come with it. The plaza for the building is another matter. One boundary of the proposed triangular site is taken up by a huge and typical structure of the mid-1950s called Bucklersbury House. To deliberately expose the full expanse of Bucklersbury House, which is the epitome of the apogee of the nadir, would be a disaster. Moreover, because of the peculiarly pointless way that Bucklersbury House is set back from the street line, the essential sense of containment for one whole side of the new plaza has already been lost.

Unlike New York, which is a massed, concentrated city, London is a low, scattered city with an even, spreading horizon marked by Christopher Wren's church spires and a large and often lowering sky. Its magnificence is due to the kind of great architecture that can make men seem great and invests their acts with a sense of nobility.

It is not the big buildings that damage this city. It is the big, bad buildings that are a London catastrophe.

London's Second Blitz

'M NOT SO SURE about London's cleaned-up buildings. The process made Paris a milk and honey beauty, but it hasn't worked that way here. Trafalgar Square, for example, has lost the dramatic contrasts of black-and-white stone that were as much a tradition as London fog. Both came from the burning of soft coal, now outlawed. Surprising that pollution should have had such extraordinary aesthetic effects.

In Trafalgar Square all accent and chiaroscuro, all soot and chalky splendor are gone. The buildings are uniformly middlin' cream, flattened out, almost two-dimensional. Without those sweeping sooty strokes and gleaming white highlights emphasizing almost uncannily the architect's intention and the city's *grisaille,* you somehow notice that the National Gallery is not the greatest of buildings, that its colonnades are weak and its domes hatlike and slightly foolish, as if they'd been bought at Herbert Johnson's up the street.

Next to the National Gallery, James Gibbs's laundered St. Martin-in-the-Fields is still splendid, but naked after the bath. In contrast, Gibbs's St. Mary-le-Strand, farther on, as uncommon a little jewel as ever stood on a traffic island, has its exquisite tempieto portico and delicately curved steps still brushed with the light and dark strokes of a painterly patina that's just right. I dread the day they clean it. Still farther east, St. Paul's is scrubbed, but unspoilable.

Trafalgar Square attracts people like Piccadilly. Its bowl-like center, surveyed by

Nelson at the elevated level of St. Simeon Stylites, its fountains and magnificently absurd, overscaled lions always with a complement of youngsters astride them, are a focus for Londoners and tourists. It is quite clear that all grand-scale plazas and grand-scale plaza life are not in Rome or points south. Trafalgar Square has a broad, epic sweep of the human panorama.

All of this activity is girdled by one of the most persistent loop traffic jams in the world. For some reason clear to the traffic people and the Greater London Council planners, you can't get anywhere in the East End without going through here first. It is London's biggest traffic circle. Congeries of tourist buses disgorging at the National Gallery ensure chaos.

But this great space has all the urban vitality and social interchange that planners admire so in theory and always want to order and regulate and clean up in practice. British planners are possessed with ordering and regulating and cleaning up. They are intensely well-meaning, rational and cerebral. Where they have ordered, etc., as in the replanned precincts of St. Paul's, the principles are orthodox and the results are lifeless. Surely there are some lessons to be learned?

London's planners' theories about what to do with tall buildings haven't worked at all. Again, the theory made lovely exposition: Spot the towers across the long, low horizon that is the historic London skyline, as vertical accents for the city's wide-skied horizontality. They stick up, not to coin an expression, like sore thumbs. They are destructive and offensive not just because they are there, but because most of them are bad buildings.

And still the planners and the Royal Fine Art Commission worry about "outlines" and "vistas," as if everyone were viewing the city from surrounding hills. What one actually sees, and what is totally destructive of the substantial excellence that is the city's real hallmark, is at eye level: atrociously ordinary building, appallingly detailed. The grandeur, strength and finesse that have been characteristic of the English architectural mind through all past periods have been replaced by the speculative mentality with buildings to match. This is how the real damage is being done.

The public debate — and it comes with every new tall building — seems to miss this point. It is always in terms of height, with proponents of the new structure forced to sacrifice a few stories as ritual service to St. Paul's and the past. New Zealand House, for example, one of the earlier and better postwar "skyscrapers" just off Trafalgar Square, should have been higher; the drama would have been well placed. It was amputated to ambiguity by aesthetic edict.

Towers are best massed as in Manhattan; they are most effective planned in groups. In London, a lone tower is an architectural and urban obscenity. A Mies masterpiece could backdrop even St. Paul's. No one debates the real issue — the quality of design.

In exasperation, one wonders if the Royal Fine Art Commission has the taste or conviction to turn down a building on design grounds, instead of just viewing from afar. It accepted the city's tallest building, the National Westminster Bank, after niggling about height — a design that I wager would have been laughed out of the planners' councils in New York. Gentlemen, it is time to stop being gentlemen.

Quality is London's basic style and continuity. Every time this quality is ruptured by some massive mediocrity it is like planting insults to Wren, Gibbs, Jones, Nash and Company in the streets. Gresham's law is in high gear; the bad is driving out the good. This time, London is being rebuilt by greed and underachievers.

In London they talk mainly about height and not the real issue — design quality. The solidity, grandeur and finesse of traditional English building are being upstaged by standard speculator construction. (Garth Huxtable)

PRESERVATION OR PERVERSION?

The Impoverished Society

THE FINAL DEFEAT for Pennsylvania Station was handed down by the City Planning Commission in January, and the crash of 90-foot columns will be heard this summer [1963]. What was not heard was the bitter and eloquent opposition at the hearings to the demolition of this New York landmark, and the Planning Commission's explanation of its action.

The explanation needs airing. What few realized, and this made all of the impassioned pleas for the cultural and architectural values of the city fruitless, was that however much the commission might be moved in the area of its civic conscience by such arguments, it was totally without power to act on them. As it pointed out in its report, it is permitted only to pass on the *proposed* use of land, not on its *existing* use, and therefore cannot rule on the value of a building that is already on the site, but only on the nature of its replacement.

The matter would not have come before the commission at all except that a zoning variance was necessary to permit an occupancy in excess of 2,500 persons for the new Madison Square Garden, which will replace Penn Station. The decision rested entirely on whether congestion would be increased by issuing the variance. The joker here, and it is a terrifying one, is that the City Planning Commission was unable to judge a case like Penn Station's on the proper and genuine considerations involved.

What this amounts to is carte blanche for demolition of landmarks. The commission's hands are tied in any interpretation of the public good that rests on evaluation of old versus new or good versus bad. If a giant pizza stand were proposed in an area zoned for such usage, and if studies showed acceptable traffic patterns and building densities, the pizza stand would be "in the public interest," even if the Parthenon itself stood on the chosen site. Not that Penn Station is the Parthenon, but it might just as well be because we can never again afford a nine-acre structure of superbly detailed solid travertine any more than we could build one of solid gold. It is a monument to the lost art of magnificent construction, other values aside.

The tragedy is that our own times not only could not produce such a building but cannot even maintain it, so that its fate is as inevitable as the Planning Commission's decision. An interesting suggestion, like Robert Zion's in the *Journal of the American Institute of Architects,* that the station's great stone vaults could have sheltered a remarkably handsome and appropriate railroad museum and that its adjoining glass and iron shell could have been converted into a public botanical garden becomes a fairy tale in terms of economic realities. It's time we stopped talking about our affluent society. We are an impoverished society. It is a poor society indeed that can't pay for these amenities, that has no money for anything except expressways to rush people out of our dull and deteriorating cities and that treats land values as the highest morality.

An even stranger kind of poverty, that of imagination and ideals, is demonstrated

---

The landmark clocks stood still when Penn Station was trucked, piece by piece, to Jersey landfill. New York's preservation law is one of the strongest in the country, but it was passed two years too late to save the McKim, Mead and White terminal. (Robert Lautman)

by the proposed remodeling of another landmark, the Times Tower, into a modern showcase for the Allied Chemical Corporation. In this case, the old building will not actually be torn down; it will be defaced. But it will be defaced in a morbidly significant way.

When it was designed in 1903 the Times Tower was a blend of progress and romanticism; it stood at the crossroads of the 20th century. Called "a valuable addition to our short list of artistic skyscrapers" by Montgomery Schuyler at the time, it was an anachronistic solution that combined the radical, still new, forward-looking steel frame with a nostalgic, backward-looking, Victorian-picturesque facade of Gothic and Renaissance details in brick and terra cotta.

In what was considered an inspired solution for the city's most important new building on the oddly shaped lot formed by the crossing of Broadway and Seventh Avenue, the architects rather fetchingly inflated Giotto's bell tower in Florence and joined it with the lower office floors in a carefully calculated, but embarrassingly inept, articulation. The result was the building's well-known, and awkward, silhouette. The Times Tower was never a masterpiece; it was ambitious, pedestrian and dull. But it was legitimately conceived for its day, and such buildings, as they embody and preserve historic attitudes and styles, actually improve with age.

The new design is also ambitious, pedestrian and dull, but without the virtue of singularity that marks its predecessor. All exterior detail will be cleaned off and the

Travelers arriving at Penn Station came through gateways of classical grandeur amid glamorous suggestions of the drama of the city and the romance of distant places. (Pennsylvania Railroad)

building "refaced" with a routine, completely faceless contemporary curtain wall. The awkward silhouette, however, will be kept, although it becomes totally meaningless once its *raison d'être* is stripped away. Thus the publicity value of the landmark is retained, while the landmark itself is destroyed.

Surely there could be no more curious confusion of values than this, no clearer evidence of the current emphasis on expedient commercial advantage over all other considerations, no sadder revelation of the architectural standards that prevail today. Anything new is categorically preferred to anything old, no matter how shoddy or undistinguished the new may be. And if the old is wanted occasionally, "reproductions" are preferred to originals, because they are newer and cleaner. It rarely occurs to anyone, as in the case of the 1905 Columbus Tower in San Francisco or the Fidelity Building of the same period, adjoining Charles Center in Baltimore, that an old building can be profitably cleaned, restored and even modernized where necessary for civic enrichment rather than civic loss.

The ultimate curiosity is the willingness, even enthusiasm, of the architectural firms employed by businessmen to wreak the damage; interestingly enough, for the Times Tower, the firm of Voorhees, Walker, Smith, Smith and Haines is successor to the partnership of Eidlitz and MacKenzie, the original designers. Architects' inhumanity to architects surpasses understanding, particularly when the earlier ones are dead. It's a good way to kill off a city, as well.

A Vision of Rome Dies

PENNSYLVANIA STATION SUCCUMBED to progress at the age of 56, after a lingering decline. The building's facade was shorn of its eagles and ornament. The last wall went not with a bang, or a whimper, but to the rustle of real estate stock shares. The passing of Penn Station was more than the end of a landmark. It made the priority of real estate values over preservation conclusively clear. It confirmed the demise of an age of opulent elegance, of conspicuous, magnificent spaces, rich and enduring materials, the monumental civic gesture and extravagant expenditure for aesthetic ends. Obsolescence is not limited to land use and building function in New York.

It was still the Gilded Age in 1910 when the building was completed by McKim, Mead and White, one of the turn-of-the-century's most gilt-edged architectural firms. There was plush in the Pullmans, crisp damask in the diners, silver bud vases on the tables, and the New York–bound traveler debouched into a Roman tepidarium.

Modeled after the warm room of the Baths of Caracalla, the station's concourse was longer than the nave of St. Peter's in Rome. Its vaulted ceilings were 138 feet high, and its grand staircase was 40 feet wide.

The soot-stained travertine of the interiors, reputed to be the first used in this country, was from quarries in Tivoli employed in building the Eternal City. Its mellow, golden cream was used in the Colosseum in the first century A.D. and St. Peter's 15 centuries later. New York could be called the Mortal Metropolis.

Six murals by Jules Guérin, huge topographical maps of Pennsy territory in sky blues, pale browns and yellow, high in the reaches of the massive walls, gradually disappeared under layers of the same soot. Generous deposits turned the exterior Massachusetts granite from warm pink to dingy gray. Now marble pomp has been reduced to rubble; stone to dust.

The proud eagles that guarded Penn Station were grounded by the demolition of New York's version of the Baths of Caracalla. Roman Imperial was replaced by Investment Modern, marble by plastic, civic grandeur by the sporting life. (*New York Times*)

Today there are new symbols for a new age. The modern traveler, fed on frozen flight dinners, enters the city, not in Roman splendor, but through the bowels of a steamlined concrete bird, as at Trans World Airlines's Kennedy International Airport terminal. Classical columns are replaced by catenary curves.

Architects' conceits may change, but businessmen remain the same. Alexander Cassatt, an extremely astute businessman and head of the Pennsylvania Railroad when the station was designed, wanted to build a hotel on the valuable air rights over the terminal.

His architect dissuaded him, arguing that the railroad owed the city a "thoroughly and distinctly monumental gateway."

As Lewis Mumford has observed, "Professional and civic pride won out over cupidity."

It was a shaky victory that lasted only 50 years. A soiled, symbolic gateway has been carted to the scrap heap, and its replacement is the Madison Square Garden sports and entertainment center connected to a 29-story office building. Land values and air rights have pushed the main concourse completely underground. The style is not Roman Imperial, but Investment Modern.

The station's decline began long before demolition. As time passed and grime gathered, life and architecture became noticeably less grand.

The Great Depression made the once-elegant terminal a home for the homeless, its increasing shabbiness and sense of inert time and the stale chill of hopeless winter nights immortalized by William Faulkner when he wrote:

In the rotunda, where the people appeared as small and intent as ants, the smell and sense of snow still lingered, though high now among the steel girders, spent and vitiated and filled with a weary and ceaseless murmuring, like the voices of pilgrims upon the infinite plain, like the voices of all the travelers who have ever passed through. . . .

With the return of prosperity, and the traveler, demolition by commercialization began. Colored ads appeared like blasphemous utterances in the marbled halls; automobiles revolved on turntables; shops and stands were added in jazzy cacophony.

In 1958 a huge, lighted plastic clamshell was hung on wires from the Corinthian columns, hovering over a sawtooth arrangement of new ticket booths. The result, according to Mumford, was sabotage, a "masterpiece of architectural and visual incongruity."

By 1963, when a group of prominent architects and citizens picketed the building to protest the announcement of the decision to demolish, it was hard to realize, with Philip Johnson, "that man can build nobly," in the light of the aesthetic debris.

Functionally, the station was considerably less than noble. The complexity and ambiguity of its train levels and entrances and exits were a constant frustration. Except for its great glass and iron waiting room, it was a better expression of ancient Rome than of 20th-century America.

But its great spaces and superb materials were genuinely noble, in a sense that architecture can no longer afford in cubage costs alone. The new terminal has nine- to 22-foot ceilings, against the original 138, all below grade. And the concept was noble, in a sense that society now tragically undervalues.

In 1906, when the $25 million hole was dug in the old Tenderloin district for the $112 million terminal and landmark, the city's and the railroad's sights were high. Now dreams of urban glory and broken Doric columns lie shattered in the Secaucus Meadows.

The Art of Expediency

T HERE USED TO BE A NEWSPAPER GAME called "What's wrong with this picture?" It was a cartoon in which there were a number of things wrong, from doors without handles and upside-down windows to pictures with mismatched halves hidden in the wallpaper. It was a world of cockeyed domesticity, antimacassared and cozily askew. The game was to find and list all the errors, or deviations from the norm.

What's wrong with this picture? The ruins of Penn Station in the Secaucus Meadows and a new subway entrance in its replacement building are not quite so simple to analyze. To begin with, what they show is the norm, in a world far from cozy and quite askew. They pose disturbing questions and touch problems that go to the core of a culture in which destruction and regeneration, art and nihilism, are becoming indistinguishable. But they say a great deal about how things are, and why, in the world that man is building for himself today.

The picture of what remains of Penn Station in its burial ground in the Secaucus Meadows shows a fragment of a classical figure and shards of columns in a setting of macabre surrealist *vérité*. The subway entrance is part of the vast Madison Square Garden–Penn Station complex.

Superficially, the message is terribly clear. Tossed into the Secaucus graveyard are about 25 centuries of classical culture and the standards of style, elegance and grandeur that it gave to the dreams and constructions of Western man. That turns the Jersey wasteland into a pretty classy dump.

As for the subway entrance, you could say, in abstract, clinical design terms, that there is nothing very much wrong with it at all: clean tilework, acceptable good graphics, a direct, nonflashy solution to a routine functional problem. And yet — it is a singularly grim picture. It speaks volumes on alienation through architecture. Kafka or Sartre never said it better. A single human figure, equally isolated in a crowd, proceeds through the chill, bleak anonymity of the 20th-century transit catacombs (ancient catacombs softened even death with frescoes) in a setting of impersonal, ordinary sterility that could just as well be a clean, functional gas chamber. The human spirit and human environment have reached absolute zero.

The easiest indictment to make is that this is a failure of modern architecture. That we have exchanged caryatids and columns for a mess of functional pottage and that Secaucus is the final resting place of our culture.

It would be simple, and false. It is the nostalgic argument of those who believe that re-creating the appearance of the past will bring back the reality of the past or the values of the past. Nothing could be farther from the truth. It is the kind of reasoning that makes well-intentioned people think it is a good idea, for example, to build Benjamin Latrobe's unrealized 18th-century theater for Richmond now, because all the drawings still exist.

At the least, that is begging the 20th century; at the worst, it is the denial and corruption of creativity in our own time. No number of archeological constructions or caryatids can put that world back together again. There is something terribly pathetic in the self-delusory belief that it can be done.

Today's architecture is the highest dramatic revelation of changes in technology, structure, style and need in a revolutionary age. It is one of the genuine revolutions in our revolution-high times. Its monuments are superb; its potential develops constantly.

What the subway image represents is simply the aesthetics of economics. The results are, as much as possible, vandal proof, dirt proof, extravagance proof and delight proof — a kind of penitentiary style. The aesthetics of economics characterize not only our common commercial construction but also the institutions and public buildings that were once meant to symbolize the shaky nobility of man. The economic standard is as accepted today as the four orders were in Rome.

Penn Station's classical shards made New Jersey's Secaucus Meadows a very classy dump. Reason prevailed in Richmond, however; Latrobe's unbuilt theater remains a paper plan. (Edward Hausner, *New York Times*)

Take, for example, the old and new Jersey City courthouses built side by side as if to deliberately make the point. The old courthouse — a solid, turn-of-the-century Beaux Arts monument of marble, murals and soaring rotunda space — has been in and out of the news in its battle for existence. Its replacement, the new courthouse, says nothing about the majesty of the law (the passion for breaking it right now simply underlines its importance) and a great deal about the society that built it. It says that society is mean and cheap and that it considers excellence a gratuitous commodity.

But the real point is that it is a dead match to Jersey City. This is the kind of city that the aesthetics of economics makes; a tawdry, formless limbo of hamburger joints, discount stores, parking lots, matchbox houses, cheap office buildings, automobile salesrooms, jarring signs and disruptive highway spaghetti. It is the environment of expediency.

Today we have politics that preach destruction and art that acts out destruction; perhaps this is the architecture of destruction. As we said about something else, society gets the cities it deserves. The courthouse only underlines the process.

Curiously, it is not the Establishment or the older generation that sees old buildings in contemporary urban terms. It is the young people, the architects and city-oriented intellectuals who have rejected the Utopian idea of an artificially imposed new order of the last professional generation and who believe in change, complexity, contrast and a multidimensional urban scene. They are not antiquarians. But they are the ones who lead visitors to Victorian monuments, early Chicago skyscrapers, cast-iron buildings in New York, old Texas houses. These are the young professionals who are testing architecture in the shifting values of a world in crisis.

"Values" is a word they avoid, but the commitment to value is there. They are not the values handed down by society or the past. They are often the denial of values as conventionally understood. Realists and futurists, the present generation finds some of its values even in the environment of expediency. Art and life always coexist.

If the wreckage of the 19th century is in the Secaucus Meadows, and the failure of the 20th century is in the landscape of alienation, the promise of the art of building is very much alive. It is not in the individual structure as traditionally designed, but in the relationships of people, land and buildings for life and use — it is in the aesthetic and human ferment that is currently called architecture.

Grand Central Tower Grotesquerie

IN THE CLASSIC VERBAL SHORTHAND by which New Yorkers communicate, the man-in-the-street response to the projected $100 million tower above Grand Central is "Who needs it?"

The Penn Central says it needs it; the English developer Morris Saady says he wants it; and the architect Marcel Breuer says he'll do it. The railroad wants it to help make ends meet, and Saady frankly wants a profitable New York monument.

The Landmarks Commission wishes it would go away quietly, and the City Planning Commission would like to wake up to find that it had dreamed the whole fantastic concept because it can't do a thing about it. The building is completely within the limits of the zoning law and needs no commission-controlled variances or approvals. Therefore, New York may very likely get it.

What the city will get, if it goes ahead, is another Pan Am Building only 221 feet from the first one and at least 150 feet higher. It will get some improved underground circulation and an architectural curiosity that could make a perverse kind of aesthetic and urban history. It would be a monument less to Saady than to the awesome value of New York air rights.

The value of polluted Manhattan air is another curiosity that will go down in history. If the air over Grand Central Terminal were not worth several hundred million dollars in building rights and income over the next 50 years there would be no Grand Central tower project. That solid gold air is there to stay, and if its superheated values continue to rise as anticipated in the coming half century Manhattan could someday replace Fort Knox.

The terminal, whatever its spacious turn-of-the-century graces, would obviously not be there to stay, measuring its land and air utilization in terms of these values, if there were no city landmarks law to protect it. And the law protects only the exterior, not the Grand Concourse.

The railroad understandably is going to persist in finding a way to tap its air rights treasure, landmark or not. The realities of this situation are not going to change. What the situation has produced is a truly remarkable shotgun wedding between sentiment and speculative economics. The result is a colossal modern office building surrealistically astride a mansarded French palace. The trick is pulled off with striking technical élan and much more suaveness than at the Pan Am, but it has inevitably created a grotesquerie. The result is no less grotesque, however, than those midtown real estate values.

Give a grotesquerie to a good architect and you are going to get a better grotesquerie, like a better mousetrap. Breuer has done an excellent job with a

---

A true landmark decision by the U.S. Supreme Court in 1978 spared Grand Central an architectural dagger through its heart and upheld New York's landmarks law, which now protects numerous interiors, including the terminal's Grand Concourse. (Ed Nowak)

The aggressive incompatibility of Breuer's proposals for Grand Central does not diminish with time. The terminal was cleaned up as part of a development deal with Donald Trump involving the remodeling of the old Commodore Hotel. (Marcel Breuer and Associates)

dubious undertaking, which is like saying it would be great if it weren't awful. Even definitions of "awful" vary today, and the awful has its advocates; to some this could be a Pop masterpiece. Icongruity is the essence of Pop art and architecture.

Entrusting such a job to a genuinely creative talent assures that ways and means will be found of doing the impossible or undesirable that would not occur to more humdrum minds. It also guarantees a thoughtful refinement of detail beyond the call of commerce.

The building, though still an oddity, is dazzlingly better than tentative proposals circulated earlier to developers by the railroad's real estate department. This improvement is chiefly in the originality of the structural system that permits the insinuation of the tower's core through the station waiting room for maximum preservation of the old structure.

Inside, the south mezzanine of the concourse would be destroyed and the dramatic shafts of natural light that still stream hazily through the unwashed high south windows would be permanently blocked.

The solution is ingenious, technically daring and very expensive. According to Breuer, going to these costly extremes to save a landmark is a romantic whim that he finds stranger than the architectural results. He would frankly prefer to demolish the terminal.

Assuming that this expensive, unorthodox construction is economically feasible for a speculative building, and Saady does not seem like a man who would risk losing his custom-made shirt, the project still raises serious questions.

There is the question of whether this spectacular construction trick within a building could be carried out without damage to the building itself. Is Breuer's stylistic trademark of cast stone, which he handles with sensitivity and skill, the most appropriate answer here, if there is any appropriate answer at all?

Would more bravura and less Breuer be better? If you are dealing in aesthetic effrontery, why not go all the way with the contrast of a sheer glass, sky-reflecting tower for maximum theatrics? For this is essentially a theatrical architecture of the absurd.

To make his superproject palatable, Saady has used a top architect, and he has taken responsibility for at least the part of public circulation with which his building is involved. Builders who do these things in New York can be counted on slightly more than one thumb. As almost irresistible bait, he has offered to rescue the concourse from its present condition as an aesthetic slum.

More important than any of this, however, is the question of whether the city has anything to say about a project that so critically affects planning and construction in one of Manhattan's most congested, focal areas.

Will these improved underground pedestrian patterns to be contributed to the city by the builder merely dump several thousand more people daily on the dead end of inadequate subway platforms and service? Is the promise of relief from new subway lines in the future enough to justify the solidification of chaos now? At what point, and by what means, can the city control its destiny? In New York only Solomon could know for sure.

Perspective on the City: Three Buildings

SOMETIMES THE BEST EXHIBITIONS are in the most unlikely places. On second thought, sometimes the most unlikely places are the best places for exhibitions. I don't know when I've seen a better architecture show in a more appropriate setting than the one called "Three Buildings," in the City University Graduate Center Mall at 33 West 42nd Street, prepared in collaboration with the New York City Landmarks Preservation Commission.

The show's unique virtue is that its subject matter is only steps, or blocks, away. One leaves the mall — a covered passageway forming the ground floor of the Graduate Center's handsomely recycled building that is a fine urban achievement in its own right — to encounter the buildings themselves. This gives the display an extraordinary dimension.

The "Three Buildings" of the title are the Fifth Avenue Library, just across 42nd Street, and Grand Central Terminal and the Times Tower, due east and west. The first two are designated landmarks; the third is not. The library is safe, the terminal is threatened, and the Times Tower has been changed almost beyond recognition.

All three buildings straddle the 19th and 20th centuries. They are all examples of progressive planning and formal, academic style. And all profoundly affected the character and development of their surroundings. Together, they are responsible to a large degree for the form and content of midtown Manhattan. And they have

Times Tower, version three, a trompe l'oeil view painted on the Crossroads Building by Richard Haas in 1979. This, too, is now gone. The old tower still stands, stripped and refaced. The Times Square project would demolish it. (© Peter Mauss, Richard Haas Inc.)

continued to serve practical and symbolic purposes well into our own time. They are, in fact, much more than buildings; these three are New York icons, touchstones of its identity, generators of function and legend, a part of the city's soul.

The library, started in the 1890s and completed in 1911, soon turned a quiet residential area into a cosmopolitan avenue of commerce and culture. Because the new building incorporated the earlier Astor and Lenox libraries for a larger, central facility — it was a time of consolidation, growth and the grand civic gesture — the library's new president, John Shaw Billings, devised an innovative and functional plan. This grand plan received a grand French classical form when a competition for the building's design was won by two young Beaux Arts—trained architects, John M. Carrère and Thomas Hastings. The murmurous sea of the huge reading room is still sanctuary for scholars and life's gentler failures; its collections are available in great rooms of marble, carved wood and bronze.

Today the building's mellowed classicism, seen from the east, is one of the city's finer vistas. The superbly planned complex of the library and Bryant Park and the set-back, green front — now designated as exterior, interior and landscape landmarks in full and wise application of the law — creates an urban space beyond price. (Try to imagine New York without it.)

There are those, however, who can imagine such things very well. For example, the bankrupt owners of Grand Central Terminal, the Penn Central Railroad. They have succeeded in having the terminal's landmark designation overturned, and the city's appeal is now in the courts.

When the terminal was built, between 1903 and 1913, it too was the result of consolidated growth and a grand civic gesture. The brilliantly functional, intricately related, multilevel plan, with the terminal built over the tracks, was connected by pedestrian routes and "circumferential drives" to the circulation of the area and the large-scale development around the station. It is one of the most stunning achievements in the history of urban design.

Ramps, passageways, subways, shops, services and offices all converge on one of the greatest interior spaces of this or any other city, the Grand Concourse — 125 feet high to its star-studded, once blue, vaulted ceiling. The planning concept, based on electrification of trains, came from a railroad engineer, William J. Wilgus; the design was the result of a competition won by Reed and Stem of Minneapolis; the stylistic grandeur was the contribution of Whitney Warren of the Beaux Arts firm of Warren and Wetmore.

The elegant facade is now black with soot, and the huge arched windows are blind with grime. Ugly leaks in the concourse quietly threaten the structure. But the worst threat is from the Penn Central and the developer. After the show's photographs of the terminal's early splendor, a picture of the proposed commercial tower for the terminal's air rights, designed by Marcel Breuer in the 1960s, is like a slap in the eye. The design shows a waffle-faced slab, obliterating the terminal's facade, supported by giant canted legs from the elevated roadway. The new tower would form one side of a huge sandwich board (the Pan Am Building would be the other side) and together they would squeeze the old building in a brutally arrogant embrace. The grand civic gesture has been replaced by the grim economic gesture.

In fact, this picture and the view of the Times Tower after it was sold to Allied Chemical in the 1960s, and its facade stripped and refaced, are the shockers of the show. The Times Tower was another turn-of-the-century hybrid — 19th-century picturesque in its Gothic detailing by the architectural firm of Eidlitz and MacKenzie, and 20th-century modern in its remarkable, early steel skeleton and underground links to mass transportation. Both the area and the brand new subway station were named Times Square shortly after the building's completion in 1904.

(Can you think of it as Longacre?) Through its special site and eccentric shape and style, the building became part of the city's cultural folklore.

The distinctive character of the old building was replaced by the lowest common denominator of nondesign; if the remodeling had set out to be artless, banal and ordinary, it could not have done a better job. There is a proposal now (the building has been sold again) to reface it with mirror glass, and anything would be an improvement. It cries to be turned into a badly needed center of tourist information and services, as part of a coordinated city plan to revitalize Times Square.

Curiously, even in its mutilated state, the structure's symbolism survives. The illuminated news banner courses around its sides in a gesture to tradition. The ball still drops at midnight on New Year's Eve. In the end, buildings are the survivors, and the barometers, of our world.

Where Did We Go Wrong?

THE FOLLOWING ITEM was not invented by some gifted pixie mentality; it is from *Preservation News,* published by the National Trust for Historic Preservation. The National Trust would not put you on. We quote:

Babe Ruth's birthplace and a few neighboring properties were recently purchased by the city of Baltimore for $1,850. The home of one of baseball's immortals is located on Emory Street, a narrow alley of humble row houses. The Mayor's Committee for the Preservation of Babe Ruth's Birthplace is now debating whether to leave the house at its present location or to move it and the neighboring houses to a site adjoining Memorial Stadium, to be part of the Babe Ruth Plaza. Vandalism in the present neighborhood has prompted the committee to resolve "to restore the house at its present location only if environmental amenities are found to be reasonable." The inaccesibility of Emory Street is also cited as a reason to move the house elsewhere. However, Emory Street is too narrow to move the house intact and dismantling would be the only solution.

It reads exactly as if Lewis Carroll wrote it.

"Leave the house where it is," said the Red Queen. "I can't," said Alice. "It's inaccessible and there's vandalism." "Then get some environmental amenities," said the Red Queen, "and be quick about it." "What are environmental amenities?" asked Alice. "Don't ask foolish questions; just move the house," said the Red Queen. "But the street is too narrow," said Alice. "Nonsense," said the Red Queen, "don't you know anything? Take the house apart and put it back together again. And move the rest of the houses with it." "Poor things," said Alice. "Where to?" "To the Memorial Stadium, naturally," said the Red Queen, "and call it Babe Ruth Plaza." "Couldn't we just leave it?" asked Alice. "If you do," said the Red Queen, "you will have to take out the other houses and put up a sign, 'No Ball Playing Allowed.'" "Mightn't 'Ballplayers Welcome' be better?" said Alice.

Alas, it is not straight out of *Through the Looking-Glass;* it is straight out of life. And if it sounds like parody, that is exactly what much of the preservation movement has become. It is game playing. The game as it is played — by a strict set of rules — is to seal off historic buildings from the contemporary environment in a vacuum of assiduous make-believe.

The process ranges from babes in Babe Ruth–land to the phenomenon of Williamsburg, where the art of scholarly self-delusion reaches the extravagantly ($79 million) sublime. It deals in "cutoff dates," which means ruthlessly destroying anything later than a certain arbitrarily selected year that interferes with the illusion desired, and "restoring back," a horrendous process of faking the chosen period by removing all subsequent accumulations of time and history. The final perversion is "reconstruction," or rebuilding things that no longer exist, and that, if you take the blinders off for a moment, merely means putting up brand-new "old" buildings, which, no matter how carefully researched and how admirable the educational motives, is a contradiction in terms and values that shows how sick the whole thing has become.

"I say the moon is made of green cheese and this is the 18th century," the sponsors of these historical "enclaves" (a favorite euphemism) of the studiously unreal tell us. No matter how you slice it, it is still green cheese, and you can slice it many ways, from Strawbery Banke to Old Sacramento. The point is that the whole idea and purpose of preservation — saving the past because it is part of the living heritage of the present, so that the process of history enriches the city and the environment — has been lost.

The result is a cross between playacting in the name of history (and the lesson being taught is curiously subversive if one still equates education with traditional values of truth and, by extension, morality, or knowing what is true or false) and a museum of period arts. The inevitable conflict set up between the forms of the past and the uses of the present — a conflict denied overtly but carefully and often comically disguised to accommodate the tourist trade — is an abrasive anachronism. It all dead-ends in a head-on clash of new, old and new-made-to-seem-old for which

In a minor preservation triumph, Babe Ruth's birthplace was not moved, but was restored as part of a baseball museum complex. A sense of reality has changed preservation from make-believe to making landmarks useful. (James Kelmartin, Baltimore *News American*)

there is no solution except playing the game harder, increasing the make-believe and the confusions of real and reproduction, not for a living lie, but for something that is a dead lie at best.

The tragedy is that this concept has become so popular that it has almost totally aborted the proper approach to the conservation of our urban heritage. The purpose of preservation is not to "re-create" the past, a laughable impossibility filled with booby traps like the lady in saddle shoes, harlequin glasses and hoop skirt who shattered this observer's first schoolgirl visit to Williamsburg. (No, changing the shoes and glasses wouldn't fix up anything at all; you really couldn't restore the lady back.)

More shattering, on a much later visit, was the lack of information from guides as to what was authentic and what was not, since obviously no distinction was made in their own minds between copies and genuine survivals. Even the survivals have been so smoothed up that the line gets fuzzy. To them, it was all real. Actually, nothing is real except those buildings that have lasted a couple of centuries, gathering a significant patina of changing American culture (stripped, naturally) and the collections of furnishings that are curatorial triumphs, deliciously arranged to simulate someone's personal possessions by a well-researched extension of wishful-think.

It is all art and artifice and the finest green cheese. It is a beautifully hollow stage-set shell, totally removed from the life-force of the society that gave it form and meaning. A little fudging for effect hardly matters. (Please don't write, oh superpatriots, to tell me that I am simultaneously sullying both Williamsburg and the American flag; it is not treason to look art and history in the eye. I value both beyond the call of tourism.)

What preservation is really all about is the retention and active relationship of the buildings of the past to the community's functioning present. You don't erase history to get history; a city's character and quality are a product of continuity. You don't get any of it with "enclaves" in quarantine. What a cut-off date cuts off is any contact with the present at all. In urban terms, preservation is the saving of the essence and style of other eras, through their architecture and urban forms, so that the meaning and flavor of those other times and tastes are incorporated into the mainstream of the city's life. The accumulation is called culture.

In New York the sentiment for preservation is a relatively new thing. The city has never preserved anything. Its nature is to destroy, build and change. New Yorkers are not antiquarians, and that is part of their pride and strength. To be successful in New York, preservation must strike a singular balance with this spirit; even the past must face the future.

The challenge is to make the city's heritage a working part of the dynamic vitality and brutal beauty of this strange and wonderful town. And above all, to make it New York.

Goodbye History, Hello Hamburger

SEE THE 116-YEAR-OLD historic house. See it being knocked down. See the hamburger stand in its place. Pow. America, of thee I sing; sweet land of Burger King.

The house was Mapleside, built solidly of sandstone with the classical graces characteristic of the mid-19th century. It stood in Madison, Wis., until it was bought

The loss of Mapleside for a Burger King headquarters taught Madison, Wis., preservationists that they needed to organize. Today the Madison Trust looks out for the city's landmarks. (Andrew Dahl, State Historical Society of Wisconsin)

and demolished by the hamburger chain, which professed to be ignorant of the building's aesthetic and historical worth. Last-minute attempts by preservationists to raise $100,000 to save it failed. Goodbye history, hello hamburger. From historic home to "home of the whopper" with a swing of the wrecker's ball.

This hamburger stand got an extra onion. It was given as part of the "orchids and onions" awards program of the Capital Community Citizens, a lively environmental action group in Dane County, Wis. The incident was reported in the *Wisconsin Architect* and *Preservation News*. As far as I know, there is no plaque on the hamburger stand.

Usually landmarks are demolished for parking lots. Blacktop without onions. This is one of the most popular sports in cities. Urban renewal has drawn its demolition lines around uncounted (has anyone ever counted?) historic buildings and districts. Waterfronts, Federal survivals, Greek Revival groups, anything that has meaning in terms of the history, style or sense of place of American communities is X-ed out first as the oldest, shabbiest and easiest to demolish.

Within the last few years, as the nature of the losses became distressingly apparent, protests mounted. Federal legislation has been passed to amend original urban renewal law so that historic preservation can be assisted in renewal areas. Local agencies have been backed, pushed and pulled into revision of plans by concerned citizens, with either overt or covert resistance. The struggle goes on, while the historic areas stand and rot, touched with the peculiar blight, stagnation and decay that comes with renewal designation and inaction.

Maybe we need the gags to relieve the despair. But the humor is pretty black.

Consider Newburgh, N.Y., for example. Newburgh is a Hudson River town in every sense: It is a product of the era when the river was celebrated in the arts and its spectacular hillside sites were romanticized by a variety of Victorian styles. Today the city has every kind of blight and problem going, and the renewal it charted for itself wrote "good riddance" across the map to its past. There is a curiously simplistic belief in troubled towns that wiping out a city wipes out its problems. Actually, the bulldozer only pushes them around, while eliminating the city's real assets.

In the midst of its difficulties, Newburgh came up with a gag that made national headlines. Demolition lines in the urban renewal plan, as usual, were drawn around one of the city's best buildings — the Dutch Reformed Church, a prime and elegant Greek Revival structure built in 1835 by Alexander J. Davis — now in the National Register. Right next to it was the line of the rehabilitation area. The rehabilitation area, it was pointed out by the *Times-Herald-Record* in a fine exposé, contained Big Nell's, the city's most notorious brothel. Big Nell's, listed as a single-family house with 16 bedrooms, was eligible for federal fix-up funds and might even get a nice new entrance street at government cost to replace one closed by the urban renewal plan. The church was eligible only for demolition.

There was enough fuss to reprieve the church and close Big Nell's, although the renewal agency, located in a building within sight of both, did some conspicuous foot dragging in remapping. The municipality has been backed, dragged and pushed toward a plan to utilize the landmark constructively. [In recent years, like many other cities and towns, Newburgh has changed course.]

In Hudson, N.Y., the same kind of senseless urban renewal plan claimed the 1837 Greek Revival General Worth Hotel. The Hudson YWCA was willing to take over the building, and the Hudson River Valley Commission, the State Historical Association and the National Trust for Historic Preservation urged that it be saved. But political heads prevailed, and Hudson demolished its National Register property. Ready for the biggest gag of all? Read it in the *Hudson Register-Star:*

"A modern Dairy-Queen Drive-In will be constructed on the site of the historic General Worth Hotel that fell victim to the bulldozers last year. The Common Council in special session voted to sell the site for $1,700. Council President Thomas Quigley said the purchase 'was a step in the right direction to develop downtown Hudson.'"

America the beautiful,
Let me sing of thee;
Burger King and Dairy Queen
From sea to shining sea.

Only the Phony Is Real

COUNTRY MUSIC got to be what it is in Nashville, as everyone knows, and it is equally well known that its temple is the Grand Ole Opry House, a Nashville landmark of considerable historical and aesthetic interest. The building was constructed originally as the Union Gospel Tabernacle in 1892, at a cost of $100,000 contributed by the public and Captain Thomas Green Ryman after his conversion by the Reverend Sam Jones during a persuasive sermon on "mother" or "liquor"; it's not certain which theme did the job.

From 1904, when Captain Ryman died, the building was known as the Ryman Auditorium. During the 1920s and 1930s, it was host to every important dance, opera and theatrical troupe that toured the country. Grand Ole Opry was established in 1925, and after a series of radio studios and smaller theater homes, moved into the Ryman in 1941. The rest, as they say, is history.

Although it was neither an opera house nor a legitimate theater, the Ryman has one of the most star-studded histories of the performing arts in the United States. As architecture, it is a vernacular version of the Ruskinian Gothic — a style with a high casualty rate because its fashionableness in the 19th century is matched only by its unfashionableness now, except with the experts. Taste turns, usually, after an entire era has been destroyed. The building is a unique combination of popular architectural and cultural history. Enough so, in fact, to be listed in the National Register of Historic Places.

Well — and this won't surprise anyone — the Ryman Auditorium is expendable. In one of those glorious cultural confusions of past and present in which only the phony is real, there is a *new* Grand Ole Opry House. It has been constructed in a $26 million amusement, or "theme," park called Opryland 10 miles from Nashville, owned and operated by the National Life and Accident Insurance Company, which includes among its corporate enterprises the Grand Ole Opry. The new Grand Ole Opry House is a modern, $15 million extravaganza containing the country's biggest TV and radio facilities, as befits a multimillion-dollar industry based on simple little country tunes.

National Life was originally politely, but adamantly, against saving the Grand Ole Opry House. This move can probably be attributed to a mixture of architectural ignorance and business astuteness. In response to considerable protest, the execution is now postponed "indefinitely," and the building stands empty. Opryland puts it all together now in one profitable commercial and tourist package. "When these good people come to Opryland and later a National Life agent calls," the company's head

It's not curtains yet for the Grand Ole Opry House, even though guitars have been replaced by tourists. One can still see the Ryman, through a glass wall, silently, of an adjacent new convention center. (Jack E. Boucher, HABS)

man, William C. Weaver, has been quoted in *Business Week* as saying, "they'll have something to talk about. We'll have ways and means of getting people's names and addresses at Opryland. I think it will be a right interesting tie-in."

A good number of people, including the National Trust for Historic Preservation, want to see the Ryman preserved. As usual, the issues are complex. The building is in a deteriorating downtown, and the neighborhood suffers, like many other downtowns, from crime. The house's discomforts are legion, and facilities for modern performances are obviously inadequate. Curved wooden pews and a "Confederate Gallery" and an atmosphere that has become a country music tradition and trademark — featured in TV presentations — are no match for superelectronics. The question of the old building's reuse is problematic, and the most compelling kind of commercial economics raises its familiar head.

"We are trying to keep an open mind," Weaver has said. But National Life has accepted no opposition reports, and it refers to preservation promotion as "agitation." Impatience, even in reply to such authorities as the dean of architectural historians, Henry-Russell Hitchcock, is thinly masked, and arguments against preservation become increasingly oblique and self-justifying. Protest is called a "media event."

In the name of reasonableness, the company has sponsored studies that have come up with the not surprising news that preservation is "economically unfeasible" due to extraordinary costs for rehabilitating the old building. This is par for the course. There is probably no landmark rehabilitation that was not called economically unfeasible before it was successfully done. And a record number have been done in the time that the Ryman has remained closed.

One study was a report by the late Jo Mielziner, who, whatever his accomplishments in the field of stage and theatrical design, was not the most qualified expert on old building renovation and reuse, to put it mildly. Mielziner concluded, comparing apples and oranges in an interesting range of non sequiturs, that because the old tabernacle served drama in a makeshift way and its design and construction are provincial rather than sophisticated, it does not deserve to be saved. The sources he quoted, such as *Antiques* magazine, refuted his inferences.

The experienced architects to call on for proper evaluation, such as Giorgio Cavaglieri, who redid the New York Shakespeare Festival Public Theater from the old Astor Library, the firm of Hardy, Holzman, Pfeiffer, the authors of a National Endowment study on the reuse of old railroad stations, Roger Webb of Architectural Heritage, or Anderson Notter of Boston, who did over the old Boston City Hall, or Hugh Newell Jacobsen, who converted the old Corcoran to the new Renwick Gallery in Washington, have not seen a sign of a beckoning finger. Beyond saying that it will welcome any solution, National Life shows no indication of actually seeking one.

The company says that it is not concerned about competition if the Ryman continues to function. Even with its discomforts and inadequacies, it would probably continue in demand. National Life is modest about Opryland's profitability, but it is a successful national tourist attraction, and it seems odd that there should be such concern, if competition is not the question, about the costs of keeping the Ryman operable. In actual fact, the company has preferred to contribute substantial funds to a new performing arts center rather than to assist the survival of a local cultural heritage. It could probably keep and subsidize the old building if it were interested in community service and public image. It might even benefit from both.

Destroying the Ryman is more than demolishing a touchstone of Nashville's past. Pulling out means abandonment of a neighborhood that needs help, and speeding the death of downtown. That's fine for the kind of redevelopers who wait like vultures to produce sterile new urban pap. But good urban design practice would have suggested long ago that the area should have been renewed in terms of historical rehabilitation and that a most important key was the Ryman and its related economic uses. There is more than one way to kill a neighborhood.

The final indignity is National Life's well-publicized plan to use the bricks and some of the artifacts of the bulldozed Ryman to build — I kid you not — "The Little Church of Opryland" in the new amusement park. That probably takes first prize for the pious misuse of a landmark and the total misunderstanding of the principles of preservation. This travesty has convinced a lot of people that demolition is an O.K. thing. Among them are Billy Graham and Tennessee Ernie Ford, who is reputed to be waiting to sing the first hymn. Well, as I said, in today's world, only the phony is real. Isn't anyone on the side of the angels?

Kicking a Landmark

THEY ARE WORRYING out in Kansas City whether Mammon will claim the Villard Houses, but they're not worrying very much in New York. Mammon is accepted, with air pollution and traffic jams, as the shaper of the environment here, and when one of the city's finest buildings stands on land currently reputed to be worth $400 a square foot, a sad shrug of the shoulders greets the news that the Villard block is up for grabs. No savvy New Yorker would give any odds on the demolition of this landmark for another Madison Avenue office building.

According to Donald L. Hoffmann, worrying in the *Kansas City Star,* New York's Villard House group — six brownstone mansions of the 1880s in the form of a single Italian Renaissance palace between 50th and 51st streets opposite St. Patrick's Cathedral — is one of the few places in the city that makes sense, visually, architecturally and historically.

Hoffmann points out that this solidly and beautifully built edifice, once occupied by Henry Villard, railroad tycoon, and his friends and in recent years the home of the Archdiocese of New York, Random House and the Capital Cities Broadcasting Corporation, ushered in New York's Golden Age. "Precious little of architectural New York can claim that much." It is a qualitative high point of the brief and glamorous period from the 1880s through the turn of the century when America's most notorious overachievers lived grandly (or bankruptly, in Villard's case) in Franco-Italianate chateaux of flamboyant magnificence, superb materials, extravagant detail and sumptuous elegance.

The cut-rate building had not yet been invented. It would not have been tolerated. The architects who built for the barons of steel and rails were men with names like Stanford White and Richard Morris Hunt who had never heard of plastic. It has taken modern corporate taste to produce the cheap monument.

The Villard House block, modeled after the Cancelleria in Rome, is one of the best things the celebrated firm of McKim, Mead and White — purveyors of palaces to 19th-century merchant princes — ever did anywhere and one of the best buildings New York could and can claim, then or now.

No one denies that the quality of the city is eroded and ultimately lost by the destruction of such buildings, of which there are so very few to leaven the ordinary commercial Manhattan mix. Not even Mammon denies it. The bankers and real estate men who have conventionally written off any construction approaching the

A palace built for merchant princes: McKim, Mead and White's Villard Houses have achieved a truce of sorts as grand entrance and elegant public rooms for a luxury hotel, as well as home for architectural and landmark groups. (Museum of the City of New York)

century mark as outmoded and uneconomic have learned to say, "Too bad." That somehow makes it worse. To destroy out of ignorance is one thing; to destroy with understanding of the meaning and consequences of the act is a sordid commentary on the values and morality of men.

All that is different or unusual about the Villard Houses' story are the expressions of polite regret accompanying the routinely ruthless real estate process. Now Mammon ostensibly has a heart. A few tears are shed. Some poignant comments are made about the past. Then the deal is closed and the wreckers move in.

The Villard Houses offer a case history of this more sophisticated method of destruction. First, no one comes right out and says that a landmark is for sale to the highest bidder; the Villard Houses are on the market by innuendo. But all the signs of the process, from abandonment to sale to demolition, are clearly indicated; the movements are as prescribed as a Kabuki dance.

The Archdiocese of New York owns all of the Villard block except the north frontage on Madison Avenue that belongs to Random House. The church rents the 51st Street side to the Capital Cities Broadcasting Corporation.

A year ago, when Bennett Cerf announced that Random House would move its still growing and scattered operations to a new skyscraper on Third Avenue, he made the appropriate remarks of ritual regret. He noted that he and Cardinal Spellman, as co-owners, had preserved the mansions and did not want to see them go. Then he opened the door just a little crack to the cold wind of inevitability — the whole process of destruction depends on the doctrine of inevitability — by saying that the buildings would probably be razed when he and the cardinal were dead.

At about that time, when, overtly, no one was selling at all but Random House had clearly cast the die, one of the city's better-known real estate men approached an equally well-known architect to work on commercial development of the block. Real estate men are not given to throwing their money away. He obviously considered it a realistic investment. The architect, who has built many of the city's blockbusters, but who has a strong professional admiration for the Villard Houses, refused the job.

Now Cardinal Spellman is dead, and Random House, on its way to conglomerate status after purchase by RCA, has moved out. In the accepted pattern of "inevitability," Cerf's protestations have shifted slightly. They take the form of a reluctant admission. "We will probably sell," he says. "It's too valuable to keep." No sane conglomerate is going to maintain a landmark. These poor little companies with their backs against the wall know where to find the butter for their bread.

The new Cardinal, Terence J. Cooke, has made no direct statement of intent. His secretary, Monsignor James Rigney, has indicated a shift of an equal number of degrees in the way the wind is blowing. He says that it would be a shame to sell, "but with all our schools and responsibilities, at some point we would have to wonder whether we are justified in keeping property as valuable as this." He has opened the door a bit farther; yes, the church might sell if the price is right.

The price is obviously going to be right at some time. There is no more prime piece of property in New York. The ritual of "inevitability" goes on as the land value goes up. Capital Cities, which has an eight-year lease, has been receiving steady calls from real estate brokers offering to buy the lease for substantial sums. "We do not want to move," a Capital spokesman says. "We'll do anything we can to preserve the building."

But the process continues inexorably. The feelers are out, the offers are being made, the principals are expressing regretful reluctance, and at some point the purchase will be consummated and the announcement made. Things will not be slowed down by the fact that although hearings have been held on official landmark designation for the block, that designation is still pending by the Landmarks Commission. [Designation was made after this article appeared.]

There are several questions to be raised now before the sellers weep all the way to the bank. They concern the church position as leader, upholder and protector of community standards and of those values that have traditionally been called spiritual, beyond Mammon. In New York the temptations of the flesh have long been supplanted by the temptations of money. With its tax-exempt status it can even be argued that the church has an obligation to resist Mammon in the interest of the city's irreplaceable public heritage, or public good. Its human commitments are incontrovertible. But that is not the only kind of community responsibility a religious institution carries.

Still, its real estate people tend to think and operate like real estate people anywhere. The merchants of cities form a watertight society. If land values ever got too high to keep the Sistine Chapel they would, of course, remove the frescoes first.

The sale of the Villard Houses is not the inevitability that the real estate fraternity makes it out to be. The church can keep and use them, as it has in the past. A prestige tenant can be found for the Random House quarters — certainly not impossible for that prime office site — with the help of the parent corporation, the church, the city and its Landmarks Commission and the business community.

It is easier and more profitable, of course, to sell. But it is a serious step to convert the dignity and beauty of the city and its dwindling heritage into cash, even for philanthropic purposes. All New York will be poorer on the profits made.

A WAY HAS BEEN FOUND to save New York's landmark Villard Houses on Madison Avenue, behind St. Patrick's Cathedral, but the solution is dreadful. That could also be known as the New York paradox: Anything worth doing is worth doing wrong.

There is the further paradox that everyone involved seems to want to do what is right. The owner of the beautiful McKim, Mead and White brownstone palazzo of the 1880s is the Archdiocese of New York. Since the Archdiocese ceased to use the major part of the building and Random House moved out of the north wing — the U-shaped Renaissance palace is actually a group of townhouses around a court — most of the building has been empty. The Archdiocese is maintaining the structures, which were designated as a landmark in 1968, at considerable expense and sacrifice. Because this must surely be ranked as one of the most elegant and tempting parcels of prime midtown Manhattan real estate, the church's dilemma is obvious.

The developer, Harry Helmsley, wants to build a new, 52-story hotel and office building behind the Villard Houses, utilizing the full development potential of the zoning of both the tower and the landmark sites. In fact, it appears that he will ask for still more size from the Board of Standards and Appeals. The Archdiocese has executed a lease on all of this property with Helmsley, as the Palace Hotel Inc., and the lease contains a number of safeguards for the treatment of the landmark buildings. But the actual design of the new building and the use and treatment of the old ones are Helmsley's baby.

The architect, Richard Roth, Jr., of Emery Roth and Sons, has worked hard to keep the landmark and give the developer what he wants. What he wants is very clearly a standard, money-making commercial formula that works — nothing risky or offbeat. It isn't so much that creative or imaginative or sensitive design is being minimized or downgraded; it is simply that this sort of design is totally outlawed by the formula from the start. Helmsley apparently also wants a close resemblance to his Park Lane Hotel on Central Park South, one of those (formula) travertine-clad, arcade-topped, easy exercises in spurious elegance.

The landmarks law requires the Landmarks Preservation Commission's approval for any alteration of a designated exterior. The alterations being requested are the demolition of the last 25 feet of a 1909 extension, including a small porch and tower and changes in the roofline in that area. Although there will be serious changes in parts of the interior — the rooms of the central section, which includes the handsome Gold Room, will be gutted for a hotel entrance — the commission has no control over this part of the plan because the interiors have never been designated. The interiors of the wings, one of which is particularly fine, would remain intact.

The plan is to "connect" the soaring hotel-office tower to the Villard Houses through the central section so that pedestrians could enter the hotel through the existing Madison Avenue court and arcade. A new hotel lobby directly behind that entrance would take the place of the demolished interiors. The Villard front would thus become a false front, because the rest of the central section would simply have a wall put behind it, making it a kind of stage-drop for the hotel. (Fire requirements make this necessary, says the architect, but others dispute it.) The wings, untouched but also unutilized, are to be rented out for whatever suitable tenants or purposes present themselves.

The ultimate paradox is that there is absolutely no attempt or pretense or inclination to use the potential of the beautifully crafted and detailed landmark structure in any way. It is a death-dealing rather than life-giving "solution." The superb Belle Epoque interiors — virtually all that are left in New York of the Vanderbilt-Astor era — are written off as so many square feet of "hard to use" space. The "solution" is total rejection. If the architect and developer had set out to kick the landmark in the pants, they could not have done a better job. (In fairness to the architect, his office is supposedly replete with earlier schemes that studied reuse, but evidently period salons are considered incompatible with commercial hotel functions.)

The net result is that the landmark is left standing, subject to finding tenants to use it. This is exactly the same problem that exists now, without the disfigurements of the new construction. Moreover, the threat still remains that if no tenants materialize and the building continues to be a financial burden to owner and lessee, application for demolition can be made under the landmarks law. In spite of the economic benefits that would accrue to owner and developer in this dubious scheme, the Villard Houses aren't home safe yet.

It is particularly hard to accept that continued hazard when the proposed design is so patently insensitive. The travertine-striped tower, with its cliché arches, is hokily pretentious. A Certificate of Appropriateness for this proposal would be a travesty.

Has everyone forgotten the lessons of the Racquet and Tennis Club (also McKim, Mead and White) and Lever House and the Seagram Building on Park Avenue? The modern, Miesian aesthetic can be handled with basic elegance, to the benefit of both kinds of classicism. New York has a right to a design of skill and sophistication as well as appropriateness; these are the qualities of the city's style.

Add the further paradox of the promise of the interior designer to furnish "in the spirit of" the rejected, original interiors, and travesty becomes a bad joke. These interiors are mint examples of the genuine grandeur that today's hotels imitate so tackily in a pastiche of token vulgarities. It takes no effort to conjure up a vision of the depressing ersatz version that will be substituted for the real thing. It is another "successful" formula.

The reasoning behind this debacle is not mysterious. It is the reasoning of the investment mind, of which Helmsley has one of the best in the business. The investment mind does things in the guaranteed no-risk investment way. It deals exclusively in how to produce the stock commercial product, no matter what peripheral interferences may intrude. A landmark is an interference. This approach does not accept unconventional challenges, even when they would deliver dividends in beauty and ambience. This could be an internationally notable hotel of cosmopolitan grace rather than a model stamped out by computer. All the ingenuity expended has been devoted to avoiding capitalizing on the landmark or sullying the formula in any way.

Ordinarily, the Landmarks Commission could engage in a little design negotiation for improvement. But the lawyer for the Archdiocese politely reminded the commissioners at a public hearing that if they didn't like the proposal, the Archdiocese might just begin to think about the Lutheran Church decision, which permits a nonprofit institution to demolish a landmark.

The question might be asked whether an outstandingly successful investor might not, just once, think in terms of the extraordinary instead of the ordinary. It is, after all, Helmsley's city, too.

WHEN THE FIRST VERSION of the Villard Houses-hotel project appeared, the Landmarks Commission sent it back to the developer for revisions. Although the interiors had never been designated, the commission also made the suggestion among others that a way be found to save the Gold Room.

The threatened Gold Room is part of the south wing, which was remodeled by McKim, Mead and White for Whitelaw Reid in the 1890s. Brendan Gill, who is engaged in a study of Stanford White, calls this "the richest and handsomest set of

The hotel tower behind the houses is a facade-saving solution, struggled over by developer, architect and civic groups. In the regilded Gold Room, musicians on the balcony play for teatime guests below. (Howard J. Rubenstein Associates)

rooms then in existence in New York and perhaps in the entire country." Nobody except Helmsley and Roth seems to feel that the Gold Room is expendable. The double-height, barrel-vaulted, balconied room with its La Farge murals, sculptured wall detail and generous gold leaf is unequivocally magnificent; it is also the last of its kind in New York. It is easy to visualize the kind of impoverished design that will replace it. The decorating clichés of the modern American hotel are vacuous, pretentious and immutable.

In fact, it is hard to figure out what anyone did in the four months between the first and second versions submitted to the Landmarks Commission. The later proposal had a new and less offensive tower, but it was far worse along the side streets, with corny, overscaled arches in fake brownstone to "match" the Renaissance Villard facades, and the Gold Room was still scheduled for demolition. By any measure except computerized investment design, the results were a wretched failure.

The New York Chapter of the American Institute of Architects, after a visit to the Roth office for a full presentation, wrote a letter of protest to the Landmarks Commission. The chapter's representatives were struck by the lack of evidence that the problem of the Gold Room had been studied with anything approaching interest or adequacy. Repeated inquiries to both the architect and the developer's representative brought the curious response that, because the Villard Houses and the hotel plan have different floor levels, no way can be found to incorporate any of the historic interiors.

Any architect worth his salt knows that this is not an insoluble problem unless someone wants it to be insoluble. Nor does the matter of protecting the old while building the new provide insurmountable costs or engineering considerations. After examining plans and elevations, the AIA suggested solutions. "How often," the

A Florentine setting of ducal richness with murals by John La Farge, stained glass and magnificent gold leaf, the Gold Room was saved and incorporated into the hotel at the last minute. (Howard J. Rubenstein Associates)

architects asked, "can a new structure so easily annex so distinguished a space?"

The impression that remains is that the hotel "experts" find it easier to stick relentlessly with stock solutions than to make the different levels work within their economic game plan. There is a brand of hotel gnomes, turned out by hotel schools, supplied with a stock of cheap clichés that is currently defacing the country, and the world. The fact that the hotel might gain immeasurably in beauty, quality and individuality, and that this could ultimately be an economic asset, is apparently beyond the comprehension or concern of anyone involved.

It might be noted in passing that the Plaza found weddings so lucrative it hired a specialist to promote them, and the Gold Room and south wing could make a superb wedding suite. As for business and style, when the Plaza returned its conventionally junked-up Green Tulip restaurant to something resembling its original Edwardian Room authenticity, business shot up.

A proposal worked out by the New York Landmarks Conservancy with the architect to make the Gold Room a bar was disapproved by Helmsley. The objection quoted was that you can walk down into a bar, but not up going out of it. No one has succeeded in eliciting a better answer. At least one observer of this exercise in Marx Brothers logic has offered an escalator.

In sum, what is being given to New York in return for a hugely profitable investment package is a particularly slick bit of real estate sleight-of-hand. It is fool-the-eye preservation. The owner of the Villard Houses, the Archdiocese of New York, and the developer could, of course, simply tear the buildings down due to deficiencies in the landmarks law, and that is their not-so-concealed trump card. But they know that this would be an extremely unpopular act that would make public villains of them both. Nor does the church deserve this, after years of conscientious, costly care of a landmark that has become a financial burden.

But this way of "keeping" the landmark, which involves some physical destruction as well as the destruction of its integrity, and no real investment in its continued life, is a spurious tradeoff. The city is being conned. For the Villard Houses are more than immensely superior architecture. Located in the city's functional and fashionable heart, they are pivotal to New York's quality and style.

One comes reluctantly to some inevitable conclusions. The architect, whatever his restrictions, has done an appallingly bad job. The developer, whatever his intentions, is inflexibly wedded to standards that he evidently will not relinquish or modify for values that he fails to perceive. He will not, in short, invest money or creativity in a superior solution. No calculations are being made in terms of image, quality and civic pride — which can also be a profitable formula. It is, alas, a state of mind. And it determines the state of the city, as well.

T HE LATEST CHAPTER of the Villard Houses saga — which seemed so hopeless a cause to so many — is something to delight the believers and confound the cynics. In the curious way of New York, which wheels, deals and compromises while managing to sustain some extraordinary standards in the face of impossible odds, a solution is being found.

After going back to the drawing board twice, against steady, mounting public pressure, the developer, Harry Helmsley, the architect, Richard Roth, and the owner, the Archdiocese of New York, working cooperatively with the Landmarks Conservancy, a private group, the Landmarks Preservation Commission, a municipal agency, the American Institute of Architects and other professional organizations, as well as the local community board, wrought wonders. They huffed and they puffed and came up with substantial improvements in interior and exterior plans. To

Helmsley, for these extra efforts, we raise a glass. (Considering that the 1886 Villard Houses are mint Age of Elegance McKim, Mead and White, it has to be vintage champagne.)

It has now been found that it is possible to keep and use the Gold Room as one of the hotel's public spaces. The library of this wing will also be incorporated. Currently, talks are continuing to see if some of the better north wing interiors can be converted to shops, rather than gutting them, as planned, to make new stores.

On the exterior of the new hotel-office tower, which will also contain apartments, the earlier cheesy design gimmicks have been dropped for a more suitable and straightforward approach. The project has gained considerably in distinction and merit, all of which can only accrue to the builder's advantage. There are possible tenants for the remaining, unused Villard interiors that the project abandoned — a still inexplicable waste of a unique resource of quality and style. But that peculiar oversight can be lived with; these rooms will stay intact, and their desirability and rental prospects will increase with the new construction.

The problem that is still to be solved is the disturbing one of the variance needed to build the tower. The developer is asking for an increase in bulk based on arithmetic that some question, a matter that usually goes before the Board of Standards and Appeals. In this case, however, the impact is so much greater and the issues so much broader than a narrow interpretation of the zoning rules would allow, and the "tradeoff" for the city involves so many critical and delicately balanced elements, from the economic boost of the new construction to appropriate preservation devices and surrounding traffic patterns, that the Archdiocese has elected to take the appeal to the City Planning Commission instead. Jurisdictionally and philosophically, this seems like the right thing to do.

In any case, it will be up to the city to decide what is proper and acceptable, probably, again, through negotiation. There is now the promise of a solution that all can abide by, that will keep the Villard Houses from demolition and in the mainstream of New York life. And that's not bad — for New York or anywhere.

The scenario relies less on heroes and villains than on increasing awareness of urban quality, a tough, sophisticated faith and sustained cooperative effort. In the end, all of the participants are the good guys. Who can ask for anything more?

Putting the Brakes on "Progress"

WHAT IS POPULARLY CALLED PROGRESS in American cities is being stopped dead in its tracks, or at least slowed to a stumbling halt in London. A strong government brake is being put on the private development of large parts of this city's older, historic areas, the kind of places and names that form a litany of London history, character and beauty for both residents and visitors.

Under the Civic Amenities Act of 1967, a law just getting into high gear, these districts can be protected as officially designated conservation areas. Town-planning authorities, who select such conservation areas, have the right either to prohibit any demolition or new construction or to control development through necessary permissions to owners and builders.

At least eight sizable London districts have been designated as conservation areas this year. They are the major parts of Mayfair, Belgravia, Bloomsbury and St. John's Wood and sections of Paddington, Pimlico, Bayswater and Kensington. A considerable part of Soho is in the process of designation now, and areas around St.

James's Place, Whitehall, Parliament and Westminster Abbey are being studied for future action.

There is no lack of desire among private developers in London to rip down whole blocks for profitable new commercial construction. The urge is international and the need of such construction is real. It is not so easy to do in London as in New York, because permission is needed from the planning authorities here for the erection of office buildings.

But as blankly depressing expanses of new office blocks have gone up in older neighborhoods, bringing with them a singular absence of style, Londoners have become angrily aware of the erosion of the past. Even with planning control, damage to the traditional fabric of the city is obvious.

The building that blew the fuse was the London Hilton's 28-story tower, which disrupted the traditional, five-story serenity of Mayfair in 1963. In the subsequent five years there has been strong public agitation for preservation of the traditional character of special neighborhoods. Popular sentiment against change is backed by the more sophisticated preservation objectives of the Georgian and Victorian societies, which enjoy a remarkable status in Britain.

Under the leadership of Duncan Sandys, a minister of housing from 1954 to 1957, the Civic Amenities Act was passed last year, adding powers of architecture and

Although the United States has protected local historic districts since 1931, English conservation areas such as Queen Anne's Gate in London's Westminster have used innovative ideas that are models for preservation on this side of the Atlantic. (Greater London Council)

urban preservation to the functions of the earlier town-planning acts.

The process of creating conservation areas is not so high-handed as it sounds. There are inquiries and hearings, and appeal of decisions is possible. Under the town and country planning acts enacted since 1947, British cities have immense planning powers and responsibilities. Land is bought and sold privately and freely. But permission for commercial development of the land, which has been generally programmed under London's master plan now being revised, must be gotten from the planning authorities. The process is frequently a compromise between the desires of the developers willing to invest hard cash and the objectives of the city.

According to Frank West, director of architecture and planning for the city of Westminster, which has been designating many of London's conservation areas, the individual whose property rights are involved cannot bring suit as he does in the United States. The matter is dealt with in London administratively, not judicially, by public inquiry, with decisions made by the local planning authorities. These decisions can be appealed to the minister of housing, whose action is final. The matter does not go through the courts at all.

There are some forms of "permitted" development that do not require government approval, such as the extension of an existing building by 10 percent of it floor space.

Under the town and country planning acts, compensation must be paid to the owner who is refused his development rights. These sums come from grants made to planning bodies by the government.

The key word to the whole preservation program is the word "amenities" in the Civic Amenities Act. As understood in England, amenities in this sense covers a civilized concept of total environmental excellence. The term refers to the complete effect of an attractive or pleasurable neighborhood, or of an architecturally or historically important district, whether its quality is due to planning or design excellence, the stamp of the past or simply a style of life.

What is involved in these criteria is what is sacrificed constantly in New York while preservationists look for "landmarks"; as they look, a street or neighborhood of less than landmark importance, but of genuine urban value, is demolished. These losses are irreparable in any city. The British concept of preservation as an act that is involved with, not isolated from, the living fabric of the city leaves United States policy on the subject in the dark ages.

London's examples of conservation areas range from a striking series of uniform, cool, clean, white streetscapes built at the same time and offering a single style, such as Belgravia's 19th-century classical facades, to the frequently architecturally undistinguished but lively streets of Soho that house equally irreplaceable small shops and services. The amenity standard can include just the grouping of compatible buildings around one of London's lush, green squares.

Under the Civic Amenities Act a builder can no longer get approval for such development as the kind of undistinguished, unrelated apartment houses with a luxury label at the south end of Montagu Square in the Portman Estates, which have shattered the square's period style and scale.

Under the act a new Soho hotel is being designed with the collaboration of the developer and his architect and the architects and planners of the city of Westminster, not only to avoid disruption of existing character, but also to reinforce the area's intimate, diversified humanity.

The big hurdle ahead will be financial compensation to those whose development plans are refused. It will take Solomon-like decisions to determine where the funds are to be given in the light of the massive designation of conservation areas, and on those decisions historic London will stand or fall.

THE FALL AND RISE OF PUBLIC BUILDINGS

Whatever Happened to the Majesty of the Law?

THE CLOSING OF THE DOORS of the stately Hudson County Courthouse in Jersey City echoed across the country. When the judges left their marble-colonnaded courtrooms for functional modern quarters in a new building next door, they made a move that is being made, in one form or another, in almost every American city. They left behind offices of solid oak and mahogany and moved into quarters lined with flexwood.

If county officials had deliberately placed the two buildings in their side-by-side position as an object lesson in the decline and fall of American public architecture, they could not have provided a better example. Never has the deterioration of style and standards been so clearly and devastatingly illustrated.

By the pragmatic measurement of population growth and space needs, the old courthouse is obsolete. No one wants a circa 1910, solid Maine granite building with bronze lanterns and crestings and a four-story interior rotunda of pearl-gray marble, opening through all floors to a central dome, embellished by murals and surrounded by polished Italian green marble Ionic columns.

Its style was "Modern Renaissance," or Beaux Arts, after the name of the school in France where this country's best architects studied at the beginning of the century. Its designer was Hugh Roberts. The buildings that the French-trained American architects came back to create, the critic and historian Fiske Kimball has pointed out, "had no equal anywhere at the time, not even in France itself."

Offered the courthouse for one dollar as a substitute for the dingy Victorian structure that has the singular historical asset of having housed the Hague administration, Jersey City Mayor Thomas Whelan replied that the city is in the process of "liquidating its unnecessary real estate holdings" and "has no need for a ceremonial city hall."

There is no nonsense about ceremony in the new Hudson County Administration and Courthouse Building that now stands next to the old one. It has been characterized as "strictly functional from top to bottom and from inside out." As the architects of the new building have observed, the rotunda of the old building is "waste space."

Instead of a soaring central well, in which the entire space of the building is caught and celebrated, there is a low-ceilinged, businesslike lobby with flat granite panel walls, standard fluorescent lighting and a terrazzo floor. Instead of four figures of Fame in the dome's pendentives by the celebrated turn-of-the-century painter Edwin Blashfield and murals of New Jersey history by Howard Pyle, Frank D. Millet and Charles Y. Turner, there is a free-form squiggle in the ordinary terrazzo floor. Plastic plants and recorded music take care of aesthetic and spiritual requirements.

Above ground level, walls are penitentiary-style structural glazed tile. In the old building there are marble railings and wainscoting for every floor and corridor. The

---

"Waste space" in Jersey City: a Beaux Arts marble rotunda topped by murals of a fleeting Fame. Abandoned, and then restored, the majestic building is once again being used for trials and court space. (Barton Silverman, *New York Times*)

A casebook study in the decline and fall of public architecture, the old and new Hudson County courthouses sit side by side, Modern Renaissance overtaken by Catalog Commercial. (Meyer Liebowitz, *New York Times*)

new walls are plaster. The new courtrooms are finished with paper-thin wood applied like wallpaper. There is vestigial marble trim. So much for the dignity of the institutions of man.

On the outside of the new building a stolid attachment of Indiana limestone makes a mock-formal entrance to a Catalog Commercial structure with a middling green, stock glass curtain wall. It is ornamented with a handy paste-on figure of Justice.

Exterior extruded aluminum mullion sections holding the glass panels have unsightly connections; glass and window sash come together sloppily and abruptly; joints are casual inside and out. The side porte-cochere that now faces a weedy field surrounding the old courthouse, with the obvious purpose of serving future parking on its site, rests on lumpily welded and painted steel beams. The noted architect Mies van der Rohe once said of building, "God is in the details." Not in New Jersey.

The materials and details of the old courthouse, according to contemporary accounts, were selected for "grace, dignity and vigor." It was meant to convey "a feeling of strength and durability." Descriptions of the new building focus on the splendors of its heating, cooling and elevator systems.

Built in two stages, from 1954 to 1957 and from 1963 to 1966, the new building cost $14 million. Its architects are Comparetto and Kenny of Jersey City. The old courthouse, one-third the size, was built for $3 million. Its replacement price would be untouchable. An additional $3 million, estimated by the architects of the new building as the cost of necessary mechanical renovation, would bring the old structure to $6 million.

Today its classical splendor looms as some surrealist vision in the peculiarly formless aesthetic squalor that is the Jersey City environment. Its gray grandeur stands aloof on a grassy rise. Children slide down the dry slope on corrugated cardboard.

The story is repeated over and over. The landmark invites the wreckers and its replacement reduces the public image to the lowest possible common denominator. Architecture has ceased to be a noble art. But it only serves man's needs and aspirations, and men and cities get what they deserve.

An Exercise in Cultural Shock

A FUNNY THING HAPPENED on the way to the new Custom House at the World Trade Center in New York. Public architecture declined and fell. The new Custom House is a seven-story glass and aluminum structure flanking the Trade Center's north tower, part of the complex designed by Minoru Yamasaki and Associates and Emery Roth and Sons. These offices, a vast functional improvement over the old ones at Bowling Green, consist of efficient, standardized accommodations with eight-foot ceilings and all the latest mechanical comforts and conveniences. They are also a paradigm of modern commercial and institutional blandness.

Sixty-six years ago at Bowling Green, the Customs Service moved into its brand new Custom House designed by Cass Gilbert. The now-abandoned 1907 Beaux Arts structure is a fruitcake of Maine granite, a potpourri of marbles, a congeries of statuary. Comparison of the two buildings staggers the sensibilities. It is an exercise in cultural shock.

The new building, like the whole Trade Center group including the giant twin towers, is an exercise in design by reduction. This is partly the fault of the times, when soaring construction costs have led to cheapness by choice and necessity, and partly because of current building systems, which substitute the technology of the neutral grid for solid, stylish stonework.

But it is more the fault of the architect, who has trivialized the inherent drama of modern engineering and nullified the legitimate and powerful aesthetic that is its true effect. He has succeeded in making some of the biggest buildings in the world ordinary and inconsequential.

Those who recognized the glories of the "surplus" Custom House battled for its retention and reuse. Several museum plans were on and off; now, plans for federal offices threaten the fine (and designated) interior. (Irving Underhill, Museum of the City of New York)

The old building is richly embellished with references to the sea. Its stone and wood carvings, bronze grilles and plaster trim flaunt dolphins, seashells, ships' prows, rudders, masts and waves. What is not nautical is classical. Forty giant columns girdle the building's substantial and ornate stone mass.

There are masks of Mercury, and the keystones of the elaborately framed windows are carved heads of the races of mankind. Tennessee marble figures in the attic represent the ancient and modern seafaring powers. Four heroic statues of the continents by Daniel Chester French flank the front.

None of this splendor could be moved to the new building's functional, featureless grid, or to the stock spaces inside. The Customs Service could not take along the huge, hanging bronze lanterns of the soaring grand hall with its rose, green and cream marbles, nor could the Service remove the Reginald Marsh murals from the vast, gloomy Rotunda that depict the stages of arrival of a ship in port, painted as a public works project 30 years after the building was completed. (Marsh received something like $90 a month for the job.)

But some things have been moved, among these a few of the 1907 and earlier Custom House furnishings. Before Bowling Green, the Service occupied the even more distinguished Greek Revival Merchants' Exchange by Isaiah Rogers on Wall Street. In 1906 Montgomery Schuyler, the great architecture critic, temporized about the new building because he liked the old one better. But he called the new one a valuable civic possession and a work of distinction.

What went along to the Trade Center are massive classical bookcases from the Merchants' Exchange, chairs from the original United States Appraiser's office that preceded the Customs Court, portraits of 16 former collectors including Chester A. Arthur and Theodore Roosevelt, miscellaneous tables and sofas and some wall sconces.

Their former setting was the office of Fred R. Boyett, regional commissioner, with barrel-vaulted ceiling, fluted pilasters and mahogany doors. Their present setting is a "ceremonial" room in the new building, but the eight-foot, two-inch ceiling — a whole two inches higher than the office ceilings — will not hold the crystal chandelier that hangs close to that length at the center of the old room; it would touch the floor.

Boyett's old office was part of a main-floor suite designed for the secretary of state. It includes a coffered and gilded ceiling with shell and ribbon motifs, a carved wooden screen and walls, and an unused, monumental stone fireplace. The new building has photolabs, projection and screening rooms, and a pistol range.

"Our people will be more comfortable," Boyett says. "We needed room for training programs and employee cafeterias and lounges that we don't have now. The Customs operation has grown and changed radically."

"But if I'd had my say 10 years ago," Boyett adds, "we'd have used the $36 million we're putting into the new building to remodel the old one to make it the show Custom House of the world."

The cost in 1907 was $5.13 million for the building and $2.5 million for the land. It stands where the original Fort Amsterdam was built, probably the most historic spot in Lower Manhattan.

Not long ago it would have been looked on only as one of the city's most valuable pieces of real estate and its scraps and shards would have been carted off to Secaucus like Penn Station in favor of a profitable, die-stamped tower. Today there is a general concern for preservation. It is an officially designated New York landmark and a listed building in the National Register.

There are serious legal and financial problems ahead. But the sponsors point out that other cities have already shown the way. Customs may have entered the age of jet transport and the functional aesthetic, but you just can't get those dolphins, masts, rudders, sails, winged wheels and cosmic connotations of commercial glory anymore.

Can Anyone Use a Nice Anglo-Italianate Symbol of Graft?

THE DEMOLITION OF New York's notorious Tweed Courthouse, behind City Hall, never announced publicly, was an early priority of the Beame administration. It has not yet taken place because of the city's financial crisis. There is no money for anything, good or bad. But the decision was simply the ultimate extension of the conventional wisdom that the building is nothing but a shoddy piece of graft.

In recent years, there have been notable changes in attitude. There are scholars in the fields of art, history and culture who see the Tweed Courthouse, with the blinders of distaste removed, both as a legitimate New York landmark on every level from architectural to political history, and as a handsome period building as well. It is, they point out, an outstanding example of the 19th-century Anglo-Italian style, extremely rare in New York — a genre introduced by Barry's Reform Club in London. Its basic aesthetic is unaffected by Tweed's celebrated gravy train.

Traditionally, guides and commentaries have vied in its denunciation. Built as the county courthouse in 1861-72, and used later as the city court, its "Corinthian architecture of Massachusetts white marble" is described in King's Guide of 1893 as a "basis of the $10-million peculations of Tweed and his associates." The later WPA guide ups the peculations to $12 million and calls it "one of the gigantic steals in the city's history."

All true. And the remarkable thing is that it is still a substantial and stylish building, its impressive interiors defaced with layers of mud-colored municipal paint. Its marble, carved wood, massive construction and profligate space could not be bought today for any rational figure. Sic transit the building art. Old Tweed would have the last laugh, in perfect, and appropriately cynical, New York style.

In spite of its obvious qualifications, the courthouse is not a designated landmark. It has been so universally repudiated for its unsavory associations that it is probably too hot a political potato for the Landmarks Commission to handle.

Ironically, public building recycling no longer represents some fantasy of the future; these reused structures are the resounding preservation successes of the present.

There are the examples of the Old Boston City Hall; historic federal building transfers across the country; the State, War and Navy Building, now the Old Executive Office Building, and the old Court of Claims, now the Renwick Gallery, in Washington; and the Public Theater in the old Astor Library and the Public Library in the Jefferson Market Courthouse, in New York — just to scratch the national list. They were all scheduled to be demolished. And they all surpass any possible replacement in style and character, with no loss in serviceability.

It was therefore suggested to the administration that the Tweed Courthouse should not be torn down without a feasibility study of the possibilities of remodeling it for the Executive Office Annex. And so, former Deputy Mayor Cavanagh, a kind, agreeable and reasonable man, whose face crumples in sad disbelief when the courthouse is praised (he displays a letter stigmatizing it as a symbol of corruption on which grounds heaven help a few Roman arches and Renaissance palazzi), ordered the study.

It was made for the task force by the Municipal Services Administration, and to

Reprieved more than once for lack of money (a fortuitous method of preservation), the Tweed Courthouse in New York is finally a designated landmark; it awaits reclamation for city offices. (Museum of the City of New York)

nobody's surprise it called for demolition. It called for it "in any event." In any event apparently meant in spite of the fact that the study found that it would be cheaper to restore and remodel the old building than to construct a new one (with a few caveats about reduced life span and maintenance costs) and that the space available would reasonably equal the space required. Former Parks Administrator Edwin Weisl, Jr., was the lone task force dissenter.

It is a report (unreleased, but relentlessly bootlegged) remarkable for its lack of preservation expertise, total absence of design visualization and failure to acknowledge any qualities except those of the most pragmatic structural immediacy. It really goes back to square one.

That old chestnut "waste space" keeps rearing its head, with the triumphant observation that a new building could have the same square footage and be one-third the size of the old one. The aesthetic rationale is that anything on that site should be smaller than City Hall — an argument with no validity at all, since everything turns on relationships, not measurements. The same goes for that other old chestnut, "matching style."

Two out-of-town experts have already come, been cordially received and delivered unwanted advice. Roger Webb, of Architectural Heritage, Inc., which turned the similar Old Boston City Hall into prime new offices, found the conversion both practical and reasonable. Hugh Newell Jacobsen, restorer of the Renwick, said he would stake his reputation on the building's soundness and the desirability of remodeling and reuse, meeting all building code and operational requirements.

But the specter that keeps rising is not Boss Tweed; it is the "colonial revival" replacement the administration wants and the aesthetic and urban damage it will do to City Hall. Honest graft is to be preferred to pseudohistorical hypocrisy. Next to that Early Howard Johnson vision, the Tweed Courthouse looks like a rose.

Anatomy of a Failure

THERE IS NO ART AS impermanent as architecture. All that solid brick and stone mean nothing. Concrete is as evanescent as air. The monuments of our civilization stand, usually, on negotiable real estate; their value goes down as land value goes up.

A typical statement of a major corporation, made with the utmost candor and the conviction of the true faith, is that land value is the whole bit. It would be irrelevant if the site contained the Kingdom of God. The logic and the mathematics are immutable.

In addition to land economics, buildings, even great ones, become obsolete. Their functions and technology date. They reach a point of comparative inefficiency, and inefficiency today is both a financial and a mortal sin.

It would be so simple if art also became obsolete. But a building that may no longer work well or pay its way may still be a superb creative and cultural achievement. It may be the irreproducible record of the art and ideals of a master or an age. Its concept, craft, materials and details may be irreplaceable at any price (yes, some things are without price and that puts them at a distinct disadvantage), and therein lies the conflict and dilemma of preservation.

Frank Lloyd Wright's Imperial Hotel in Tokyo was an extraordinary record of the coordinated architectural and decorative arts of a single period, carried out in 1,009 days of on-site work by one of the great architects of all time. Fifty years later it was obsolete by current standards, as land use and as an operating hotel. It took less than four months to demolish what took four years and an astronomical, for that time, $4.75 million to build.

What is the point in writing about it now? Does it have any more than the grisly fascination of postmortem? Actually, it is a terrifyingly revealing chronicle of some of the preservation problems of our time. It could be called the anatomy of failure.

The wrecking ball swung from 8 a.m. to midnight from November 15 until almost the day that ground was broken, with appropriate Shinto rites, for a new, 17-story, $55 million, 1,000-room hotel, on February 28, 1968.

Furnishings, including some of the famous Wright-designed fittings, were rushed without notice to a Nagoya department store and sold as second-hand goods. It all went in 45 minutes, cheap; Wright's peacock chairs sold for a dollar. Almost everything else, with classic Japanese neatness and efficiency, was baled, wrapped or tied in piles of copper (cornices, lighting fixtures), wood (grilles, trim) or whatever, and sold as scrap. The heavier rubble made landfill. Some carved stone was saved; examples will go to the State University at Buffalo, where Wright's Martin House of 1904 is being restored.

As a result of desperate preservation efforts that read like a bad script, part of a central section of the building may be re-erected in the Meiji Village 15 miles north of Nagoya. This is a 128-acre outdoor museum of 18 reconstructed buildings of the period from 1868 to 1912. (This equivocal triumph hung fire for awhile because the Wright building was too late in date, but it was finally accepted.) Even that gesture is contingent on raising funds.

For once, everyone had been well alerted by the press, beginning with Tokyo newspapers in March of last year. After some initial difficulty in getting interested persons together, the Committee for the Preservation of the Imperial Hotel was organized and met in July. In October Mrs. Wright arrived on the scene, as head of the American branch of the committee. She was followed by a stream of visitors who came with everything but money.

Even as late as November, the committee's pitch was for retaining the whole structure on its site. In November the Architectural Institute of Japan supported the cause with a report and resolutions also urging *in situ* preservation.

No one had spoken officially to the hotel management, which was understandably skittish. A meeting was finally arranged in November through the Ministry of Education's National Committee for Protection of Important Cultural Properties. Imperial President Tetsuzo Inumaru was adamant. The hotel was coming down. The committee proposed an alternative: move the whole structure to another site. Estimates were over $4 million. The committee was given until January 15 to arrange to move at least part of the building; after that date demolition would be completed.

The timetable, of course, was impossible. So were the economics. Less than $10,000 had been raised internationally by the committee. Even the cost of saving 97 carved stone samples came to $135,000, or about $1,350 for each piece, and the committee could not cover that.

The first failure, therefore, was one of objectives. At too late a date, totally unrealistic goals were being pursued. A hard look should have been taken at the facts of the situation and a feasible plan established. Some of the vast rambling building's interiors with their remarkable architectural and sculptural details and furnishings — the peacock alleys, parts of public spaces — might have lent themselves to selective preservation. Under the pressures of time and money, this was the only sensible procedure.

There was a failure of communication, as well. Japanese bureaucracy is rigid; different government agencies that controlled land or museums or other possible

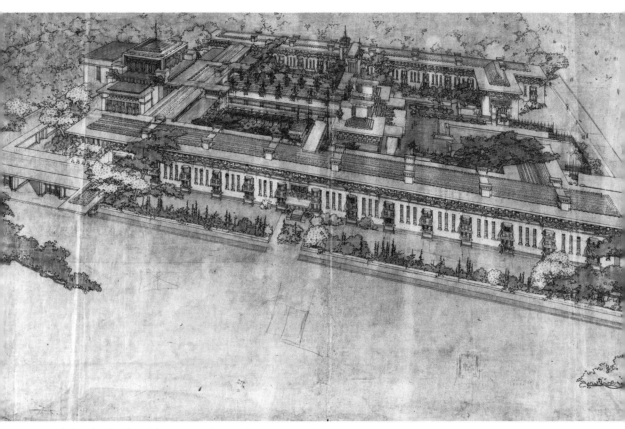

A Frank Lloyd Wright masterpiece, Tokyo's Imperial Hotel, exists solely in memory, except for fragments and a partial section rebuilt at Japan's own Disneyland-like Meiji Village. (© 1962 The Frank Lloyd Wright Foundation)

aids simply did not negotiate. Moreover, as Professor Bunji Kobayashi, an architect closely involved in the preservation effort, points out, bureaucrats control the government tightly and "the voice of the intellectual community is seldom heeded. Some government figures feel that they lose face if they follow such outside voices."

There were also procedural failures. As the deadline approached, the committee found that it did not have the legal status to accept donations beyond small gifts. It was helpless either to take over the building or move it to another site, even if time or money had made either more than the wildest dream.

But the most tragic failure is of the whole American art and cultural establishment. It seems incredible that not a single foundation, not a single major museum, not a single large university, not a single cultural institution or agency, not a single philanthropist saw the opportunity to select and preserve one part of one major spatial element, with its crafts and accessories, of one of the major works in American art history.

It was an unparalleled opportunity. While museums squabbled over acquiring the not-quite-prime glories of the Temple of Dendur and grants were given for still more theoretical studies, all were blind to the chance to add a meaningful part of a work of American creative genius, by one of the masters of the modern movement, to an American collection, at a moment in time when it could have been plucked for posterity. In the final analysis, the worst failure of all was the total absence of vision and value judgment where it should have existed, a serious and shameful indictment of our most illustrious institutions.

Anatomy of a Success

THERE IS A GHOST in the New York Shakespeare Festival Public Theater at 425 Lafayette Street in New York, a most un-Shakespearean ghost with the unlikely name of Austin L. Sands. Sands was a 19th-century New York merchant and insurance man. As reported by the diarist George Templeton Strong, "old Sands' spook" appeared to Joseph Cogswell, director of the Astor Library, now Joseph Papp's New York Shakespeare Festival Public Theater, three times in 1860.

By rights, Sands and Cogswell should have been present at the opening of Papp's theater. This opening was a very special occasion. It marked the transformation of the old Astor Library into the new home of the Shakespeare Festival — the first structure saved and remodeled for reuse under the New York landmarks law.

The merits of Papp's plays and the technical qualities of the theater are the drama critic's responsibility. But as architectural preservation — that combination of civilized sentiment and historical sensibility that makes cities rich and real and has nothing to do with real estate values that make cities rich and sterile — the new theater is a heart-warming hit.

In the Astor Library's former main hall, a handsome, 50-foot-high, skylit chamber with a two-tiered row of classical cast-iron colonnades built in 1851 and scheduled for demolition in 1965, there is now one of the most delightful small theaters in New York.

(House seats, Mr. Papp, for John Jacob Astor, who left $400,000 in his will to construct the original building on then-fashionable Lafayette Street, for William B. Astor, who added the south section in 1859, and the later John Jacob Astor, who built the north wing in 1881.)

The theater seats 299, not counting ghosts, and cost $445,000, roughly the same price as the original building. "We were going to have an 800-seat theater," Papp says, "but we got to love that room. We were showing everyone that room and then we were showing the plans that destroyed the room and we decided against it."

Under the landmarks law, the exterior of a landmark building must be preserved, but there are no restrictions on interior remodeling.

Program credits should read architecture by Giorgio Cavaglieri; mechanical engineer, Nicola Ginzburg; structural engineer, James Hufnagle; contractor, Yorke Construction Company; theater designer, Ming Cho Lee; theater lighting, Martin Aronstein; acoustical consultant, Christopher Jaffe.

In what is now called the Florence Sutro Anspacher Theater, steeply ranged red velvet seats lead down on three sides of the virtually intact main hall to a floor-level stage. Cream-white Victorian balustrades and columns with leafy cast-capitals have been restored and picked out in real gold leaf. "A quality decision," Papp explains. "The building kept forcing us into quality decisions." (Sorry to add one more crack to the tiresome total about Lincoln Center, but most of the gold leaf there is fake.)

The old skylights in the gently curved ceiling have been cleaned and lit softly from behind. Red velvet curtains draw on motorized tracks backing the second-level colonnades.

On the fourth side of the room, behind the stage, two of the classical columns have been stripped down to their iron shafts and made part of a supporting structure for lights, sound baffles and a second-story catwalk.

All this "working equipment" is left bare and painted a deliberately contrasting black: modern structural "brutalism" played against genteel Victorian propriety. It is a theatrical exercise in the aesthetics of contrast, and it works. The theater has beauty and charm. It says a lot, in succinct architectural terms, of change and continuity in slightly more than a century — one of the most fascinating centuries in the history of

The successful adaptation of New York's Astor Library as the Shakespeare Festival Public Theater continues over the years in a fine relationship between drama and architecture that enriches the city's cultural life. (George Cserna)

the adventure called civilization. Why does New York continue to throw it away?

During that century, visiting celebrities toured the Astor Library as one of the city's chief cultural attractions and found its skylit halls "bright as a house of glass." The building closed at sundown because it had no artificial light. Sands came later.

The book collections, according to a guide of the period, did not contain "all the treasures of the British Museum and the Bibliothèque Nationale," but, it added sanguinely, "that fact is not easily discovered." It scarcely matters now. The 200,000 books are scattered to other library branches, and the thousands of refugees are gone who passed through the building's halls from 1920 to 1965, when it served as headquarters for HIAS, the Hebrew Immigrant Aid Society.

What remains is the continuum called culture, the mixture of past and present, of art, history and humanity, of creative experiment and monumental elegance, that brings people to cities like lemmings to the sea. The strong survive and add to the urban heritage; the weak disappear forever into Uris buildings.

In January 1966, just after the Shakespeare Theater had arranged to purchase the Astor Library from an apartment house developer who had bought it from HIAS, with the 18-month-old Landmarks Commission as intermediary, this writer stood in the bone-cracking chill of the deserted and grimy north hall. There is nothing colder than death, and a dead landmark is no exception.

For $2,535 the north hall has been given fresh paint, gold curtains and new life. Some $61,490 will turn it into a fully rehabilitated rehearsal and recital hall. The almost identical south hall, still grimy, is a shop for sets. Both are acoustically excellent, spatially extravagant period gems, unreproducible now, with the same skylit ceilings and double-tiered rows of classical colonnades as the new theater in the central hall.

In the partly refurbished lobby, brick arches at the rear are left pointedly bare. That will be $71,590 more. Below, carved out of solid masonry piers and arches, is the shell of a second 299-seat theater, shored up by wooden scaffolding while it waits for funds. With structural steel needed, it will cost $784,713. Approximately $1 million of an estimated total of $3 million has been spent; one year of a three-year restoration job is complete.

Outside, the solid brick and brownstone structure is untouched. It has been called "Italianate," "Byzantine," "Rundbogenstil" and "German Renaissance" by 113 years of scholars, admirers and detractors. Call it anything, but call it a success.

Culture Is as Culture Does

AFTER 50 YEARS OF LIFE and 20 years of death the great Adler and Sullivan Auditorium in Chicago is back in business again. Orchestra Hall, also in Chicago, was beautifully spruced up for its 68th birthday. In St. Louis a 1925 movie palace has been successfully transformed into Powell Symphony Hall, complete with handsome bar from New York's demolished Metropolitan Opera House.

In New York a few years ago, Carnegie Hall was rescued from the developers and refurbished. A lot of musicians would still rather play there than in the new, acoustically and aesthetically controversial Philharmonic Hall that almost sealed its doom. In Brooklyn the Academy of Music is being quietly restored to its original turn-of-the-century elegance.

Sentimentalism? Hardly. This is no more than a practical coming of cultural age, a belated recognition that fine old buildings frequently offer the most for the money in an assortment of values, including cost, and above all, that new cultural centers do not a culture make. It indicates the dawning of certain sensibilities, perspectives and standards without which arts programs are mockeries of everything the arts stand for.

The last decade has seen city after city rush pell-mell into the promotion of great gobs of cultural real estate. It has seen a few good new theaters and a lot of bad ones, temples to bourgeois muses with all the panache of suburban shopping centers. The practice has been to treat the arts in chamber of commerce, rather than in creative, terms. That is just as tragic as it sounds.

The trend toward preservation is significant not only because it is saving and restoring some superior buildings that are testimonials to the creative achievements of other times, but also because it is bucking the conventional wisdom of the conventional power structure that provides the backing for conventional cultural centers to do it.

That wisdom, as it comes true-blue from the hearts and minds of real estate dealers and investment bankers, is that you don't keep old buildings; they are obsolete. Anything new is better than anything old and anything big is better than anything small and if a few cultural values are lost along the way it is not too large a

"To honor Louis Sullivan for the original design of this building would be superfluous," said an AIA awards jury about the revival of the Auditorium Theater; "the restoration itself is the homage paid to him." (Richard Nickel)

price to pay. In addition, the new, big buildings must be all in one place so they will show. They'll not only serve the arts, they'll improve the surrounding property values. Build now, and fill them later.

At the same time, tear down the past, rip out cultural roots, erase tradition, rub out the architectural evidence that the arts flowered earlier in our cities and enriched them and that this enrichment *is* culture. Substitute a safe and sanitary status symbol for the loss. Put up the shiny mediocrities of the present and demolish the shabby masterpieces of the past. That is the ironic other side of the "cultural explosion" coin. In drama, and in life, irony and tragedy go hand in hand.

Chicago's Auditorium is such a masterpiece. With its glowing, golden ambience, its soaring arches and superstage from which whispers can be heard in the peanut gallery, it became a legend in its own time. One of the great 19th-century works of Louis Sullivan and Dankmar Adler and an anchor point of modern architectural history, it has been an acknowledged model of acoustical and aesthetic excellence. (Interestingly, it is a hard theater to "mike" today, and many modern performers, untrained in balance and projection and reliant on technical mixing of sound, find it hard to function in a near-perfect house.)

Until October 1967, the last performance at the Auditorium was of *Hellzapoppin'* in 1941, and the last use of the great stage was for USO bowling alleys during the war. Closed after that, it settled into decay for the next 20 years. Falling plaster filled the hall, and the golden ceiling was partly ruined by broken roof drains.

Last fall the Auditorium reopened, not quite in its old glory, but close to it. The splendors of the house were traced in the eight-candlepower glory of carbon filament light bulbs of the same kind used in 1889 when the theater, and electricity, were new. Their gentle brilliance picked out restored arches, balcony curves, frescoed lunettes, stenciled traceries and plaster friezes in warm gilt and umber.

The story of the Auditorium's death and resurrection is another of life's little cultural ironies.

In 1904 the Chicago Symphony moved to the new, smaller Orchestra Hall. In 1929 the Chicago Opera pulled out for Samuel Insull's opera house on Wacker Drive. A 4,237-seat house, minus symphony and opera, was hard to fill, then and now. But the Auditorium was never meant to be profitable; that was why Adler and Sullivan encased it in a hotel and office structure to carry it commercially, and this did work for a while. Then only the Auditorium's formidable granite walls kept it from being torn down.

In 1957 the building was acquired and the commercial parts used by Roosevelt University. In 1960 the university created the Auditorium Theater Council, a legal act that made it possible to turn the theater over to a private group for restoration and operation. The council was headed by Mrs. John V. Spachner, whose lifelong dream it had been to bring the Auditorium back to life.

It took seven years, against all kinds of odds, to do the job. It had to be done on a hard cash, pay-as-you-go basis, because the council, in order to protect the university, its trustees and council members from liabilities due to loans, contracts or theater operation, is prohibited legally from spending anything except money actually in hand. This is a continuing impediment.

Fund raising ran into trouble immediately when it was announced that the new McCormick Place convention hall would include a 5,000-seat theater. When it was built, it turned out to be an acoustical dud, and the whole thing subsequently burned down. But the biggest blow came in 1962, with the feasibility study of the council's architectural consultants, Skidmore, Owings and Merrill. For a fee of $50,000 they told the group that it would cost $4.25 million to restore the building and that it was structurally unsound.

Another Chicago architect and Auditorium buff, Harry Weese, who has also refurbished Orchestra Hall, was certain that the building was solid. He wrote to the council, offering to help without charge, and his answer was his appointment as head of the building committee. The final answer, with theater and engineering consultants George Izenour and Fred N. Severud, using valuable information in the SOM study and historical research by Crombie Taylor, is a sound, functioning house for just over $2 million. It raises a healthy skepticism about other it-can't-be-done preservation studies.

Pay as you go has left some gaps. Originally, almost every inch of flat wall was covered with Sullivan's characteristic laced, gold stencil ornament, and the luster of the house is considerably dimmer without it. Mechanical features are incomplete. But the work will go on.

In New York the same kind of thing is being achieved without fanfare at the Brooklyn Academy of Music. A quasi-public institution, it is being restored over a 10-year period by a team of young architects, MacFadyen and Knowles, with city money, under Parks Department aegis.

We have never had greater technical means or expertise to make our landmarks bloom. The question is no longer whether we can bring old theaters back to new brilliance but whether we can fill them when they're done. As with the new centers, that will be the acid cultural test.

Coming of Architectural Age

T EN YEARS AGO, the two square blocks of solid sandstone, granite, brick and marble built and rebuilt as the Patent Office by Robert Mills, William Elliot, Edward Clark and others from 1836 through the 1880s, a monument in the noblest of Washington's classical styles, were scheduled to be pulverized and replaced by blacktop. To a lot of people, particularly parking lot operators, blacktop is the most beautiful thing in the world.

Ten years ago, the choice between landmark preservation and parking was made almost automatically in favor of the latter, and the ghosts of monuments past occupy parking lots in every American city. But the Old Patent Office cheated fate. Today it houses the Smithsonian Institution's National Collection of Fine Arts and the National Portrait Gallery.

In 1958 the Old Patent Office was given to the Smithsonian Institution. Six years and $6 million after conversion to a museum began, give or take a few unhappy Government Issue design details, the orphan Smithsonian art collection has acquired a stunning home, its first since the collection's founding in 1846.

To architectural historians, the building is a fine example of 19th-century style from Greek Revival to Victorian Renaissance. To management experts, whose pragmatism is usually matched only by their spiritual poverty, the name of the style is Waste Space.

Corridors, used as galleries, average 17 feet wide and 17 feet high. Where cool abstractions now hang, beds for the wounded and dying were improvised on the marble floors after Antietam and Bull Run.

The Lincoln Gallery, named for its use as the promenade for Lincoln's second inaugural ball, is approximately 60 by 300 feet and has 64 white marble columns and pilasters rising in cathedral-like groined vaults.

The present library, three stories high, elaborately balconied, colonnaded and

Slated to be pulverized for parking, Robert Mills's Patent Office was refitted, instead, as the newly renamed National Museum of American Art and National Portrait Gallery. The building's dignity survives a discordant and inappropriate mall. (Jack E. Boucher, HABS)

skylit, is sumptuously Victorian; the kind of waste space (*vide* also the high-rising, marble-clad, mural-decorated rotundas of old courthouses and city halls) that makes men at least seem noble.

The building had been unbelievably abused. The great spaces were cut up into small federal offices. One-eighth of an inch of government green paint had to come off those marble columns. The Granite Gallery, now used for sculpture, has heavy, square, gray granite columns and architraves that support solid brick barrel vaults, rediscovered in the paint-removing process.

The graceful stairs had elevators rammed in the stairwells. Marble floors were all but destroyed by partitions and electrical and heating conduits.

In the restoration and conversion, the government almost ruined the building again. As the federal agency in charge of construction, the General Services Administration had the job of turning the Old Patent Office into a museum for the Smithsonian. Most of its work has had to be undone by the museum administration and its architectural consultant, Bayard Underwood.

The GSA knows how to build the world's most banal office buildings. It has cornered the market on all of the ugliest standard features made anywhere, and no matter what architect designs the buildings it constructs in any city of the country, the G.I. equipment appears and covers them like a slow ooze. The thought of its warehouses is numbing.

As work proceeded on the new museum, office clocks were suddenly and mysteriously smacked into the center of 60-foot exhibition walls. Fire hoses, alarms

A three-story skylit and balustraded library and granite-colonnaded picture galleries serve their new uses in the Patent Office with handsome Greek Revival and Victorian style. (Smithsonian Institution)

and air grilles were dotted about like Pop art in prime exhibition spaces. Standard anemostats for the air conditioning appeared like tin platters as the focal point where the handsome groined ceiling vaults meet.

But what should really be preserved in some branch of the Smithsonian (they were removed as rapidly as possible) is the all-purpose monster of a museum ceiling fixture devised by the GSA that runs on by the mile embroidered with endless outlets for plugging in the worst of everything ever designed for museum use. Its greatest feature was instant and total interior sabotage.

The new museum, therefore, is virtually a rescue operation. The clocks were pulled out and safety equipment moved when possible. Fluorescent fixtures by the yard have been replaced by curved lighting tracks that follow the line of the vaulted ceilings to hold a variety of incandescent spots. Considering the building's conversion history, the majority of the struggles between archeology and adaptation to modern use have been resolved successfully.

Until recently, mere magnificence was no reason for keeping an old landmark around. The Smithsonian has not only brought this prime Robert Mills building back to life (he was also the architect of the Treasury Building and the Washington Monument) but has also undertaken the restoration of James Renwick's original Corcoran Gallery, the old Court of Claims, on Pennsylvania Avenue.

This may not be a preservation avalanche, but in government circles, where change comes like treacle and culture is often equally sticky, it is an indication that the United States is coming of architectural age.

Victoriana Lives

VICTORIAN TASTE is still as exotic and unfathomable to most Americans as the puberty rites of far-off tribes, but the Smithsonian Institution's Renwick Gallery, a restored 19th-century structure, is a noble preservation success. In a classic struggle for survival, it is nice to report that the good guys have won.

Formerly the Court of Claims, and originally the first Corcoran Gallery, the building was scheduled for demolition in 1958, when shards of disintegrating ornament threatened passersby and the kindest word in a congressional bill of particulars calling for its demolition was firetrap.

One hundred years earlier, the red brick and sandstone structure, commissioned in 1858 by William W. Corcoran, the banker and art patron, and built 1859-61 at Pennsylvania Avenue and 17th Street, burst on classical Washington like an ornate Technicolor pastry. It was the city's most avant-garde expression of the arts.

Today it is a $2.8 million restoration miracle, an example of the civilized reuse of the past to enrich and inform the present, and the nation's official showcase for the arts of design.

Between, it was sold to the government when Corcoran built his new gallery in 1897, stripped, partitioned, thrown to the judges and the pigeons, and abandoned to the General Services Administration and general decay.

Demolition of the building was to be part of a gigantic renewal booboo that would have gutted Lafayette Square and its environs of art, charm and history. In place of the old court and Federal houses there were to be matched marble mastodons.

Under the Kennedy administration, the plan was scrapped, and architect John Carl Warnecke began the restoration and rebuilding of Lafayette Square and the rescue of the old structure. In the Johnson administration, it was given to the Smithsonian. In 1969 Hugh Newell Jacobsen, the Washington architect, took on the completion of the interior.

The refurbished building, which will be used for public functions as well as providing display for American design, crafts and decorative arts, is named for its distinguished 19th-century architect, James Renwick, Jr. Renwick also designed the Smithsonian's first building, the turreted proto-Disney structure on the Mall.

Renwick's design for Corcoran was in the latest French taste, modeled after Lefuel's addition to the Louvre in Paris under Napoleon III, known stylistically in this country as Second Empire. It was complete with monograms and portraits of Corcoran in friezes and cartouches. Humility hadn't yet been invented for the rich.

Corcoran sat out the war in Paris with his gallery unfinished and his money in gold bars, and did not open the building until 1871.

What the visiting awestruck public saw then was a giant staircase leading to the main picture gallery, which contained Corcoran's choicest paintings, hung in tiers on a plum-colored wall. They rose to a 24-foot-high cornice, below an elaborately decorated ceiling that soared to a 38-foot-high skylight. A "modern" continuous gas fixture circled the room.

Below the paintings the effect was more spartan: a wood dado, wood floor and benches, and a projecting brass rail protecting the wall. Opposite was the Octagon Room, designed for the most notorious art object of its day, Hiram Powers's titillating naiad, the Greek Slave.

Today the visitor climbs the stairs to the Grand Salon, and lo, there are many of the original paintings, borrowed from the Corcoran collection, "tiered" on plain walls.

The ornate ceiling is gone. The dado, wood-grained in the 19th-century fashion, has been rebuilt. The magnificent room — this is actually a small building of great spaces — is now furnished with velvet island settees topped by gigantic urns from the Philadelphia Centennial Exposition of 1876, a pair of 10-foot eagle commodes from New York's Metropolitan Museum that obviously needed a 95-by-42-foot home, and an assortment of chairs from the Smithsonian collections.

It is all, of course, a "tasteful" reconstruction. It does not pretend to "accuracy" or "facsimile" status. Ninety percent of the woodwork and almost all of the detail was gone. The $2.8 million question was how to "restore" a building that was meant, by Renwick, to have white marble with white china-gloss trim inside and was never carried out that way, served as a warehouse for uniforms during the Civil War, was completely redone in the gravy-stain-and-ormolu taste of the 1870s before it opened and was subjected to creeping GSA green and toilets tucked in corners for the next 55 years.

You do it, in Jacobsen's words, "by getting it back to the spirit of Renwick," not by seeking literal reproduction. "The guy was awfully good," Jacobsen says. "He picks you up on the street, takes you into the building, there's that roll of drums on the stairs, and then you're up there — in the great space."

For exterior restoration, there were Mathew Brady photographs; for interiors

In a suitable cycle, the old Corcoran Gallery is now the Smithsonian's Renwick Gallery, after a stint as the Court of Claims. Because the "miracle" material used to rebuild exterior details crumbled faster than the original, restoration continues. (Smithsonian Institution)

Upstairs, the Renwick re-creates the spirit, and part of the first collection, of the Corcoran, "skying" the paintings in vertical rows. The Grand Salon recalls the early gallery, with a bit more Victorian opulence. (Smithsonian Institution)

there were hundreds of design pattern books of the day.

The exterior was painstakingly cleaned, patched and repaired by the Washington firm of Universal Restoration, Inc. More than 90 percent of the original detail had to be reconstructed in a special molding, casting and carving process using a stonelike composite with a sandstone aggregate finish.

Inside, 20th-century technology — air conditioning, heating, wiring and plumbing — had to be threaded through a 19th-century structure, hewing to the thin, dangerous line of appropriateness. Tons of GSA lights, anemostats and wall clocks that had popped into place unbidden with mysterious speed had to be replaced.

But if the Smithsonian knew exactly what it was doing with the building, it seems to be totally at sea about its function as a display case for design. The exhibits suffer from ambivalence, torpor and clichés. Given a concept, which it clearly lacks, the new Renwick Gallery can, and should be, a superb and civilized setting for the arts of design.

The Bizarre and the Beautiful

HE PENNSYLVANIA ACADEMY OF THE FINE ARTS, a quintessentially Victorian building by Frank Furness, the Philadelphia master of the style's boldest extravaganzas, opened on April 22, 1876, for the nation's centennial year. The cerulean blue ceiling of its grand stairhall was studded with silver stars, the walls were a gilded geometry of stylized flowers on a rich, red ground above incised floral patterns on Natrona, a sandstone-brownstone blend. Ornamental bronze stair rails boasted bouquets of clustered-globe gaslights sprouting from elaborate, spiky stems. Arcades of Gothic arches surrounded the court and galleries, accented by polished columns of Pennsylvania blue or rose crystal marble. Doors and woodwork were of golden oak; floors were carpet or intricately patterned encaustic tile. Colors were plum, blue, gold, sand and olive green. There was no brown anywhere.

Exactly 100 years later to the day, for the Bicentennial, the Pennsylvania Academy reopened. It had been closed for two years for restoration. By the time the doors were shut, a century of neglect and renunciation of the Victorian aesthetic had reduced its showy glitter to genteel mud. What had not been suppressed by changing taste had simply succumbed to grime. If the academy had been a Furness bank or insurance building, or one of the many Furness works in the path of downtown renewal around that super-Victorian fruitcake, Philadelphia's City Hall (which proved too solid and too expensive to demolish), it would be gone. More than half of Furness's Philadelphia buildings have been destroyed, and much of the rest of his legacy has been severely mutilated. No architect has risen to higher favor in his own time or plunged to greater depths of rejection in later years.

By 1973 the fate of the academy hung in the balance; it was saved by a vote of the board, advised by art experts and preservationists. The reopened building is spectacular; the colors glow again, the gold glitters, and all is radiantly diffused with the light of the double skylit roofs that make the structure a giant greenhouse. A little inevitable dust will serve to dim the brand-new luster and place the building and its style more legitimately in time. But the original intent of its superb spatial organization and intricate decorative arts is revealed with clarity. This is not only the rehabilitation of a building, and of an extraordinary architect's reputation; it is also a pivotal step in the reevaluation of this country's Victorian architecture.

The $5.1 million restoration was carried out by Hyman Myers of the architectural firm of Day and Zimmerman. It involved meticulous research, including scrapings, archeological-type digs, study of old photographs and an obvious devotion to the cause. (That spread to the workmen, as well.)

Construction of the building, which housed both the galleries and an art school founded in 1805, was the last word in fireproofing in the 1870s: shallow brick vaults carried on cast-iron beams, combined with cast-iron columns, trusses and solid brick bearing walls. New mechanical systems have been inserted into the ample spaces provided by Furness's ingenious original arrangement for heat and ventilation. There are new skylights and lighting, and some discreet remodeling has added extra levels for the school and a restorer's studio. Polychrome iron columns have been uncovered where encasing plaster was stripped away, as well as chamfered rooms that had been paneled over. Purists will find some fudging where missing, heavy cast-iron parts were replaced by lighter, modern materials. But the 20th century has been as true to the 19th century as it is realistically possible to be.

The timing of the restoration, ostensibly for the Bicentennial, actually coincided with a growing consciousness of the excellence of the best 19th-century architectural design. The zeal of preservationists, based largely on sentiment and history, is being matched by a sharpened and increasingly knowledgeable appreciation of the virtuosities of Victorian work by both practicing architects and architectural historians.

In fact, it is not without significance that the installation of the building's opening show, "In This Academy," which included the excellent choice of temporary gallery colors from clear white for contemporary work to plum, sand and gray-blue-violet for older pictures, was the work of the Philadelphia firm of Venturi and Rauch, simultaneously embattled for its colors and backgrounds for the Whitney's "Two Hundred Years of American Sculpture." (The academy's refurbishing was started under Tom Armstrong, who moved on to head the Whitney, and was completed under the current academy director, Richard J. Boyle.) The younger "Philadelphia school" architects, in today's vanguard, find much to support the Venturian theme of "complexity and contradiction" in the rediscovery of the Victorian richness that the modernists rejected.

In the past few years there has been a rising tide of interest in Frank Furness's work from the 1870s to the turn of the century, led by a coterie of Furness buffs. The Philadelphia Museum held a Furness show in 1973, accompanied by a fine book and

Frank Furness's High Victorian Pennsylvania Academy of the Fine Arts was too original and eccentric for proper 20th-century taste. Beautifully refurbished, it glows with color and pattern and dramatic light and space. (Gutekunst, Pennsylvania Academy of the Fine Arts)

checklist by James F. O'Gorman, working with George E. Thomas, Myers and Cervin Robinson. Professor O'Gorman has characterized Furness's buildings as "among the most boisterous and challenging in an age noted for aggressive architecture." This exuberant, colorful style died of "good taste" by the end of the century, killed by the proper palazzi of McKim, Mead and White.

The Furness oeuvre is bizarre and eccentric. He was an original, in the sense of a talent that takes the taste of his time and transforms it into an overwhelmingly personal expression. That taste, as the historian Carroll Meeks defined it some time ago, was for the "eclectic picturesque." In the work of Furness, it became, in O'Gorman's words, "a bedlam of heterogeneous parts."

Turrets, textures, polychromy, rounded and pointed arches, mansarded and decorated pavilions, dwarf columns, diapered brick patterns, strangely placed windows, warped levels and fulsome ornament were combined in compositions of almost volcanic intensity. Deliberate oddities of arrangement and scale created explosive visual pressures. This is not the naive "bad taste" that has been so simplistically disdained by later generations; it is a deliberately manneristic style that richly rewards the informed eye. The facade of the academy, done early in his career when the firm was Furness and Hewitt, is actually one of his more restrained works.

All of these features can be traced directly to the dominant creative strains of the 19th century. Furness's originality is an amalgam of English Ruskinian Gothic, Butterfieldian ecclesiology, French neo-Grec classicism, the parallel urges for structural rationalism and decorative romanticism, and the elegant ornament of Owen Jones. His work fuses and transcends it all.

The point to be made is that this remarkable architecture has much to teach us — and surprisingly, perhaps, it is the younger architects who are most aware of it. The danger is that these lessons must be learned without falling into the trap of an eclectic decorative revival or of sacrificing the salient lessons of the modern movement. But those "modern" architects who work on the restoration of these Victorian monuments are particularly impressed. Hugh Jacobsen speaks respectfully of the grand stair in Washington's Renwick Gallery as "that roll of drums, getting you up to the great space." The stairhall at the academy is clearly one of those great spaces, with involved, rewarding relationships to the rest of the building that are both striking and subtle. The plan is an outstanding example of the Beaux Arts *parti* (Furness studied with America's first Beaux Arts–trained architect, Richard Morris Hunt) in which the function and progression of spaces create the architectural whole.

On entry, the stairhall is experienced on three physical levels; the eye and body and expectations are directed along the architectural *marche* up to the galleries and through them, led on by the pattern of natural light from the skylights and by the color and ornament, all as calculated as they are dazzling. (The artificial light flattens and deadens the building's contrasts and subtleties; it still needs work.) It must be emphasized that this is not decorative excess for its own sake. Each detail is used to enhance, accent and differentiate, to create spatial flow and unity. These are tools manipulated with full awareness.

What we experience in the academy is not nostalgia; it is architecture. The Victorian building is only beginning to be recognized as good architecture, and even, on occasion, as great architecture. Its richness is a complex system of symbols and meanings, of visual devices and sensuous effects that may have titillated a nouveau riche culture, but that also formed an extremely sophisticated and skillful, erudite and brilliant, highly manneristic 19th-century building art. Many of its monuments have been destroyed out of ignorance. Much of what remains is an abused and irreplaceable heritage.

URBAN SCENES AND SCHEMES

Manchester, N.H.: Lessons in Urbicide

T HE STORY OF THE DESTRUCTION of the Amoskeag mill complex that has formed the heart of Manchester, N.H., for over a hundred years has a terrible pertinence for the numberless cities committing blind mutilation in the name of urban renewal.

Demolition is under way of one of the most remarkable manifestations of our urban and industrial culture. The historic, but still functioning, planned mill community of Manchester, faced with adjusting to changing economics, is being indiscriminately bulldozed for a researched, consultant-approved and officially adopted urban renewal scheme consisting almost totally of parking lots that mocks the quality of vision and design now being ruthlessly effaced.

The Amoskeag plan, conceived and started in the 1830s by the Amoskeag Company's 19-year-old engineer, Ezekial Straw (later governor of New Hampshire), united factories, waterways, public buildings and public commons, housing and commerce in an integrated design. The famous mill town's simple, handsome, vernacular red brick buildings, constructed for the textile industry from 1838 to 1915, stretched for more than a mile along the Merrimac River, flanking canals and mill yards. The excellence of the complex has made it an acknowledged monument of American industrial history and urban design.

"Monuments don't pay," says Manchester's urban renewal director, Cary P. Davis, quoted in *Time,* as he handed them over to the bulldozer. Still, the tragedy of Manchester has not gone unremarked. *Time, Fortune* and *The Architectural Forum,* representing the professional press, have added their voices to the usual ones of the historians. Maybe that is a good sign. By slow drops and trickles in the pool of public information and opinion, a force that exerts considerable political leverage, an awareness of our losses may develop before the country is stripped bare of its urban art and history.

It is significant in this context that the term "industrial archeology," a phrase employed by historians, is beginning to break into more popular usage. Industrial archeology is the study of the buildings, plans and structural and social complexes developed by the forces of commerce and industry that have conspicuously shaped this country in the 19th and 20th centuries. Manchester is, or was, a prime example. The term covers a large, important and varied body of building that makes special technological, functional and aesthetic contributions to the American environment. But its monuments are largely ignored. We have a way of sweeping under the rug art and history that do not conform to accepted, preconceived notions of cultural achievement. We tear down those genuine and often strikingly handsome monuments while we build meaningless reproductions of the domestic and official 18th century. There is a game, for example, that could be called "Who's got the real Independence Hall?" played cross-country.

The Amoskeag mills of Manchester, N.H., have been burned and bulldozed, but the mill town of Lowell, Mass., is enjoying a renaissance, thanks to National Park Service, state and local action. Industrial archeology is now part of American history. (HABS)

Industrial archeology is concerned with a great deal of the American scene —
significant, strong, tradition-shattering structures and plans that tell more about
American civilization than many of the conventional touchstones.

Randolph Langenbach, a Harvard graduate who has spent several years
documenting the Amoskeag-Manchester story for the Smithsonian archives and on
his own, writes that Manchester's "role in the growth of American society is really
more important and symbolic than the role of Williamsburg. Although much
venerated, Williamsburg was more English than American in style, and its
significance did not last through the greatest period of America's industrial and social
growth, as did Manchester's." This was written in an article for the Harvard Alumni
Bulletin. (Harvard grads, community leaders all, supporters of culture, read and
remember.) But in the preservation script as it is written today, Williamsburg and its
imitators get all the lines. And all the money. They are rebuilt and refurnished to
expensive, improbable perfection, while the wrecker's ball swings freely in the
country's Manchesters. What a splendid $75 million Rockefeller restoration and reuse
demonstration project this could have made. Development problems of this
magnitude and of this historical importance probably cannot be solved by any city
without foundation aid.

The tragedy cannot be blamed on lack of information. John Coolidge's book on
the Utopian 19th-century planning of Lowell, Mass., *Mill and Mansion,* has become a
classic in the field. The Lowell buildings no longer exist. William Pierson's studies of
New England mill towns are standard literature. Between this competent scholarship
and the politically appointed agencies that run urban renewal there is an
unconscionable communications gap that could most kindly be called ignorance.
The results of ignorance are urbicide.

Langenbach is now documenting Manchester's self-destruction. Ninety of the
buildings will go for parking lots and access to still-functioning factories. The canals,
now polluted, will be filled in for sewers. What is being destroyed for some of the
most limited and discredited aims of urban renewal, he points out, is the "unity and
impact of one of the most powerful urban scenes anywhere in the world."

How did it happen? The same way that the heart and soul are being cut out of
uncounted American cities to be replaced by faceless clichés. First, an outside
research firm is called in to analyze the community's problems and make
recommendations. The extremely respected, internationally known firm of Arthur
D. Little, Inc., produced such a consultant survey for Manchester in 1961. While
making numerous economic suggestions, the report offered the information that
"even with extensive improvements and upgrading, the millyard will never be an
asset from the esthetic point of view."

Well. The blind telling the blind what to do. Say that to any architectural historian
or urban designer worthy of the name and watch the fireworks. The real catastrophe,
however, is that it is exactly this kind of seriously inadequate, damaging nonsense
that is being sold successfully to municipalities countrywide. The researchers, the
planners and the surveys themselves are close to identical, ignoring any indigenous
character for formulas of repetitive, profitable sterility.

The conclusions thus offered and received as gospel are much like the grotesque
solutions of incompletely programmed computers. They are wretchedly wrong. No
one has remembered to put in the factor of environmental design sensitivity based
on recognition of its characteristics through knowledge of its forms and appreciation
of its history. On those well-known research and planning teams collecting fat fees
for a depressingly standard product ground out in town after town, there is rarely a
contributor of this essential expertise. The tragically faulty recommendations that
result from this basic omission are then translated into action by renewal agencies,

most of whom are urbanistic amateurs. Surgery is carried on by plumbers.

What is being produced is a kind of urban Pablum. We are making a dull porridge of parking lots and cheap commercialism, to replace the forms and evidence of American civilization. The buildings despised and sacrificed today are, or would have been, tomorrow's heritage. We have forgotten, to quote Langenbach again, that "economics is a social science." We wonder why the economic formulas produce inhuman cities.

This is the certain way to the blight of the future. In Manchester, where the memory of the mills as a poor and oppressive way of life is still alive, nobody really cares. And that is the most tragic indictment of all.

Syracuse, N.Y.: Ugly Cities and How They Grow

THE CRISIS OF OUR CITIES can be stated in very simple terms: They are becoming insupportably hideous. Underneath the ugliness and often causing it are many real ills brought on by overwhelming social and economic changes and population pressures since the war. The cities are sick, and urban renewal is government-applied first aid.

One suspects that the doctor's cures may be killing the patient. Visit almost any city in the United States and its most striking aspect is apt to be a bulldozed wasteland in its heart. Out of the wasteland, more often than not, rises another dreary wasteland of new construction.

The story is the same for private redevelopment. Only one sure fact emerges — the new is replacing the old indiscriminately, as a kind of sanitary cure-all, often without satisfactory rationale or results. All too frequently, good is replaced by bad.

These remarks could apply to almost any American city, since most share the same ills and cures, but they are prompted by a visit to Syracuse, N.Y., a community of approximately 216,000 afflicted with all of the symptoms of a city this size, at this particular time.

In spite of a general effect of spotty disorder, Syracuse is rich in good architecture of all periods. In addition to a range from great Greek Revival to high style High Victorian, it has the most magnificent "modernistic" fruitcake that this observer has ever seen, in the Niagara Mohawk Power Building of the 1930s. What is happening to all of it, however, is so typical and so deplorable that Syracuse can stand as a case history.

Clinton Square, the former downtown center from which business has now moved southward, is, or was, a well-scaled public space surrounded by fine vintage buildings. The Syracuse Savings Bank of 1876 by Joseph Lyman Silsbee, who later trained Frank Lloyd Wright in Chicago, ranked as a Victorian Gothic masterpiece. Flanking it is, or was, a splendid Second Empire structure, the Gridley Building of 1867, and the third Onondaga County Courthouse of 1856, a landmark of high quality by Horatio White. Opposite is a competent Classical Revival post office of 1928. Each is a top example of its style.

Between them are more recent structures, dull beyond credulity, but still not destructive of the complex. The old buildings relate perfectly in size and scale to the square; they offer rich stylistic variety to the city. The rub, of course, is that most of them are obsolete.

This is the tragedy and the problem of urban "progress." The savings bank has existed by grace of a previous owner who prized it. The courthouse, which has had

The Gridley Building in Syracuse, N.Y., a fine Second Empire fruitcake, has been saved and restored for architectural offices and a restaurant. The courthouse is still in use. (HABS; Board of Realtors)

"temporary" government uses for 50 years, faces demolition with the removal of the adjoining police headquarters to a new building in Syracuse's chief urban renewal area, where a combined civic and cultural center is rising. This area has produced at least one structure of special interest — the Everson Museum by I. M. Pei.

Syracuse is wearing those peculiar renewal blinders that make it fail to see the possibility of the present conversion of a historic structure for a concert hall, for example, rather than marking a nebulous future X in the new cultural center.

The city wears blinders in many ways. It fails to appreciate the superb cut granite mass and steeple of St. Paul's Church. It ignores the numbing object lesson of the contrast between its strong, rusticated, 19th-century Richardsonian city hall and the flat, pusillanimous, 20th-century state office building next to it that wins some kind of booby prize for totally undistinguished design.

In cities like Syracuse, new and old coexist as bellicose, resentful strangers. There is a curious, Martian mixture of almost surrealist strangeness; Queen Anne gingerbread next to cantilevered steel. The old waits grotesquely for the new to sweep it to destruction, and the all-important lesson of urban design is still unlearned. You don't wish the old city away; you work with its assets, allying them to the best new building for strengthening relationships for both.

As long as architects reject the past and fail to deal in continuity, cities like Syracuse are doomed to self-destruction.

St. Louis, Mo.: Success and Blues

THE SUCCESS OF POWELL SYMPHONY HALL in St. Louis is probably going to lead a lot of people to a lot of wrong conclusions. In a kind of architectural Gresham's law, the right thing wrongly interpreted usually has more bad than good results.

The first wrong conclusion is that Powell Hall represents the triumph of traditional over modern architecture. False. The correct conclusion here is that a good old building is better than a bad new one. Powell Hall represents the triumph simply of suitable preservation. And, one might add, of rare good sense.

This conversion of a 1925 movie palace represents the intelligent reuse of an old structure that was, and is, a stagily handsome theatrical setting. It has the added advantage of having started with conventionally satisfactory conditions for good acoustics. It is quite fair to conclude that this involved less of a gamble than a new design solution.

The building's elaborate, unreproducible, Silver Screen Versailles features are a fortuitous "architecture *trouvé*." The result is a concert hall of suave elegance, beautiful sound and stunning economy (about $2.5 million total cost instead of the $10 to $20 million required for a new building) with a maximum of glamor and glitter. As St. Louisans danced to Strauss waltzes on the stage and in the Grand

One cultural center that never became a camel: Powell Hall in St. Louis. This handsome movie theater-turned symphony concert hall is an early example of preservation through appropriate reuse. (St. Louis Symphony)

While decimating its historic downtown by razing a number of National Register and other historic buildings in the path of the 21-block Gateway Mall, St. Louis has used more than $1 billion in rehabilitation tax credits for center-city renovation and construction.

Foyer after the opening concert under 11-foot chandeliers in a cream-white, crimson and gold-leaf setting, leaders in other cities were crying quietly over their multimillion-dollar, superstatus, superbuilding plans.

Most of those cities are engaged in the absurd cycle of tearing down irreplaceable old structures while they promote expensive new projects of depressing vacuity. Perhaps the sheer rationality and taste of the St. Louis venture may set some kind of badly needed example.

A pertinent conclusion that is being systematically evaded would be that we are putting up a lot of bad new buildings in the name of the arts. Somehow cultural centers turn into camels. (A camel, it will be remembered, is a committee-designed horse.)

The well-meant efforts of community groups lead to few artistic triumphs or architectural masterpieces. They lead, instead, to those big, miserably ordinary new houses tricked up with depressing applied art that fall flat on the eye and ear. They lead to compromise and caution (Lincoln Center), and great art is never cautious. They lead to pretty mediocrity on a colossal scale (the Kennedy Center) and pratfall bows to tradition (the Metropolitan Opera House.) They produce a comfortable conservative culture, without a single *frisson,* in both package and product. Most depressing of all is the fact that so much power and prestige stand behind these failures of nerve and style.

It is not that modern architecture has failed. It is that we have yet to use the dramatic beauty or unparalleled design and structural potential of our age. It is not that we are already tired of contemporary halls. We have hardly experienced one, in the proper creative sense of the word.

Any discussion of success or failure in St. Louis leads inevitably to the city's major downtown renewal program. (The decision not to put Powell Hall downtown was motivated partly by the fact that the new Busch Stadium preempts all parking and traffic facilities — a curious shutout for a new plan.)

The completed St. Louis arch, soaring 630 feet at the river's edge, is magnificent. Its superscaled, stainless steel curve soars grandly enough to justify any questionable engineering rationale. It offers surprising attitudes of contemporary abstract grandeur from almost every angle, and if you must share in the great American tourist compulsion to get to the top of everything big, you can be shot up in a purple capsule, like one of five peas in a pod, to see the view from its gently swaying apex.

This may be the only way you will see the Mississippi and its historic levee. They are lost to the eye and to the ordinary pedestrian, although it is possible to get to the river if you know how. The stunning, slow rise of textured rose-gray granite that once provided a working slope for riverboat cargo is, as a prominent St. Louisan pointed out, as handsome as a city-size Nagare sculpture. The level of the park created for the arch when the old waterfront with its priceless cast-iron architectural heritage was bulldozed hides river and levee. The park is still desolately unlandscaped.

The arch stands in a curious kind of limbo called urban redevelopment. It has no setting, and this is meant less in terms of planting or vistas than in its relationship to the city at its feet.

Waterfront St. Louis was a case history of a dying downtown. It can now be judged as a case history of commercially sponsored renewal.

Except for the arch and the old courthouse, which form some genuinely provocative urban views, downtown St. Louis is a monument to chamber of commerce planning and design. It is a businessman's dream of redevelopment come true.

There are all of the faceless, characterless, scaleless symbols of economic regeneration — luxury apartments, hotels, a 50,000-seat stadium and multiple parking garages for 7,400 cars. Sleek, new, prosperous, stolid and dull, well served by superhighways, the buildings are a collection of familiar profit formulas, uninspired in concept, unvarying in scale, unrelated by any standards, principles or subtleties of planning or urban design. They just stand there. They come round, rectangular, singly and in pairs. Pick your standard commercial cliché. The centerpiece is the Busch Stadium, big and banal, smoothed up by the aesthetic ministrations of Edward Durell Stone.

There are none of the traditional values of vitality, variety and humanity that make cities challenging and great. Sensing something lacking, St. Louisans thought the answer might be to add a kind of Disneyland for those whose interests are not

The magnificent 1894 Union Station in St. Louis, long a silent, mammoth ghost, is now a Rouse shopping center. Its reincarnation benefited from federal rehabilitation tax credits, like hundreds of other recent rebirths in St. Louis. (Artega Photos)

bounded by baseball and football, an idea that was fortunately abandoned.

There was a competition for a mall leading to courthouse and arch, won by Sasaki, Dawson, De May Associates, but no one sees much point in building it, since malls are for people involved in pleasurable urban activities and what is pleasurable or interesting about a promenade bounded on one full side by a parking garage? This will not be helped environmentally by the reerection of the Spanish Pavilion from the New York World's Fair, a building more meaningful for its interior display than its exterior architecture.

The new St. Louis is a success economically and a failure urbanistically. It has the impersonal gloss of a promotional brochure. A prime example of the modern landscape of urban alienation, it has gained a lot of real estate and lost a historic city.

Saratoga, N.Y.: Losing Race

SARATOGA, N.Y., is a community known for horse racing, a historic Victorian heritage and its new cultural center.

The city's past is firmly linked with hotels — some of the most luxurious of the Gilded Age. This is a community still rich in fine late 19th-century houses, and those who look can find the celebrated Canfield Casino, now shabby-elegant, a semi-museum and a preservation problem. Not much more remains of Saratoga's vanishing record of high Victorian society, a historical and aesthetic phenomenon that few cities anywhere could match.

The extravagant hotels, with their baroque opulence, elaborate gingerbread and 11-course dinners, have gone the way of the dinosaurs that they grew to resemble. It is not without significance that on the site of one of the greatest hostelries, the Grand Union, there are now a Grand Union supermarket and parking lot that have stamped Saratoga's once-great main street with a back-alley look. It is impossible to get more environmentally ordinary than that.

Ironies abound in the Saratoga saga. As the old hotels were bulldozed and the new cultural center was built, a shortage of hotel space developed. The timing was bad in more ways than one. Now that it no longer seems impossible to restore and modernize old buildings — we are seeing a small, swelling groundwave of striking preservation successes in several cities that would have been called pie-in-the-sky projects 10 years ago — it is probable that not everything of the past had to be sacrificed. The supermarket-motel image doesn't do a thing for Saratoga except downgrade it. Some of its unique heritage could have been fitted into the city's cultural renaissance by sensitive, civilized planning.

It has been touch and go since 1957 for Saratoga's park and casino that still stands in it, when a referendum was passed approving the leasing of park space for a hotel, which did not materialize at the time. Instead, a hotel was built just outside the park. But the authorization is still on the books.

Unfortunately, there is no such thing as an appropriate design for the destruction of a public park. And in front of the hotel that was built instead of the one in the park, as beacon, focus and image of the new Saratoga, is the Holiday Inn sign, the granddaddy horror of them all.

This visual monstrosity poisons the environment wherever it is, and it is everywhere because the Holiday Inn corporation insists on it as identification all over the country. The sign seems to be a prime clause of the franchise. A coast-to-coast atrocity, it could undo a dozen natural-beauty programs. It would have been a

Reflected in the spring that gave the town its name and raison d'etre, Saratoga's casino has been adapted for museum and community use. The great hotels are gone, one replaced by a supermarket. (Saratoga Springs Preservation Foundation)

hole-in-one triumph for Lady Bird Johnson's campaign if all Holiday Inn signs had disappeared, outlawed in the public interest.

This does not mean that all signs everywhere are bad, or that they must be in discreet or quaint 18th-century script to be okay. Public graphics is another environmental subject that needs clarification.

Subway advertising, for example, is generally excellent. It gives brightness and scale and an emotional and visual lift as well as waiting-time distraction to a dreary setting, and it seems rather sad that the new Washington subway, in an excess of architectural purity, will have none. The ads on New York's buses, also bitterly fought by the purists, add a flash of moving color and wit to the city's tense, gray streets.

What one of the professional magazines, *Progressive Architecture,* calls Super-graphics, a highly imaginative public use of bold lettering, image and color, can be an environmental pickup. Even those telephoto shots of highway vulgarization with their shoulder-to-shoulder neon and plastic, used as arguments for beautification, become quite smashing graphic compositions in their own right — the photo result, curiously, is an art form in itself.

There is a thin line everywhere today between art and accident, or even art and atrocity; it is a characteristic of our time. Current architectural theory calls for complexity and disorder (in a kind of tastefully arranged, properly evocative counterpoint of aesthetic experiences, of course), using the happy accidents of unplanned construction as examples. The unhappy accidents don't count. There is a perfectly good case to be made for subtleties and variations of design outside of Cartesian order, but the idea is already being carried to extremes of heady intellectual irrelevance.

Billboard blight is fought by concerned citizens in a losing battle against a powerful business lobby, and yet billboard art, as sophisticated abstraction and out of environmental context, becomes Pop art, translating the punch-in-the-stomach assault of the highway into the aesthetic punch in the eye of the gallery. The line grows steadily thinner.

But even with this precarious balance of values, there is still simple environmental malpractice — and the theorists of the new chaos be hanged. When an Indianapolis-based store chain called Vonnegut's (to take a typical, all-American example) gets a pat on the back from a trade publication for its "new look" — one of those totem pole accretions of towering mix-matched and mismatched humdrum graphics to lure the helpless driver — it is archetypal bad. It is really bad because it isn't even bad enough to be good enough for the new chaos.

Certainly Saratoga is no more confused or much worse off than any other community today; its "new look" is national. It is only that Saratoga's unique architectural history makes its transgressions a special study of environmental abuse. What the next abuse will be is always a gamble, although the outrages and odds are reasonably predictable. But that's what makes horse racing, anywhere.

New York: Sometimes We Do It Right

WHEN IT IS GOOD, New York is very, very good. Which is why New Yorkers put up with so much that is bad.

When it is good, this is a city of fantastic strength, sophistication and beauty. It is like no other city in time or place. Visitors and even natives rarely use the words "urban character" or "environmental style," but that is what they are reacting to with awe in the presence of massed, concentrated steel, stone, power and life. It is a quality of urban greatness that may not solve racial or social tension or the human or economic crises to which a city is prone, but it survives them.

In this sense, one small piece of downtown Manhattan is very, very good. For a demonstration of New York at its physical best, go to Broadway between Cedar and Liberty streets and face east. You will be standing in front of the new building at 140 Broadway, one of the handsomest in the city, and you will not be able to miss the 28-foot-high vermilion steel cube by Isamu Noguchi that balances on one point in front of it, at the north end of a travertine plaza.

Look to your left (Liberty Street) and you will see the small turn-of-the-century French pastry in creamy, classically detailed stone that houses the neighboring chamber of commerce. To your right (Cedar Street) is a stone-faced building of the first great skyscraper period (pre–World War I through the 1930s.)

Move on toward the East River, following the travertine plaza that flows elegantly on either side of the slender new shaft, noting how well the block size of the marble under foot scales the space. Surprisingly, the site and the 52-story tower are trapezoidal in shape.

At Broad Street, the 140 Broadway plaza stops and Chase Manhattan Plaza begins. There is an unfortunate wall between them, due to abrupt changes in ground level and the fact that the architects of both buildings, Skidmore, Owings and Merrill, had no idea when they did Chase in the early 1960s that they would be doing the adjoining building less than a decade later.

But the open space continues, even with this barrier. Closing it and facing Chase's gleaming 60-story tower across Liberty Street is the stony vastness of the 1924 Federal Reserve Building by York and Sawyer, its superscaled, cut limestone, Strozzi-type Florentine facade making a powerful play against Chase's bright aluminum and glass. A more conventional masonry-faced structure walls the plaza to the south.

There will be still more open space west of 140 Broadway, following the same axis. Just opposite the new building is the U.S. Steel site, where the Singer Building stood. That landmark loss to New York's skyline will be replaced by a skyscraper by the same architects who have done Chase Manhattan and 140 Broadway, Skidmore, Owings and Merrill.

The architects and owners have received approval from the City Planning

The urban drama at its best: A bright Noguchi cube balances in front of a suave, dark "skin" building — part of an ensemble of new and old that creates a rich 20th-century vista in downtown Manhattan. (© 1968 Ezra Stoller, ESTO)

Commission to adjust the zoning of the two-block site to extend the present pedestrian channel farther toward the Hudson River. The Liberty-Cedar block west of Broadway will be another open plaza, paralleling the existing one. The new skyscraper will be constructed on the block to the north.

Still farther west, slightly off this axis, will be the giant World Trade Center twin towers and plaza. For much of this, underground connections are being planned.

The result, a striking slice through one of the densest, most dramatic cityscapes in the world is a stunning success in terms of urban design. For once, the losses, such as the Singer Building, are at least being balanced by rational gains. For once, there has been intelligent, sensitive capitalization on one of this century's most fantastic urban phenomena. Instead of thoughtless destruction through new construction, there is a calculated relationship between past and present and between buildings and spaces.

This small segment of New York compares in effect and elegance with any celebrated Renaissance plaza or baroque vista. The scale of the buildings, the use of open space, the views revealed or suggested, the contrasts of architectural style and material, of sculptured stone against satin-smooth metal and glass, the visible change and continuity of New York's remarkable skyscraper history, the brilliant accent of the poised Noguchi cube — color, size, style, mass, space, light, dark, solids, voids, highs and lows — all are just right. These few blocks provide (why equivocate?) one of the most magnificent examples of 20th-century urbanism anywhere in the world.

Not the least contribution is the new building, for which Gordon Bunshaft was partner-in-charge at SOM. One Forty Broadway is a "skin" building — the kind of flat, sheer, curtain wall that it has become chic to reject. Younger architects, off on a wild, Arthurian search for the *nouveau* picturesque, and an uninformed public that never understood or accepted what was happening have turned their backs on one of the miracles of modern building: the skyscraper wall reduced to gossamer minimums of shining, thin material hung on a frame of extraordinary strength through superb contemporary technology.

The significance and beauty of this achievement are not dimmed by the instances of its commercial prostitution as the unjustly denigrated "glass box." It is still one of the great developments and most remarkable expressions in all of architectural history from Stonehenge to the present. It has produced some masterpieces and made a lot of commercial building palatable. One Forty Broadway is a commercial building, not a monument. Here the skin is handled with suave expertise.

It is New York's ultimate skin building. The wall is held unrelentingly flat; there are no tricks with projecting or extended mullions; thin and flush, they are used only to divide the window glass. The metal spandrel facing, in one smooth piece, echoes the placing of structural steel and seeks no "artful" plasticity. The taut, shiny-dark sleekness of matte black aluminum and gleaming bronze glass is an architectural statement of positive excellence as well as a foil for the ornate masonry around it. The quiet assurance of this building makes even Chase look a little gaudy.

What next? Probably destruction. One ill-conceived neighboring plaza will kill this carefully calculated channel of related space and buildings. Seagram was semisabotaged by the recent construction on its south; it can happen here. It takes only one opening in the wrong place, one "bonus" space placed according to current zoning (read "business") practice, to ruin it all.

Space is meaningless without scale, containment, boundaries and direction. The fabled massing of the Wall Street skyscrapers has been given masterful urban definition by the architects' ordering of these few blocks of new construction. This is planning, whether it is merely fortuitous or foresighted. It is the opposite of nonplanning, or the normal pattern of New York development. See and savor it now, before it is carelessly disposed of.

Lower Manhattan: Where Ghosts Can Be at Home

THERE ARE NO FLAGS FLYING TO MARK IT, but a battle has been won in New York. After years of callous wholesale destruction of the city's architectural heritage, there is now a near-total reversal of official policy toward the past. The Housing and Development Agency, the city's superbuilding department, has asked for and is currently getting from the Landmarks Preservation Commission reports on what should be saved, historically and architecturally, in the city's 25 urban renewal areas. The City Planning Commission has selected a waterfront site for urban renewal designation in Lower Manhattan, with preservation as a prime objective.

In its lucid, readable report on the Washington Street renewal area, the Landmarks Commission makes this statement: "The report itself is a landmark. This is the first time in New York City that a government agency charged with the task of historic preservation has been required to report to the agency in charge of urban development."

Asking for professional guidance sounds about as simple and logical as coming in out of the rain. But although expertise has always been generously available in New York, it has been conspicuously unwanted in city circles.

The city's action comes only after 20 years of ruthless and indiscriminate bulldozing of Manhattan's most historic areas carried out with a singleminded insensitivity compounded about equally of bureaucracy and ignorance. It took 15 years of that time to get a landmarks law and commission, an achievement that surprised a lot of professional New York cynics.

Remember Brooklyn Bridge South? The city crushed the life and color out of it and handed the wreckage to the developers for urban renewal superblocks. We won't bore you with the losses again; they are recorded in New York histories and architectural textbooks. They are also preserved on hundreds of feet of underground movies and uncounted photographs by artists, historians and observers of the New York scene who roamed the rosy brick rubble — there is no brick quite as handsome as that of the 18th and early 19th centuries — with recording film and grim despair.

Where ghosts are no longer at home: South Street Seaport, a growing "festival marketplace" that mixes old New York with new money (Rouse, federal, city and state). *In situ* preservation can become a commercial stageset. (© Steve Rosenthal, Benjamin Thompson and Associates)

(You meet some of the most interesting people on demolition sites.)

In the old, established order of things the Washington Street site, which included the Washington Market, would have gone exactly the same way — and most of it did.

It may be an indulgence to point out, for that useless thing called history, that the old Washington Market, now semidemolished as part of a 38-acre renewal area, was a very special place, like Covent Garden in London or Les Halles in Paris, the latter also on the way out. (There is already a frozen-food teeny-bopper generation that never knew it.)

Not only were its shabby "genteel" brick houses and commercial buildings, which ranged from the 18th through the mid-19th centuries, similar in material, scale and style, but they had accumulated an extraordinarily handsome set of spontaneous graphics in the signs painted on the old houses.

The area was "redolent," in the Landmarks Commission's word, of old New York, and equally redolent of garlic and pearly onions, and gleaming with the fresh color of avocados, tomatoes and eggplants. It was filled with the bustle of early dawn activity for a city still stonily asleep. Hopelessly nonfunctional for the 20th century and, we assume, now happily transferred to safe, sanitary and totally sterile in every sense of the word new accommodations in the Bronx, the old market had Hogarthian energy and Georgian style.

The Landmarks Preservation Commission has recommended strongly that a group of six virtually intact early 19th-century houses in the market — some of the oldest in New York — be preserved and utilized in any redevelopment scheme.

They are at 29, 31 and 33 Harrison Street and 327, 329 and 331 Washington Street, between Harrison and Jay. They form a corner and an almost complete block. It has also suggested that three more houses, 314, 315 and 317 Washington Street, on the block below, be moved, if possible, to fill out the block. It has further been urged that the city's earliest remaining cast-iron front, erected in 1848 by New York's innovating builder James Bogardus, be dismantled and reused in some fashion.

The Housing and Development Agency has accepted these recommendations. It has announced officially that any "sponsor" will be required to find a use for the Harrison-Jay Street row and must restore the houses as part of its bargain with the city.

Certainly the houses are shabby and derelict to the average eye. But even to the average eye it is clear that this group of buildings, again in the words of the Landmarks Commission, suggests "an earlier time and a different way of life." Behind the grime and commercial remodeling are the dormered roofline, the domestic two and a half stories, the Flemish bond brick, the dentil cornices, splayed double keystones and incised block lintels that are the delight of those who collect rare examples of the stylistic past.

Just across Lower Manhattan the City Planning Commission is including an 11-block, 38-acre site for renewal that will focus on the early 19th-century Schermerhorn Row at Fulton and South streets on the East River. This group of buildings is one of the few that still evoke sailing-age New York. In this case, preservation is not incidental to the project; it is its purpose.

The restoration area, to include a South Street Maritime Museum and sailing ships anchored at the foot of Fulton Street, is being sponsored by the South Street Seaport, Inc., a private preservation group. The city's renewal role will be to make land assembly possible. The kind of faith, hope and civilized vision that New Yorkers are not supposed to have got the ball rolling, and now the city has picked it up.

We need both the South Street and Washington Street projects. They are only a drop in the bucket of what has already been destroyed. Both have the singular virtue of being *in situ* preservation — original buildings still on their original sites.

Nothing beats keeping the old city where it belongs and where its ghosts are at home.

But unless enough instances of the old city are integrated with new construction, there will be no real urban continuity or economic reality. We will simply have acquired an occasional embalmed architectural freak. The objective of preservation is the retention of the full range of styles, sensations and references that record the city's history and achievements visually and environmentally, to keep them in the city's vital mainstream.

So please, gentlemen, no horse-drawn cars, no costumes, no wigs, no stage sets, no cute-old-stores, no "re-creations" that never were, no phony little-old-New York. There is a tendency in American restoration for corn to conquer all. In Europe old buildings are used naturally and normally, not reduced to cultural kitsch. That is perversion, not preservation.

The past becomes real by its legitimate and handsome contrasts with the present. Give us the best of contemporary style, life and uses in the old buildings. Now that we have won the battle, let's not lose the war.

The Blooming of Downtown Brooklyn

GENERALLY, IT IS EASIER to get New Yorkers to cross the Atlantic than to cross the East River. Still, the blooming of downtown Brooklyn should not really take them so very much by surprise. It wouldn't if they didn't keep looking the other way. A walk across the Brooklyn Bridge on a magical early spring day or evening reveals more than its accustomed romantic beauty. (How spoiled we New Yorkers are; but this is part of our dubious charm.) Downtown Brooklyn is still fraught with real and continuing problems, but there is enough visible accomplishment in terms of design, development and the creation and reinforcement of community and amenity for a dozen other cities.

Brooklyn's lessons in architecture and urbanism — which largely involve informed efforts to turn around an area decimated by a residential and commercial flight to the suburbs of the 1950s and 1960s — are heartening. And so are the role and achievements of the city agency in charge, the Office of Downtown Brooklyn Development, under the direction of Richard M. Rosan, working in collaboration with exceptionally strong and dedicated local groups. This is one of those on-the-spot mayor's planning offices that have done more for New York in terms of positive development policy than any single idea or action initiated by city government in the last decade.

You don't have to be a closet Brooklynite to know about Brooklyn's brownstone revival, but the first thing that strikes the visitor is the startling dimensions of the residential renaissance. These neighborhoods go on literally for miles, ringing downtown Brooklyn. They have an incredible population of 275,000 — at least as big as three medium-size cities. Beginning with Brooklyn Heights, the revival moved to Cobble Hill, Boerum Hill and Park Slope — four areas that have been declared historic districts. Still another, Fort Greene, is in the process of designation.

Almost all of these seemingly endless, superb streets of 19th-century row houses were once slated for the bulldozer brand of urban renewal. That figured, of course, since the easiest thing to demolish is a treasury of intimately scaled, rich architectural styles of exceptional craftsmanship and quality. The revival that took place instead was a spontaneous, snowballing, bootstrap operation of individual and collective gut faith, born of a dedication to the principle that New York is livable, made by a young, committed, urban middle class.

If you want to know the extent of such faith, it is worth noting that with the exception of a few local Brooklyn institutions, New York banks would give no loans or mortgages on any of these houses in any of these areas. Has anyone ever estimated the disastrous impact of such "sound banking policy" on cities, even when street wisdom was in the act of proving the bankers wrong? They have a lot to answer for. (They'll handle the buildings now, at quintuple markups in sound, marketable neighborhoods.)

This charm, comfort and beauty, from tree-lined streets and blooming back yards to Eastlake parlors and sun-filled kitchens, is within a stone's, or a subway's, throw of the Big Apple. Transportation facilities are excellent, although they need upgrading like the rest of New York's mass transit. Everything converges on downtown Brooklyn. And if the natives don't want to cross the river, they have an over-

Brownstones, once again a bargain in Brooklyn, have been reclaimed by the mile in downtown neighborhoods the size of a small city. Brooklyn Union Gas Company demonstration projects have transformed several rows into Cinderellas. (Brooklyn Union Gas Company)

whelming concentration of their own cultural and educational institutions.

Again, if one stops to think about it, the score is stupefying. There are at least a dozen educational institutions, with 45,000 enrolled in them, as compared to 26,288 students in Cambridge, Mass. Baruch College is now moving toward realization on 13 acres of the Atlantic Terminal renewal site after 10 years of backing and filling. There is a small, steady, loyal stream to the dance programs (outstanding) and exhibitions (ditto) of the topflight Academy of Music and Brooklyn Museum. (One draw, even with Manhattan's easy riches, is dinner at Gage and Tollner's landmark restaurant, an island of authentic food and atmosphere in the expensive *ersatzschmier* of New York dining.)

And that's not all, as they say in boostersville. Just beyond the bridge is Brooklyn's civic and commercial center. About 67,000 people, divided between the public and private sectors, work in its businesses, courts, government agencies, law and insurance offices, and retail enterprises. And these are not just buildings — we are also talking about architecture. From the solid granite Romanesque Revival Post Office and the neoclassical Borough Hall to the nifty Art Deco of Corbett, Harrison and McMurray's 185 Montague Street (headquarters of the Office of Downtown Brooklyn Development), there is more substantial, stylish, top-quality building in downtown Brooklyn than one can shake an architectural historian at. Block for block, it is some of the best, most underpublicized landmark territory in New York.

Most of the pivotal change and the concentrated redevelopment effort have taken place in this central business district, around Fulton Street. There has been commercial spillover beyond, from the brownstone neighborhoods, revitalizing Atlantic Avenue as well, with its older ethnic strengths and burgeoning antique and specialty shops. Atlantic Avenue is now surprisingly reminiscent of New Orleans's Magazine Street in both character and renewal. The development office has devised a special Atlantic Avenue zoning district to protect just those urban and architectural features that would be lost, without controls, in the regenerative process.

With the Downtown Brooklyn Development Association, the planners have made steady progress in the Fulton Street area. Abraham and Straus and May's have held on, while the famous movie houses died and traditional shopping turned into a redundancy of fancy shoes and wigs. But even with suburban defection and social change, this section still has the sixth largest sales volume of all U.S. central business districts, and one of the planners' proposals is a Fulton Street pedestrian mall. This seems about to go ahead. (Not the least problem is the repeated political, social and commercial mobilization needed, year after year, as every project inches forward one hearing at a time.)

A good deal less visible remedial action has also been under way. The Livingston-Bond garage that opened recently does more than provide parking space; it is a coordinating facility for off-street unloading, goods handling and new shops. Two handsome new, key buildings have been completed by the firm of Skidmore, Owings and Merrill — for Con Ed and the New York Telephone Company. Under careful planning persuasion, they feature such mandated urban assets as arcades and new subway entrances as well as far-above-speculative-quality design.

There have been disappointments. Dreams of large amounts of new office space have died with the real estate market. Housing plans have collapsed, brought on by the failure of UDC. But nothing is too big or too small for the Brooklyn planning office. A clear indication of its eye and attitude is a series of tidy, tiny, "traffic island" parklets throughout the area — carefully repaved, with trees and benches. The strength of a local planning office is that, unlike a centralized agency, its attention is focused on every street corner. This is the only kind of planning that really works.

We have saved the best till last. Downtown Brooklyn not only has the unparalleled view of Manhattan, it has a wonderful waterfront. The development office's Fulton Ferry waterfront plan ranges from the building of a small park and ferry slip, almost complete, to a pair of imaginative schemes to use a fine "modernistic" factory for the Brooklyn Museum Art School and the city-owned Fire Boat House for a Brooklyn Bridge Museum. (One of New York's secret treasures is the set of Roebling's inch-by-inch watercolor renderings of the bridge in the original wooden file cabinets.)

Long-range plans would link the area with the South Street Seaport on the Manhattan side. But it isn't necessary to wait for that to happen to explore the architectural marvels of the dramatic brick Empire Stores with their griffins and eagles and arched gates at the water's edge. Last one over the bridge is a loser.

Salem, Mass.: Renewing It Right

I AM NOT ONE FOR SILVER LININGS or Panglossian optimism; I deal too much in the darker sides of people and cities. I am as aware as anyone that the world, or a good part of it, is teetering on the brink. It may even seem odd at such a time to suggest that a few things are going right. One small thing that is going very right, very quietly, and that will have noticeable long-term effects, is the consciousness that cities have developed about themselves. This self-discovery, brought about by calamitous renewal and the recognition of something called the environment, is barely 10 years old. It has been a largely unheralded urban revolution. But it is now generally acknowledged that an active awareness of a city's character, amenity and style, of its cultural and architectural tradition, of its ambience and quality of life, are as essential to its prosperity and health as the tax base.

In some American cities, drained by the automobile, suburbia and social change, this awareness has been linked to survival. Salem, Mass., is such a city, a small, encompassable community of 40,000, particularly rich in history and architecture. It is the quintessential example of the older American city that must "renew" itself to keep itself alive.

Salem has had all the problems of the aging physical fabric and the slipping economic base that unite failing metropolises of every size, plus the special concern of how to deal with a substantial national heritage. The difference between this city and others is that Salem is carrying out its renewal successfully and sensitively. It was not done without some disastrous backing and filling and radical changes of signals in the last 20 years, but that is illuminating too. And it still has a long way to go.

The message beginning to come out of Salem is that it is just those "uneconomic" assets of history and style that must be used as the basis of rebuilding to achieve the kind of quality and interest that attract the sort of money and activity that add up to the elusive creation of an attractive urban life.

The city's core of handsomely recycled old buildings complemented by excellent new buildings, united in an inviting network of green pedestrian passages, puts its emphasis on the human dimension and the highest standards of urban design. Its economic base is being reestablished on restored streets and in landmark buildings containing an emerging kind of personalized, specialty store with which the ubiquitous, standardized shopping center cannot compete. Salem's results promise to be a stunning rebuke to every community that has ever thought the only way to revitalization lay through imitation of those shopping centers or by mutilation of what was often a unique identity for shoddy-slick, newly jerrybuilt anonymity.

But it was not always thus. I might as well confess here that I was the original

The restoration of communities that had not been totally mutilated by urban renewal is a phenomenon of the 1970s, sparked by a realization of what had been lost. Salem has employed a sensitive approach to the past and the future. (Laurence Lowry)

witch of Salem. In 1965 I wrote a passionate indictment of Salem's then-proposed rape by renewal. Traffic and construction were its blind priorities and demolition its hallmark. That first plan was the product of the bulldozer mentality of the previous decade and of early federal renewal policies that ignored or penalized conservation. The article brought national notoriety to Salem, and a visit from the national Advisory Council on Historic Preservation. It also prefaced a drastic change in course.

Preservation, rehabilitation and reuse became top requirements; to date, over $3 million in public and private funds has gone into redoing old buildings. Developers were invited to submit schemes for preservation-related new construction that they were willing to build; Mondev International of Montreal, collaborating with architect Nelson Aldrich of Boston, won this critical assignment. Robert Kerr was hired as resident planner, and John Barrett, who has headed the Redevelopment Authority through all of its swings, coordinated some outstanding teamwork.

Particularly high marks must go to Nelson Aldrich and his firm and Mondev's subsidiary, the Salem Corporation, for their part in planning and design. Also notable is the work of the Collins, Dutot Partnership of Philadelphia, who have detailed and landscaped the pedestrian-park framework that sets so much of the style and amenity standards for the whole. Credit must be given to Bob Kerr, a planner-preservationist of persuasive sensitivities, who died before he could see the results, and to the banks and business community who have backed the process.

I shall not go into the technicalities of the unconventional devices such as historical and scenic easements that were manipulated as creative financing tools. Or of the intelligent planning that is putting the automobile where it belongs (in a convenient and compatible parking garage and strategic open areas) while providing the servicing of stores through courts and alleys behind streets. These are all ingenious and sensible solutions.

Nor shall I quibble about degree and kind of restoration, or inevitable errors or miscalculations, or the complexities that dictate compromise. The lovely brick and granite buildings of a pedestrianized Front Street, restored by James H. Ballou, have evidently been held for too-high rentals in a sluggish economy, slowing the renewal process. The rebuilt public market facing a beautifully reinterpreted Derby Square with its Bulfinch-style town hall of 1816, now successfully reunited with the surrounding brick vernacular buildings (they were to be torn down in the first plan), has simple new market sheds bridging past and present. But it will need subsidies to bring back the produce merchants, and it clearly runs the danger of an artsy-craftsy fate.

The point is that the rebuilding is all being done well, with a strong and yet delicate balance between centuries. What the visitor experiences now in the 40-acre central business district is still a tentative mix. There is a lot that is seedy, and one neither wants nor hopes for a total prettying up. Salem never promised anyone a Williamsburg, thank heavens, and the restoration of a fine, abused historic fabric has been a rational tool of contemporary reuse.

There are no design bows, or pratfalls to the past, just proper relationships and details. A new office building called One Salem Green, for example, by Campbell, Aldrich and Nulty, is sleekly modern and still a perfectly calculated foil for surrounding 18th- and 19th-century structures, including the restored Lyceum Building (site of Tom Thumb's wedding and now a fine French restaurant). The new offices are the focus of a small city hall plaza, a pocket park where before there were only the shabby backs of buildings behind a main traffic street.

The central parking garage, also by Campbell, Aldrich and Nulty, is one of the few genuinely attractive, nonjarring structures of this type ever to be dropped in the middle of a historic commercial district. There are handsome brick and patterned concrete pavements, sharpened vistas, and trees and seats everywhere.

When Mondev starts the new shopping block on the central commercial spine, Essex Street, the linchpin of the plan will fall into place and everyone will breathe a lot easier. HUD has committed an "urgent need" grant of $1.47 million under the Community Development Act to complete the pedestrian network by turning Essex Street into a landscaped mall. This promising commercial project, another by Campbell, Aldrich and Nulty, would create a functional and delightful East India Square at its heart.

Also at that heart are the Peabody Museum and the Essex Institute, two of the country's most distinguished institutions, forming a wonderfully rich blend of commercial and cultural activities. The exterior of the Peabody's new wing is a bit bleak and brutal, something that might have been ameliorated by more design finesse, but its urban intentions of street scale and placement are impeccable. The Peabody alone is worth anyone's Bicentennial visit, as one of the world's most enchanting and absorbing collections of Americana and Orientalia, mined from the exotic maritime history of early New England and the China trade in which Salem starred.

To those who treasure the ship captains' homes with their delicate McIntire doorways on Chestnut Street, the spacious common with its elegant bandstand, the

Bulfinch custom house on the harbor, the rewarding streets of bowdlerized but real architectural history, the news out of Salem is good. And for all who consider the culture and continuity of cities surpassingly relevant, the Salem plan signifies a country come of age.

New Orleans: The Old American City

A SMALL, OVERBOUTIQUED SECTION of the hundred-odd blocks of the French Quarter is about all the tourist ever sees of this remarkable city, except for an occasional foray into the Garden District. Fanning out around the Quarter are seemingly endless neighborhoods of uncommon stylistic richness, in various stages of regeneration and decay. The sheer architectural quality here is astounding.

But it is not all as safe and sound as the visitor— lulled by the protected and publicized Vieux Carré — believes. The central business district right next to the Quarter, a treasury of noteworthy structures, is currently fighting for its historical life. Rows of Greek Revival commercial buildings, of the kind New York ruthlessly demolished in Lower Manhattan in the 1960s, still stand, often enhanced by the characteristic iron filigree galleries added from the 1850s on. But many are gone and more are being knocked down almost daily, as are the later Italianate, Renaissance and cast-iron structures nearby that make up the 19th-century commercial city.

What has happened is that delayed "development," sparked by the new downtown Superdome, is currently hitting New Orleans like Hurricane Camille. Without the Quarter's legal district protection — incredibly, this is all that has protection in the city except for some National Register listings — the historic commercial area is now being savaged by speculators. The "demolition derby," as it is billed locally, goes on virtually within eyeshot of the waiting lines of pilgrims to Antoine's.

One out of every five buildings that stood in the central business district in 1970 no longer exists. Fifty-five new parking lots have been created, largely through old building demolition, and 42 percent of the district's land is now either vacant or used for parking. Except along Poydras Avenue, a central artery of the area where the "Manhattanization" of New Orleans is now taking off from the Superdome, building owners seldom have construction plans when they bulldoze, and are merely gambling on rising land values.

A growth management program has been studied by the Philadelphia firm of Wallace, McHarg, Roberts and Todd for city hall and the chamber of commerce. The consultants have indicated that there is more than enough vacant land to accommodate any future development needs. It is just a step across Canal Street from the Quarter to the gaping holes.

Pending completion of the study, a nine-month moratorium on further demolition was put into effect. When the moratorium hearing was held by the city council, it drew an immediate and overwhelming rash of before-the-deadline demolition requests from landowners. In a desperate and commendable response, Mayor Moon Landrieu called a special council meeting and imposed a temporary moratorium on all demolition permits until the formal proposal could be acted upon. But enough permits had already been granted to blitz some of the best remaining blocks.

Curiously, while this tragic destruction takes place, other New Orleans neighborhoods are being spontaneously salvaged. In-city residential districts, each one a marvelous potpourri of characteristic regional housing styles, are coming back

Nine blocks of Canal Street have become New Orleans's newest historic district, the fourth downtown. Designation followed destruction and some property owners' objections, but the law providing control over demolition and new design is working. (*Times-Picayune*)

spectacularly. Just beyond the central business district is the Lower Garden District, stepchild of the neighboring Garden District. Almost every street there seems to be undergoing extensive restoration. The antebellum houses, ranging from modest to quite grand, are mixed with later Victorian houses and industrial and commercial buildings.

The restoration boom is solidly entrenched in New Orleans's older residential sections, which seem to go on mile after fascinating mile. The old house revival is due partly to the execrable quality of the city's suburbs and the New Orleanian conviction that New Orleans is a fine place to live.

Success, however, breeds uneasy questions. How does the city propose to keep already mixed neighborhoods integrated as they are upgraded? How does one balance the problematic equation of poor and black displacement against rescue and revival of sound housing stock? Some answers are being sought in a neighborhood conservation study by the New Orleans firm of Curtis and Davis.

On the other side of the French Quarter are two very old districts as fascinating as the Quarter itself, but without any of the creeping preservation slickness. In Tremé, to the northwest, and Marigny, to the east, buildings range from the oldest house type, the dormered Creole cottage, to the raised cottage and the post–Civil War "shotgun" dwelling (railroad plan flat) with limitless lacy jigsaw filigree and brackets.

Then there are the long avenues, such as the incomparable Magazine Street, with its vital commercial mix in modest structures sometimes arcaded or galleried for the length of a block or more, and Tchoupitoulas, with its miles of cotton and other warehouses along the river. And there are also, of course, St. Charles, where the streetcar has been placed in the National Register, and Esplanade, and farther afield, Bayou St. John.

The tourist sees little of all this unless he has city-proud friends or family. New Orleans as a whole can only be sampled in the average visit; it cannot be fully seen or savored in weeks, months or even years. And so New Orleans is not at all what it seems from the souvenir shops of the Quarter's Chartres Street or the antique shops along Royale (moving out to Magazine as the fashionable rents get too high) — but something vaster, more complex and infinitely more varied and real.

Not that the Quarter isn't real; its charm is just somewhat glossed. It is a rare and genuine slice of cultural and urban history. But at this moment there is some recognizable handwriting on the wall. It is more than the commercial veneer of tourism. The Morning Call — traditional home of French coffee and beignets for generations — has left to move to an improbable suburban imitation called, equally improbably, Fat City. The open French Market is being prettily glassed in to house still more candle shops. There has been such a rash of hotel construction — the real Trojan horse within the gates — that new ones are no longer allowed to be built in the Quarter, although they can still be assembled out of old blocks.

With hindsight it is obvious that hotels should never have been added to the Vieux Carré or even placed at its immediate edge, as witness the visual bomb of the new monster high-rise Marriott. The city's mistake has been in treating the area primarily as a business bonanza rather than as an environmental trust, something not achieved automatically or guaranteed by aesthetic restrictions. It would draw tourism just as profitably without building it in. There are more ways to destroy than with the bulldozer.

But this is quibbling in the face of the demolition crisis in the adjoining business district. The new skyscrapers do little to curb one's distress. One Shell Square, a properly pristine tower by Skidmore, Owings and Merrill, must be credited with the unlikely achievement of looking totally deserted day or night. There is no visible life behind its obscure, dark glass windows or on its equally blank and formidably formal stepped plaza, graced only occasionally by a casual wino.

Philip Johnson and John Burgee are scheduled for another high-rise directly next to it on Poydras Street — already being called Park Avenue — the Pan American Life Insurance Building. Considering the sensitive urban and aesthetic nature of their recent work, that sounds promising. But it is less promising when one realizes that the architect and the client have knowingly destroyed one of New Orleans's irreplaceable "alleys" at the rear of the site, in spite of local pleas to save it, with the intention of "replacement" street level activity. For those who have walked the intimate alleys with their humanly scaled old structures, there is no replacement for the real thing, even in the most suave big-city style. [This building was cancelled because of the 1974 recession.]

Beyond that, there are the conventional horrors: a Hyatt House supercomplex scheduled to tie in with the Superdome; a 56-story office building and hotel grouping to zoom past everything for the site of the historic and handsome St. Charles Hotel, recently demolished. It is possible under existing zoning to build a larger structure on an equivalent piece of land than is permitted in Manhattan right now and someone is obviously about to do it in a no-win game of can you top this. The sad irony is that recent technical innovations have made the sky the limit in spite of marshy soil.

What price New Orleans? Only a few hundred million in local, Texas and other investment dollars. *States-Item* reporter and columnist Jack Davis has raised the critical question. Does anyone really have the right to destroy a city because he owns the land it stands on?

Marblehead, Mass.: Spirit of '76

T'S STANDING ROOM ONLY in this pre-Revolutionary town, but then, it always has been. "Old Town's" narrow streets were built up early, a clapboard-to-clapboard sequence of colonial, Federal and Greek Revival houses of stern simplicity in the best New England tradition, to which little could be added or subtracted. Things have remained crowded, austere and beautiful for several hundred years.

It seemed as if age and density were a natural protection against anything except normal, evolutionary change. But Marblehead's closeness to Boston has inevitably made it a bedroom community and suburbia has expanded its historic heart, bringing assorted domestic architectural atrocities common to the rest of the country. Density and demand have sent real estate prices zooming into the ludicrous range, with builders' banal worth $30,000 jacked up to $90,000 if it has any suggestion of a view. For $100,000 upward you can get a rather nice waterfront place. [Now there is virtually nothing under $100,000, and that nice waterfront place will cost you from $400,000 to a tidy million.] There is no shame.

If there is a handkerchief of land anywhere, people build. Streets that seemed permanently settled into a close mix of classical and Victorian suddenly sprout intruders in someone's garden; speculators seize the edges of the town dump and the cemeteries. Zoning and historical controls are fairly recent concerns. The "sold" sign goes up before construction is finished, and the only way to get a historic property is to become a close friend and caretaker to a dying native.

The old houses are beauties and the new ones are bastards. Among the latter, the precut "colonial" model with overhanging, 17th-century-type second story for shooting Indians is very popular with traditionalists. For the more "progressive," there is quasi-modern. The developers' product has moved from the sinking-into-the-ground number, with a kind of half story at the bottom that looks as if its windows are just disappearing into the earth, permitting a story-and-a-half "decorative" phony pedimented entrance, to an extraordinary combination of fake mansards and lally columns.

The false mansard disease is the current epidemic in and out of town. It seems to have infected the entire Northeast. It appears on everything from domestic to commercial structures, as a shingled (usually higgledy-piggledy imitation handmade) horizontal box topping supermarkets, gas stations and homes for the aged. The ever-proliferating roadside eating places, from pancake houses to "pubs," are all fake-mansarded on the outside and real plastic on the inside, food included. Shopping centers (mansarded) split and multiply where woodland stood. Roadside farm stands (no mansards) with native produce dwindle every year.

This instant vernacular is not a builder's rational simplification of clearly understood, more aristocratic styles, as on the streets of historic Marblehead, for a result of logic and elegance. It is a builder's shrewd invention of a cheap gimmick meant to evoke the older, legitimate vernacular with consummate shoddiness of execution and intent.

While building booms, traffic increases. Marblehead's one-way, winding streets that accommodate nothing larger than a Volkswagen have always been a potential driver's nightmare. "Casual" country driving habits include wrong side of the street parking and blithe ignoring of stop signs. Private ways are like Route 128. Bucolic lanes have bumper-to-bumper parking. The town recommends bicycle use as an alternative to car use, and that compounds chaos.

As a gesture to order, at least for the lost and strayed, there is a travelers' information booth in the center of town. After several seasons when it was manned by students, the radical innovation was made of using senior citizens. Complaints have dropped, absenteeism on good beach days is no longer a problem, and the new staff is a mine of local lore. It may be the beginning of a trend. So much for the youth cult.

You have to be middle-aged, at least, in Marblehead to remember Abby May's homemade candies (caramels not made in damp weather). The shop gave way to a pizza parlor long ago. Cameron's local breads have been gone for many seasons, and the Bide-a-Wee restaurant, where little old ladies have come in vintage hats for luncheons of broiled scrod and grapenuts pudding since time began, has turned into a gift shop. (The signs were clear when Bide-a-Wee succumbed to cake mix.) The old hardware store, where a night-blooming cereus on the sidewalk outside was a once-a-summer Marblehead nocturnal event, is a handprint fabric shop. Boutiques proliferate.

But Marblehead is not without its bucolic aspects. There is a miniature farm next door to us, the source of neighborly contributions to our table, and animals have been depleting the vegetables. The owner, assisted by Marblehead's finest, spent several of summer's most glorious weeks trapping and shooting skunks. Try that under your window. Mornings dawned with an anxious inspection of the trap to see if an execution was imminent. The police arrived at breakfast time, lights flashing, guns at the ready. Not exactly one of your urban problems.

One suspects, from glimpses of an unprecedented influx of Beautiful People, that the very worst may be happening to Marblehead: It may finally be getting chic. There is also a lot of sharing of houses in tight-packed Old Town by young Boston workers and airline employees, the congestion made worse by a car for every tenant. At the other end of the scale, the tourists who usually bypassed Marblehead are increasingly finding their way to its intimate waterfront in cruiser-size station wagons and Martian sport clothes.

They are also trekking to nearby Salem to line up en masse at the "Witch House," an over-reconstructed 17th-century landmark, complete with cafe curtains, at a corner marked by maximum heat, seedy commercialism and an endless traffic impasse. There is little waiting at the handsome McIntire and other historic houses in which the city abounds.

Salem, which now assiduously advertises itself as "historic Salem," just as assiduously destroyed or sabotaged a good part of its past before it saw the light. A series of demolition sites, mudholes and dust-pockets have finally turned into a prize-winning preservation-renewal plan. The pieces are coming together handsomely.

The pieces are still intact in Marblehead; they are just being elbowed briskly. The tiny gardens bloom brilliantly, the High Victorian red brick tower of Abbott Hall tops a low skyline of Federal and Grecian graces, and sunrises and sunsets are magical over one of the most breathtaking of small harbors, bridged by sailboats from shore to shore. A stroll along the streets (never on Sunday) is a lesson in history, art and taste, and the continuity that is genuine urban life. This is one of the wonder spots of the world, but the spoiling has begun.

OLD FRIENDS AND DELIGHTS

Jefferson's Virginia

THE UNIVERSITY OF VIRGINIA, built from 1817 to 1827, is probably the single most beautiful and effective architectural group of its kind in this country, or in the history of American building. And since it is a work so distinctly from the heart and mind of Thomas Jefferson, the great statesman and humanist whose art and politics shared a common philosophy and culture, a trip to his "academical village" is a fine way to touch base with the beginnings of the new nation.

I paid a first visit on a day in late winter, in soft rain. For February, the temperature was mild, and the even light and gray sky set off the Jeffersonian formula of red brick and white colonnades with a singular clarity and serenity. The wet weather enhanced the color of clay-red earth; the green of the grass was pre-spring muted.

As it was conceived and still stands, the heart of the University of Virginia consists of two rows of continuous, connected pavilions and colonnades facing each other on the east and west sides of an approximately 750-foot-wide lawn. Called the east and west lawns, these rows are backed by a second, arcaded row of dormitories known as the east and west ranges. There are gardens between the rows, enclosed with serpentine brick walls. At the center of the main axis of the group, at the north end, is the Rotunda. The complex is set on a ridge, so that the modern university recedes below it.

The three-sided rectangle was meant to be open ended, for a spectacular view of the valley and mountains beyond. With a sublime stroke of insensitivity, the vista was closed with new construction in the 1890s by McKim, Mead and White. If the vista were open now, however, the view would be of motels, shopping centers, gas stations and the random signs that are the totems of the 20th-century environment. To get to the world of Jefferson one must go through the world of Venturi — a traumatic, time-tube trip from the Pop landscape of the 20th century to the neoclassical architectural elegance of the early 19th century. Motels to Monticello, it might be called, or subtitled, how the rolling hills and rocky ridges of the beautiful Piedmont, sweeping to the Blue Ridge Mountains and the rim of the sky, became the world of the schlockbuilt fast buck.

The university's heart is literally centuries away. The classical pavilions, of which there are five on each side, are joined by the colonnaded student dormitories between. They were used originally for instruction and the professors' residences. Although the effect is unified, each one is different, as is frequently pointed out, because Jefferson wanted the various classical orders illustrated to serve also as teaching models. They range from the Doric of the Diocletian Baths and the Ionic of the Theater of Marcellus to the orders as found in Palladio.

The colonnades between pavilions gradually grow longer from one end to the other, a fact that is noted less frequently. The one exception to the Roman or

---

A $10 million campaign is under way at the University of Virginia to restore the pavilions and ranges on the lawn of Thomas Jefferson's "academical village" and to create an endowment for their maintenance. (University of Virginia)

Palladian orders is a maverick pavilion with a recessed arch that seems to derive from the latest thing in France at that date — the work of Claude Nicholas Ledoux —a not surprising architectural adventure for Jefferson the Francophile. This use of the new French style was as avant-garde as some of the other sources were doctrinaire.

But there is nothing doctrinaire about this architecture as a whole, and that is the reason for its beauty and importance. Although it gives the appearance of uniformity in the classical totality of its composition and details, it is still rich in calculated variety. There is something in man that loves order and unity; they are virtues that induce serenity. But the unity of this complex is never static, because of the differences in its never-identical parts and the subtle device of the changing measure. The architecture is a kind of paradox: at once didactic and free, monumental and humanistic, aristocratic and pragmatic, romantic and rational, formal and hospitable. It combines an intimate human scale with controlled, universal vistas. The result is consummately lovely, with a quality of grace lost to our age. These are lessons that have escaped the modern monumentalists.

But it was far from perfect. Roofs leaked, chimneys smoked, the orientation that produced such handsome effect also exposed the rows to burning western sun in summer and driving east winds and rains in winter, and cut off southern breezes in the heat. The pavilion lecture rooms were inadequate and the professors' quarters didn't work for family life. The proximity of the students to faculty was a cause for complaint. But whatever is, or was, wrong seems to be forgiven today for the impact and pleasure of the whole. Students compete avidly for the cell-like rooms with their (unchanged) outdoor facilities. Firewood stands neatly stacked outside the doors.

It may be somewhat ungrateful to examine the role of Jefferson more closely in this design. The concept was clearly his; it had surfaced shortly after 1800 in earlier proposals. And his adjustment of the plan and relationships of the parts are sensitive responses to site, function and form. But there is a tendency to magnify the considerable talent of a man who was essentially a gifted amateur.

Jefferson was "fixated" on books and on "fishing" his designs out of them, according to Benjamin Latrobe, his friend and America's outstanding architect at that time. Latrobe was a man of sophisticated professional training and taste. Jefferson turned to Latrobe for advice on the Virginia scheme, and the suggestions he got from both Latrobe and from William Thornton, the first architect of the Capitol, are exactly what turned the design from a skilled amateur concept into a professional masterwork.

He must have been a bit of a nuisance, as so many well-intentioned amateurs are. To both Thornton and Latrobe he wrote for "a few sketches, such as may not take you a minute . . ." — a request that always makes the pros groan. But Thornton suggested columns instead of piers for the arcade, which adds much to the power of the scheme. And Latrobe crystallized that power with the proposal for "something grand" at the north end, in the form of a great dominating building, where Jefferson had just intended to continue the rows. This gives the composition its full force and definition. And Latrobe anchored the plan with the pavilions at the corners. These changes were catalytic improvements. Jefferson chose the Pantheon as the model for the Rotunda, and made able adjustments in scale.

When Jefferson worked alone, as at Monticello, he produced an extraordinary, eccentric, half-failed building. It is not a really beautiful house, inside or out. There are splendid starts and inept stops and passages that mismatch intention and result, demonstrating at every unresolved turn how his spatial and structural knowledge failed to keep up with his ideas. Architecturally, that house is in trouble everywhere, but the vision that comes through was exceptional. More than a cultivated classicist, more than an expert Palladian, Jefferson had already embraced the bold "new" expressionistic neoclassicism of Soane in England and Ledoux in France. The two-story-high rooms, the strange second floor disguised as part of a single story, all grope passionately for the new spatial expression.

Jefferson experimented and overreached magnificently — another characteristic lost to our cautious, computerized time. He never played safe, and he avoided, in the words of the historian William Pierson, "the sterility of the absolute." His architecture reveals him as a "humanist and poet concerned with the goodness of life."

The Jefferson design for the University of Virginia suggests the whole range of values to which American democracy aspired: unity in variety, the subordination of the parts to the whole, a humanistic order and the dignity of the individual. Delight was also there; where has delight gone in 150 years? What has happened to the values that infused the life, art and politics of the new nation?

Beaux Arts Buildings I Have Known

MANY OF MY EARLIEST AND MOST PERSISTENT architectural memories are of the Beaux Arts in New York, but I was unaware of it, like Molière's bourgeois gentilhomme who didn't know he was speaking prose. When I did become aware of it, I found out I wasn't supposed to like it. Alas, it was too late. Those buildings were as much a part of my life as my family, and I could neither dismiss nor neutralize my feelings toward them, which were intimately involved in the process of growing up.

By a curious coincidence, one of the institutions that taught me that they were all wrong now tells me that they're all right, and I'd be confused if I weren't delighted. The Museum of Modern Art, in a scholarly reversal of its own tradition as keeper of the flame of modern architecture, has featured a large and beautiful show of 19th-century French academic drawings called "The Architecture of the Ecole des Beaux Arts." The Beaux Arts style, in its variations from ornate French classicism to cool Roman and Renaissance revivalism, is to be found in this country's major monuments from 1890 to 1910 and later. The Architectural League has prepared a tour list of some of the best local Beaux Arts buildings, available at the museum. In connection with these activities, I would like to present my own list. It might be called Beaux Arts buildings I have known and loved (or hated) in New York.

I grew up, all unwittingly, in a Beaux Arts structure called the St. Urban, whose style and substance were light years away from today's architectural con-game known as the "luxury" apartment house. All the milestones of my childhood and adolescence are colored by Beaux Arts experiences. I think of Grand Central Terminal, not in its present grimy state, battling for its life, but as I remember it on Friday afternoons when we would take the Merchants' Limited — crisp white damask and roses in silver bud vases in the diner — to visit family in Boston. The trip began in the Grand Concourse, which seemed to hold all the nameless promises of pleasure and adventure of travelers past and present in its constantly moving, muted rhythms beneath the great sky-blue vaulted ceiling with its illuminated constellations. (Tomorrow, the universe.)

Grand Central's monumental richness and superb efficiency were accepted without question by New Yorkers; in fact, it was fashionable only to question its style, considered inferior to European models and somehow tainted with American utilitarianism. I can see now that it is absolutely one of the best things of its kind

The Metropolitan Museum is conspicuously engaged in superbuilding for supercollections. Although one still enters via Hunt's grand (and now glossy) Beaux Arts *marche*, an attempt was made to eliminate the grand stair to the second floor. (Museum of the City of New York)

anywhere in the world. The facade from Park Avenue South is quintessential Beaux Arts — immense arched windows and paired, fluted columns rising building-height above the girdling roadway like a triple triumphal arch, fronted by a bronze Commodore in his astrakhan-collared coat directing taxis to the other side. It is hard to imagine New York without Mercury, Hercules and Minerva atop Jules Coutan's monumental clock; it is part of the city's essential image and remaining elegance.

There were trips from Penn Station too — McKim, Mead and White's Roman extravaganza of 1910 in cream travertine and pink granite, later soot-darkened, where the traveler debouched into the tepidarium of the Baths of Caracalla. It was demolished in 1966. "One entered the city like a god," Vincent Scully has written, ". . . one scuttles in now like a rat."

When I was allowed to roam New York by myself, I went first to the Museum of Natural History, where I spent spellbound days in the old J.C. Cady wing of 1877, a dark, blackish-brown pile later cleaned to a surprisingly frivolous pink. The blue whale suspended from the entrance ceiling became my friend. So did the building. When the museum built its new centerpiece in 1936, an archeologically correct Roman monument in retardataire Beaux Arts by John Russell Pope, I hated it, and still do. Not because anyone told me to hate it (by then I knew), but because those pompous, forbidding, overscaled steps led to huge, cold, tomblike halls, vast, dim, dead spaces in which one felt depressed and diminished. This is a kind of building totally devoid of joy. I cannot make myself go there now, but I am glad that lots of other people do.

The world really opened for me across town, at the Metropolitan Museum. It was true-blue Beaux Arts (Richard M. Hunt, Richard H. Hunt and McKim, Mead and White, successively, from 1895 to 1906) and its grandeur worked. The steps invited rather than repelled, in that formal Beaux Arts *marche,* or moving progression of spaces, that invited one into the high-ceilinged hall with its tapestries, chandeliers and stray knights in armor or oversized antiquities. (I have never been able to reconcile myself to its current "restoration," a slick cross between IBM and I. Magnin glamor.) In the best Beaux Arts fashion, these spaces either beckoned you up the grand stairs (if you were young and supple) to the painting galleries, or led you left or right, to the worlds of Egypt, Greece and Rome. It is no exaggeration to say that this building shaped my life.

So did the 42nd Street Library (Carrère and Hastings, 1898-1911), when my art studies began to take me there for research. Another beautiful Beaux Arts building became a friend. It made no pretense at chumminess; it was intended to impress, but again, it worked. A sense-expanding spatial sequence from the arched and colonnaded portal to more marble and massive stairs and richly detailed rooms inside provided both grace and grandeur and suggested that man might be noble, after all. Or at least that he knew quality from junk.

Walks around town left indelible impressions. There was the New York Yacht Club on West 44th Street (Warren and Wetmore, 1889), a baroque extravaganza with flowing water carved below galleon-shaped windows — what child would not adore it? I was a post–post graduate student before I knew that this was *architecture parlante,* defined in the Architectural League's guide as "architecture whose function is literally articulated by its form and decoration" — here ships and sea in stone.

A woman still does not enter New York's great Beaux Arts men's clubs, except as a pariah through designated areas. I remember visiting the University Club (McKim, Mead and White, 1889), a Renaissance superpalazzo, and making an instinctive, architecturally propelled rush for the great, gutsy marble columns visible from the

Indirect lighting and lavish corporate-style furnishings have replaced the old chandeliers, stone benches, Assyrian reliefs and odd suits of armor in the Met's Great Hall. Facilities have been streamlined to handle today's museum-going crowd. (Carleton Knight III)

door. None of that, now. I was peremptorily turned aside into a pusillanimous "ladies" dining room. The insult was as much architectural as personal.

At the Battery, I found the U.S. Custom House (Cass Gilbert, 1907), 40 giant columns around its sides, embellished with dolphins, rudders, tridents and winged wheels, guarded by Daniel Chester French's Four Continents. Farther along, on Liberty Street, was James Baker's 1901 Chamber of Commerce Building, a particularly rich fruitcake of dormers and bull's-eye windows, colonnade and copper-crested roof, frosted with garlands. Delighted by their outrageous assurance, I adopted them both.

From my office window, as I write, my constant companion is a small Beaux Arts skyscraper directly across on 42nd Street. It is elegantly composed and decorated, with three elongated, vertical bands of round-arched windows dominating a delicate, five-bay arrangement, topped with a crown of carved stone. The street at its feet is porn-country; the neighborhood around it is a disaster area. But the finesse with which the building proposes that skill and order are not only justifiable but desirable is somehow reassuring. I raise my eyes for an architecture break in a city that is as heartbreaking in its beauty as it is in its poverty and decay. It is still a city of dreams — promised, built and broken.

A Hard Act to Follow

I HAVE HAD TWO CONTINUING LOVE AFFAIRS with Beaux Arts buildings in New York, the Metropolitan Museum and the 42nd Street Library. Both institutions have opened doors to the discovery of the wonders and beauties of the universe for me as a child and an adult, something the big city is supposed to do — and does.

High school, college, graduate work and professional research have led me to the library's elegant French classical pile of Vermont marble on Fifth Avenue, past E. C. Potter's lions of 1911, through the Corinthian columns of the triple-vaulted entrance and the rich, bronze doors to the noble foyer, up the monumental stairs into the half-acre vastnesses of the reading rooms as gently sounding as trees by the sea.

One can, of course, rise directly to the treasures of the third floor by elevator, now efficiently if somewhat banally automated, but I remember the open bronze cages run by autocratic ladies in sweaters on stools who took grim delight in closing the doors in your face. When you missed them, you waited, and waited, and waited. You walked, then, along corridors as wide and splendid as ballrooms lined with displays of rare prints on the way to the imposing stairs and the skylit silence of History and Genealogy and the Fine Arts.

I can do it blindfolded, but except for the section of the second floor where the addition of ugly fluorescent lighting fixtures strikes a harsh, false note, I wouldn't want to. I'd hate to miss that prime example of sentimental Victorian pictorial history by the yard, Munkacsy's *Blind Milton Dictating Paradise Lost to His Daughters* on the second floor landing. But it is not for nostalgia or memorabilia that I sometimes detour to Fifth Avenue. It is for substance, style and quality in a city and world that are hard put to provide such commodities today and hardly know how to evaluate them. I am not weeping for the past; I am concerned for the future.

For me, the building has always worked well. I have found it an excellent tool, and much, much more. I could not be persuaded to admire a monument that does not work, not even the beautifully detailed elegance of Carrère and Hastings's Beaux Arts masterpiece of 1902-09. No building is admirable that abuses function.

Like going back home: The New York Public Library at 42nd Street has been painstakingly restored rather than fashionably refurbished. In a rare but deserved honor, the architects, Carrère and Hastings, are enshrined in niches in Astor Hall. (© Peter Aaron, ESTO)

Some turn-of-the-century commentators thought the library forfeited claims to architectural greatness because its classical grandeur had been fitted to function as the designers' primary concern, with some sacrifice of approved monumental formulas. Later it was fashionable to admire only the rear of the building, where plain, vertical slit windows light the stacks and lighten the structure's mass with protomodern simplicity. How temporal are the standards of critics!

It must be remembered that this is one of the last of the great 19th-century buildings. It was actually conceived and planned in the 1890s. Still, it has consistently filled 20th-century needs. In spite of its formal grandeur, the experience of the building is intimate and emotional. In spite of its scale, it is never cold or tiring. For me, it is always like going home.

The library's Fifth Avenue facade is both magnificent and welcoming. The fact that the terrace and park behind have become a mugger and drug dealer's oasis was never part of the Beaux Arts *parti*. (New York Convention and Visitors Bureau)

The New York Public Library receives support from two sources. The citywide circulation system is paid for by public funds from city and state. The research collections, of which the 42nd Street branch is the heart, are sustained by private funds from the Astor, Tilden and Lenox foundations, the three sources united in 1895 to create the New York Public Library, plus gifts and annual fund raising.

The Mid-Manhattan Library, an addition across the avenue, increases the availability of general research and circulation material. The new facility represents a careful jigsaw of city, state, federal and public and private funds, and it is wonderful to have it. But did it have to be so depressingly ordinary in design? The trip across the street was all downhill. It makes one hope that the furniture of the mind is what really counts. I don't, of course, believe that for a minute; you can't be literate, or educated, and nonvisual at the same time.

Across the street Carrère and Hastings keep their backs politely turned. Carrère is in bronze by Jo Davidson, and Hastings is in marble by Frederick MacMonnies. Both are in niches at the foot of the north and south stairs.

They got the commisssion by competition in 1897, a process that has produced some of the country's best public structures. The building was authorized by the city on the site of the old Croton Reservoir in the same year.

The completed structure cost $9 million and is virtually unreproducible at any price. Pressed for a description, Hastings called it a modern building. It was meant to serve the needs of its day, he explained, by an evolutionary use of the Renaissance forms that he believed most suited the tastes of Western man. He was rumored to be less than satisfied with the Fifth Avenue front. Some thought the building overly rich in decorative detail. That was before craftsmanship died.

As urban planning, the library still suits the city remarkably well. A stepped terrace on the Fifth Avenue side offers a balustraded, tree-shaded space skillfully separated from street traffic. An "esplanade" at the rear, between the building and Bryant Park, from 40th to 42nd streets, arched over by giant trees and bordered with ivy, is one of the best and earliest examples of the block-through pedestrian passage now stressed by New York's planners. Compare this gentle monumentality and knowing humanism with the pompous aridity of the new street treatment of the library's sister Beaux Arts monument, the Metropolitan Museum. Someone should have looked 40 blocks south.

The library's white Vermont marble, cleaned in 1950 and hosed down early Sundays, is mellowing to a pale Athenian gold. "It is one building in the spring morning with the new green of the lindens," wrote David Gray in *Harper's Monthly* of March 1911, "another in the autumn rain, another in the snow-suffused winter twilight, and others under the moon or the night sky, or under the low-hanging yellow mist tinged with the city's lights." That is the enduring magic of New York.

The Skyscraper Style

T HE ART DECO AVALANCHE IS ON. The period and its products are being flirted with by the popular press, puffed by dealers in nostalgia and apotheosized in a series of books. Finch College's exhibition (1974), called "American Art Deco Architecture," has put the movement into proper focus in the broad terms of American building of the 1920s and 1930s with emphasis on what is increasingly called the Skyscraper Style.

No style has been more neglected, undervalued, misunderstood or camped up. No style has been more vulnerable to the bulldozer, egregious remodeling or the disdain of contemporary scholars. In the peculiar terms of the growing popularity of Art Deco (named after the Paris Exposition of Modern Decorative and Industrial Art of 1925), kitsch is being given equal standing with high art. And so the selective scholarship and qualitative standards imposed on the subject by Elayne Varian, who organized and installed the exhibition and wrote the catalog, are exactly what is needed at this moment.

It is as easy to be entranced by this style as it is to miss its genuine substance. There is immense visual pleasure in its fantasy world of ziggurats, sunbursts, zigzags, waves, stepped triangles, stylized machines, abstract suggestions of energy and speed, and the exotic natural wonders of waterfalls, tortoises, condors and doves. One marvels at the superb craftsmanship in marble, bronze, glass, bakelite, monel metal, plastics and rare woods.

The appeal of this vintage modernism — naive, romantic and upbeat — is enormous. The American work is a sizable production by men of notable talent, among them Eliel Saarinen, Paul Cret, Raymond Hood, Bertram Goodhue and others who have not yet received their due. But what is most clearly and heartbreakingly revealed in any presentation is that the buildings shown represent the last great period of decorative art. We are struck with the poignant reality that it

The demolition of the Richfield Building in Los Angeles — an Art Deco masterpiece of oil-related themes such as automobiles and airplanes executed in bronze and marble and the zigzags of a mythical Machine Age — was a serious architectural loss. (Marvin Rand, HABS)

will never be possible to do this kind of work again.

Art Deco, or Style Moderne, is primarily the art of the skyscraper age. As such it is extraordinary that these structures have been systematically excluded from the modern architecture textbooks, or relegated to footnotes. They are among the biggest and best buildings in a country that has earned its place in architectural history in large part through skyscraper development.

Because they failed to conform to the tenets of the International Style — a rigid "functionalism" with a "technological" aesthetic that equated ornament with "crime" — they have been blacklisted by the official historians of the International Style, which had a valid claim and stake in the 20th-century architectural revolution. The International Style is, in fact, correctly perceived as the prime base of modernism, but to make the point propagandistically its promoters were rigidly exclusionistic. These exclusions, particularly with hindsight, have become ludicrous.

The essential difference between the International Style skyscraper and the Art Deco skyscraper (and there were hybrids, such as Raymond Hood's 1931 McGraw-

Hill Building in New York) is that the International Style struggled to reveal the expressive visual power of the structural frame, and Art Deco simply took the technology for granted and embroidered the result.

It is quite possible to read structure and function in the column and spandrel facade of the 450 Sutter Building of 1930 in San Francisco by Timothy Pflueger and James Miller. But beyond that the spandrels are decorative fantasies, and both glass and metal are angled for a richly plastic facade. One of the least recognized factors of these Art Deco skyscrapers is the extremely successful plasticity of the building as a whole, aside from the applied ornament; there is a great preoccupation with planes and volumes and sculptural effect. Such effects are further dramatized with light, often in the form of lit glass tubes — another element of the Deco vocabulary. The Niagara Mohawk Building in Syracuse, N.Y., is a spectacular example.

Most of these characteristics aim at a frankly surface appeal that is highly suspect within the puritan ethic (aesthetic?) of modernism. To International Stylists, this approach, tied as it is to tradition, is original sin. Still, the ornament is often extremely beautiful. It is perhaps hard to grasp the fact that elevator lobbies can be historic interiors; Art Deco turned them into incredible 20th-century art forms. These examples are disappearing, however, persistently destroyed by marble-slab "modernization." A radiator grille, a mailbox or a doorknob can be, and is, a collector's item. When a building is torn down or remodeled, the discarded parts are so prized that the vultures close in.

It is worth noting that Art Nouveau and Art Deco have much in common: They both emphasize the primacy of a new vocabulary of ornamental forms of a remarkable creativity and strong sensuous pleasure, bypassing structural innovation. If one style is valid, so is the other. And yet the former is accepted as part of the

Another example of the style, 60 Wall Street in New York, is gone, but in Oakland, Calif., the Paramount Theater, decked out in a splendid array of lavish Art Deco theatrical motifs, has been saved for a concert hall. (Jack E. Boucher, HABS)

official 20th-century aesthetic and the latter is not.

These buildings are rarely designated as landmarks, and even their documentation has only begun. So far, their fate is in the hands of speculators. Los Angeles's Richfield Building of 1928 by Morgan, Walls and Clements was demolished in 1967. The Cities Service Company, which moved from Wall Street to Tulsa recently, has torn down an assortment of its Wall Street properties in spite of New York's official pleas to save them, leaving only Clinton and Russell's 60 Wall Street tower built for Cities Service in 1932. It faces an uncertain future. In a more welcome move, Oakland, Calif., has converted Timothy Pflueger's Paramount Theater of 1931 into a home for the Oakland Symphony.

Those who can should take a few field trips in New York and other cities. The elevators in the Chrysler Building, for example, are a special aesthetic experience; each cab is an elaborately different marquetry and metal Deco garden of delights. The best exhibitions of the art of architecture are still in the streets. It will be tragic if these buildings end up as fragments in a museum.

Art and Nostalgia and the Great World's Fairs

WHETHER YOU DEAL IN FIRST-HAND MEMORIES or trendy revivalism, a small show called "1930s Expositions" (New York Cultural Center, 1973) is an enchanted bit of nostalgia. It memorializes an innocent and romantic world that idealized past and future on the pleasure principle in an art form of equal innocence and romanticism that reached its apogee in a single decade.

The display, which consists of enlarged photographs, reconstructed models and wonderful campy souvenirs from the collection of Lawrence G. Zimmerman, was organized originally by Arnold L. Lehman for the Dallas Museum of Fine Arts.

These were the American world's fairs of legend, illusion and fantasy, spawned by the London Crystal Palace of 1851 and spun off by Chicago's white plaster extravaganza in 1893. There was a Century of Progress in Chicago in 1933, the California-Pacific Exposition in San Diego in 1935, the Texas Centennial Exposition in Dallas in 1936, the Golden Gate International Exposition in San Francisco in 1939 and the World of Tomorrow at the New York World's Fair in an absolute orgy of excess in the same year.

I came in at the end of the decade for the last one, as a schoolgirl, so my responses are both personal and academic. But the sight of the Trylon and Perisphere and the Futurama brought memories crowding back of fireworks-illuminated Courts of Honor, sleek, levitated soap statuary and color-washed fountains on summer evenings, with the particular bittersweet poignancy of lovely, lost times.

It is a historic era now, and the style it embodied was pure futuristic fairy tale, made of the hopes and dreams of hard times, when many needed hopes and dreams to stay alive. There was no cynicism. There was no black humor. The human condition, or one's awareness of its problems and inequities, had not reached the point where a sense of the absurd became salvation. It was an absurd world, in its own way, but we loved its flashy, streamlined promises of better things.

These glorious, overreaching efforts, Lehman's exhibition text tells us, were "all eagerly anticipated and intensely debated during the planning years, enormously successful in terms of attendance and all generally financially unsound. Like the movies and baseball, fair going became a recognized American pastime. In a decade of economic depression, fairs offered an escapism similar to but more tangible than

Hollywood palliatives [that] easily outdrew the reality of contemporary life. . . . Great, white, magical, temporary cities thrilled millions of awed visitors."

And no wonder. Chicago's three-and-a-half-mile lakefront site in 1933 was committed to "advancement through technology" in theme and style. Its plywood and plaster buildings owed much to the Moderne mode propagandized by the Paris Exposition of 1925, with its flat, faceted and striated surfaces, shallow ornaments of Art Deco inspiration and smoothly curved and striped vertical and horizontal forms.

It was all style, even its technology, and it reached its peak in the Travel and Transportation Building by E. H. Bennett and Hubert Burnham, where ostentatiously cable-hung, dark and light prismatic panels and a stunning Art Deco sunburst entrance were obviously the impeccably modernistic *dernier cri*. (Modernistic, we remind our nonhistorian readers, is not a synonym for modern; it specifically identifies this 1920s-30s style, currently adopted as fashionably high camp.)

The federal government had a Busby Berkeley special of three triangular, striped, concave-sided towers rising suavely from a globular base sprouting stepped projections and heroic statues like department store dummies wrapped in carefully folded napkins, theatrically floodlit from below. The whole fair was bathed in brilliantly colored light by Joseph Urban. Raymond Hood and Paul Cret were on the architectural commission.

San Diego in 1935 devoted the 1,400-acre Balboa Park to an orgy of Spanish

The Travel and Transportation Building at Chicago's 1933 Century of Progress was a high point of 1930s expressive style and technology. In Dallas, remnants of the 1936 exposition in Fair Park are being restored. (Bill Hedrich, Hedrich-Blessing)

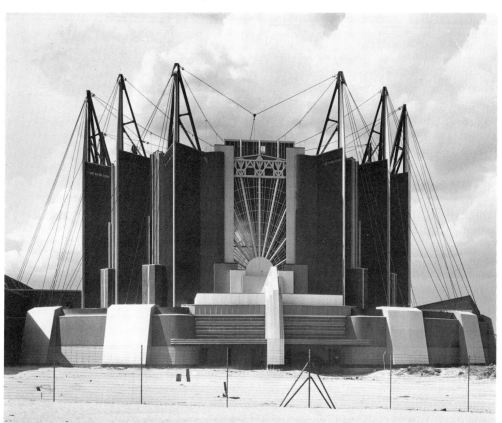

colonial *modernisme* in its California-Pacific Exposition, based on the remaining
Bertram Grosvenor Goodhue buildings of the Panama-California Exposition of 1915.
Stylized and imaginary Aztec and Mayan motifs were flattened into friezes and
borders and all-over patterns on massed and pyramided structures. The automobile
companies added their characteristic white stuccoed facades.

Dallas in 1936 orchestrated a monumental celebration of Texas under six flags, and
60 percent of the buildings were permanent, to serve as exhibition halls for future
state fairs. A contemporary description of its style serves best: "Severe and
monumental, interpreted as modern, flavored with the condiments of Egypt and
Archaic Greece, and finally seasoned with the warmth and sunshine of the
southwest."

Again, this supereclecticism relied on bold, modernistic massing and formal
geometry. The entrance was an enormous Lone Star, and the searchlight-striped sky
at night over the huge, symmetrical Esplanade of State and its central reflecting pool
must have made a stage set Hollywood couldn't match. Sculpture, in all of the fairs,
was universally unsurpassed trivia. Here archaic-visaged maidens with pastry-horn
Greek hairdos and smoothly inflated bodies trailed cut-paper draperies over
extruded cactus plants and other native flora.

San Francisco in 1939 exploited its Pacifica motif for a kind of orientalized
modernistic fantasia on the 400-acre, man-made Treasure Island in the Bay. The high
points were "elephant towers" of stepped, abstract geometry on soaring pyramidal
bases and fountain courts where oversized plaster goddesses dangled stars.

The combination of futurism, exotica and streamlined classicism, in various
formulas, was Everyman's vision of tomorrow. It was the last gasp, in Lehman's
words, of the grand space-making schemes of the Beaux Arts planners and the
adolescent excesses of the industrial designer's art.

Apart from its evocative delights, this show is a conscious departure from the
approved art-historical way of looking at exposition architecture. Superficially, it is a
bow to high camp, an ode to kitsch and an example of the current fashionable
preference for period corn. It breaks with the tradition of Sigfried Giedion, which
traces exposition building as a series of dramatic exercises in progressive technology,
from the glass and metal of the Crystal Palace to the increasing spans engineered for
various Machinery Halls. This led finally to the circuses of tortured experimental
techniques in recent years.

The approach was valid and the structural history it taught was real; it was just
hopelessly one-sided. The pictures in the history books are carefully selected for
timeless technical details, and the taste of the time is just as carefully finessed.

There is now a new and rising art historian's view of the international exposition
as a catalyst of taste and style. Its function as a prime cultural indicator has been
passed over for real or imagined cosmic significance. It tells about society at a certain
moment, which is the role art and history play best.

And so there is more to the sudden passion for the memorabilia of the recent past
than mere nostalgia. Nostalgia is a sadly desperate game, an instinctive gut reaction
to the fact that we have gone through, and are still going through, a period of
shattering change, a destructive, antiheroic, antibeautiful phase of smashing beliefs,
idols and ideals, in a world that offers none of the certainties and standards that kept
earlier generations stable in adversity.

It is a clutching at the symbols of romantically remembered pleasure — we forget
the boredom or pain — for those who experienced it, and a kind of cultural role
playing for the young. It is the regret, conscious or visceral, for a simplicity and
optimism that can never come again. Art is part of this, and today life and art are
complex and anguished, and you can't go home, or to the great world's fairs, again.

Friends in Public Places

I AM NOT THE PERSON TO JUDGE the statues in the Metropolitan Museum's show on "New York City Public Sculpture" (1974) as art, because they are all my friends. Besides, my competence runs more to how public art affects public space.

I have been a street wanderer since childhood, and most of these heroic bronzes and marbles are familiar individuals for whom I feel a surprising warmth. It wasn't until I developed "taste" and studied art that I found I wasn't supposed to like them — not really. The Union Square equestrian statue of George Washington by Henry Kirke Brown is not the Colleoni, and Bernini would have laughed at the Maine monument. The standards of verisimilitude and representation of virtues larger than life had become aesthetic unmentionables.

And so the reviewer of this 19th-century public sculpture by American artists is in trouble. He can have a ball with it as camp or a problem with it as art, since it is impossible now to approach it in terms of its original intentions. It is hard to accept it philosophically and grossly unfair to judge it any other way, even while applying the absolute yardstick that the critic must carry. Skills serve philosophy, and the simplistic promotion of heroic ideals and the perfectable nobility of man as beloved by the Victorians and considered the perfect accent for city spaces has succumbed to the realities of the age of the antihero.

That is why attempts at representational heroic sculpture today are instantly doomed; without belief there is no art. And it is therefore a wrenching effort to evaluate the success or failure of these 19th-century monuments as sculpture alone. Even though it has become fashionable to admire and admit the emotional impact of the Lincoln Memorial — we now acknowledge the moving quality of Daniel Chester French's giant seated figure within Henry Bacon's classical temple — few fully embrace the genre, the period (which extended well into the 20th century) and the product.

This step has been taken wholeheartedly, however, by the director of the museum's show, Lewis I. Sharp, who is also responsible for the commendable catalog (produced with a grant, quite properly, from the Plaza Hotel, on whose doorstep both Augustus Saint-Gaudens's General Sherman and Karl Bitter's Pomona, Goddess of Abundance, stand).

This most sensitive and delightful presentation of 22 examples of New York statuary ranges from the handsome totality of the architecturally planned space at the entrance to Brooklyn's Prospect Park by Stanford White, with the collaborating effort of a galaxy of sculptors, to John Quincy Adams Ward's Horace Greeley brooding over City Hall Park in a fringed chair.

In some cases, the public spaces were designed or carefully considered at the same time. In others, the statue was placed almost arbitrarily, with much debate over site. In almost all instances, the architect was commissioned for the base as carefully as the sculptor was commissed for the figure and was a man of equal reputation.

Saint-Gaudens, for example was consistently partnered with Stanford White, and Ward and Richard Morris Hunt were a repeated team. And until you've seen a really bad base, like the awkward high-rise of the equally awkward Daniel Webster in Central Park (whose pomposity affords a certain delight), you may not be aware of the difference this can make.

To consider this work in terms of urban design is a distinct relief. Although I must confess to an increasing admiration for Saint-Gaudens, whether it is inspired by his ladylike Victory leading Sherman appropriately toward Bergdorf Goodman's, or by any number of his masterful figures and friezes.

The Plaza, properly called Grand Army Plaza, just south of Central Park at 59th Street and abutting Fifth Avenue, is a close-to-perfect city space. Even the unpardonable mutilation provided by the General Motors Plaza across the street, an object lesson in a plaza in the wrong place and in contrasting commercial banality, has failed to destroy its integrity.

Bergdorf's now stands in place of the Vanderbilt mansion, but its classily unpretentious modern style is a fine backdrop for Bitter's Fountain of Abundance, with its serene Renaissance basins. To beat a marble horse, the General Motors building, with its provincial posh, is the only fall from grace. It replaced the Savoy Plaza.

The fronting plaza itself is the work of the architect Thomas Hastings, of Carrère and Hastings, who completed it in 1916. He united the concept of the sculptor, Karl Bitter, and the presence of Sherman. The result is eloquent proof that excellence and elegance — elitism if you will — can also be popular. No public space in New York City has more universal appeal.

The monuments count as much as the spaces. They create the ambience, the character and sense of place. People flock to them. At the least, they are places to sit down; for the more thoughtful, they are places to contemplate change. They also offer certain kinds of enduring human presence and intimations of glory and pleasure. It does not matter if the glory is hollow (Sherman left the South in ashes, after all) or if the pleasure is evoked in stone (abundance may only be in Bergdorf's windows). One does not live by art alone.

Today's plazas are made as much by zoning regulations as by the architect's creative impulses. And what the architect puts in — for he almost universally controls the urban and aesthetic product — may elevate those voids to fine public spaces or be gratuitous decoration. But that was true in the 19th century, as well.

The difference now is that the vision is coolly abstract and the philosophy rests on the beauty of geometric elementals rather than with the evocations of natural form. There is no warming recognition, no identity of human purposes. Sometimes, however, the result is excellent, full of the absolute power of successful spatial and sculptural relationships.

The scale and style of the plaza of Gordon Bunshaft's sleek 140 Broadway, with its dramatic accent of Noguchi's upended red cube, is a fine example of architect as patron. Bernard Rosenthal's large work at Astor Place elevated its ordinary "found space" setting from mere traffic flow to public space. Louise Nevelson's handsome piece is meaningless on upper Park Avenue, because it neither creates nor complements space worthy of the name.

When the pool in front of the Vivian Beaumont Theater at Lincoln Center has water, the Henry Moore provides that essential, fulfilling element of style and definition that raises the whole complex to urban art. Not least is the strong, evocative sensuosity of the work, as opposed to geometric abstraction. There is an extra dimension of implied human reference that does much to make people relate to the space. The all-important result must usually be achieved in the modernist aesthetic by finesse of proportions and scale.

The use of space and sculpture is traditionally one of man's most creative contributions where it counts most: as a three-dimensional part of the functioning city scene and of the activity of life. More people experience art here than in galleries and museums. The art of the city is the most pervasive art of all.

Saint-Gaudens's statue of Victory leads General Sherman not to the sea, or to the vanished Vanderbilt mansion, but toward Bergdorf Goodman's upscale shop across Grand Army Plaza. One does not live by art alone. (© 1980 Philip Trager)

THE NEAR PAST

Rediscovering the Beaux Arts

T HE MUSEUM OF MODERN ART'S MAJOR FALL EXHIBITION, "The Architecture of the Ecole des Beaux Arts," is clearly meant as an object lesson to architects (particularly to young ones) and a question raiser for everyone. These questions are serious and heretical ones about the doctrine and dogma of modern architecture — the movement that the museum was sublimely instrumental in establishing. They are part of a broader questioning of the whole modern movement reflected in a rising interest in the work of the rejected Academy, the Establishment mainstream in all of the arts against which the modernists rebelled.

The Modern's show is, therefore, an extremely significant polemical and art-historical event. It follows the Metropolitan's eye-opening and ground-breaking display of 19th-century academic French painting last spring, which proclaimed the Academy's return to respectability in powerful, tastemaking art circles, and its assumption of the position of a kind of reverse avant-garde. That show was also a brilliant act of scholarship.

All this is equally true of the Beaux Arts show. As everyone who follows events of the art world probably knows by now, this is a whopping, more-than-200-item presentation of architectural drawings produced by the students of the Ecole des Beaux Arts in Paris from the late 18th to the early 20th century, representing the kind of building (and training) that was specifically rejected (and despised) by the leaders of the modernist revolution.

The concept of the exhibition, the painstaking selection of material from forgotten and neglected archives, the application of rigorous research and a knowing eye, must be credited to Arthur Drexler, the director of the museum's Department of Architecture and Design; his achievement is an impressive one. His collaborators in organizing the exhibition and preparing its catalog, which will be augmented by an important, profusely illustrated book of detailed and murky scholarship later this year, are David Van Zanten, Neil Levine and Richard Chafee.

There is considerable shock effect for the viewer entering these galleries, so long sacrosanct to the modernists' cause, now filled with huge, precisely and exquisitely rendered classical and eclectic facades of monumental, palatial and arguably unnecessary casinos, cathedrals, conservatories, water circuses, royal residences and reconstructions of Greek and Roman antiquities. It is even more of a shock to realize that these frequently superb, if occasionally wildly overreaching, exercises in grandeur were largely the work of students in their late teens and early 20s, responding to a discipline of the hand and mind absolutely unknown today.

While each student progressed individually, his development was rigidly controlled by the *concours* given at every stage of advancement, and by the expertise with which he executed his competition entries. (The Beaux Arts system, with its indentured ateliers copied from France, dominated architectural education in the

---

One of America's richest buildings, the Library of Congress, a competition-winning design by Smithmeyer and Pelz built 1873-92, is a busy compendium of Beaux Arts elements — grand stair, colossal classical details and monumental symmetry. (Jack E. Boucher, HABS)

United States from the 1860s to the 1930s, until the advent of Gropius and the Bauhaus. It led to the establishment, in emulation of the Prix de Rome and the French Academy, of the American Academy in Rome — a gentlemen's club for creative and scholarly research that is only now facing extinction.) The basic solution to an architectural problem had to be set down in a 12-hour *esquisse* and then adhered to in the *projet rendu,* which took three to six months to execute. The architects were relentlessly separated from the boys right at the start by the ability to devise a solution immediately, and then to execute it with the highest degree of skill — a painstaking, perfectionist rendering of plan, section and elevation in a style and technique formularized over two centuries.

The drawings, just as drawings, in ink and colored wash, are magnificent. They are at once grand and delicate, detailed and abstract. In their finished precision, they parallel the Academy in painting, but the similarity stops with the care of execution. The detail was there not to satisfy a 19th-century taste and sentiment for verisimilitude but because these were professional architectural renderings upon which the next step, the production of measured working drawings for construction, would be based — if they had not been student projects. Literal, perspective renderings were disdained as less-than-accurate, unprofessional illustrations of the architect's intent, and although they were pushed by Viollet-le-Duc during his aborted Ecole reforms, they never caught on. This careful drawing, therefore, does not approach the polished or licked surface *("le fini")* of Academy painting, in part because the work was never meant for the public, which judged by realism and finish, but for the professional architectural juries that evaluated them in the endless Ecole competitions. In fact, this is probably the first time that the public has seen these drawings at all, at least in a coordinated display.

A point that Drexler doesn't mind making with the show is that few architecture students can draw today, any more than they can spell or write; there is no requirement for this level of skill. Model making has become a substitute for draftsmanship. It also frequently substitutes for thinking, and even for design, because it so drastically cuts down the range of conceptualization that can be achieved with the far more flexible pencil in hand. Drexler frankly hopes that this fact will not go unnoticed.

What he hopes most of all is that people will be startled and even seriously upset by the show, which does not — in the museum's customary fashion — present its historicism as protomodern, but as countermodern. Because Drexler is hellbent on counterrevolution. "History," he says, "is written by the victors, and what they leave out is the losers." In fact, what the architectural modernists attempted to do was to bring history to a halt. Not only was the past rejected out of hand, but the present was to have nothing to do with it. Unlike modern painting, in which a sense of continuity with the past can be traced, however tortuously, from, say, Courbet and the Impressionists to cubism, architecture attempted to make the break absolute. The Bauhaus and its successors succeeded in jettisoning history — the Futurists had only hoped to destroy museums and their contents. They were aided by the fact that the industrial and technological revolution made the materials of their art, unlike paint and canvas, totally new; so by abandoning masonry for steel and concrete and a new structural-aesthetic potential, a new vocabulary of forms was made legitimately possible. In one very real sense, this made history and its lessons irrelevant, although they were lessons that the early, Beaux Arts–trained modernists were never able to forget.

A new absolute was invented — timelessness — and its justifications were ruthlessly edited. For the orderly progression of civilization a false kind of scientistic myth of art-as-technology was substituted, married to the quasi-religious morality of the machine aesthetic. And to make that aesthetic more complex, a new kind of relationship was established with painting. In spite of vows of structural functionalism, both new and old materials were used in building to create a romanticized resemblance to the flat, painterly, geometric abstractions of cubism. Although modernist painting and architecture shared the rejection of the Academy and both contributed to the distortion of the past, only architecture abolished it. But history did not pack up and go away; it stayed, all too solidly, in the cities, and the new buildings violated their historical context with an unprecedented vengeance.

And so the exhibition is first of all a revisionist reconsideration of history. But Drexler brusquely rejects any idea of it as an incentive to revivalism. He does not, however, reject the idea of eclecticism as a next step in architecture, although he claims no clairvoyance about the forms it will take.

It is therefore possible to enjoy the display just as a treasury of 19th-century styles and standards — revelations of a now unreal world. The drawings are all competition winners, from the lesser *concours* to the coveted Prix de Rome. The consistent theme is the now discarded classical tradition, the underpinning of the French Academy. But the examples cover everything from late 18th- and early 19th-century romantic classicism to the exotic revivals of the later 19th century and the final, consummated, official Beaux Arts style.

Official meant more than Establishment. This is all official architecture in a sense we no longer comprehend — it was not just that it was concerned with public buildings, which was how the Beaux Arts defined architecture, but that it was state architecture, taught, commissioned and controlled by a central government authority. The Ecole was a state school, an outgrowth and affiliate of the Academy established by the monarchy in the 17th century. The Academy dominated teaching and practice. Its graduates went on to do all official, state-sponsored construction, and private construction simply followed along. Ecole graduates automatically received the prominent or prestigious commissions, and were eventually elected to the Academy, a position from which they continued to dictate style and practice to the Ecole.

The exhibition selection begins with the 18th-century work of Peyre and Vaudoyer, who influenced so much of the Ecole's teachings, and goes through a galaxy of 19th-century ornate and eclectic modes. The arcades of Louis-Ambroise Dubut's Granary of 1797, stretching to near-infinity, recall the almost surreal serenity of Boullée and Ledoux (Debut was a pupil of Ledoux), and they prefigure Durand's prototypical classical solutions for France's civil engineers. Charles Percier, later one of the chief architects for Napoleon and the Empire, is present with a student project for a colonnaded Menagerie of a Sovereign in 1783. Louis Duc's Colosseum studies (1829), Marie-Antoine Delannoy's Restoration of Tiber Island (1832) and Edouard Loviot's Parthenon Restoration (1881) contributed significantly to the 19th-century's lust for classical (not to say imperial) antiquities. François-Louis Boulanger's Library of 1834 could be the work of an ancestor of Louis Kahn (and is, in a sense, since Kahn and other early modernists were Beaux Arts products) in its "served and servant spaces" and love of courts and walls.

By the end of the 19th century, as projects grew ever larger and more elaborate, Louis-Hippolyte Boileau's Casino of 1897 offered a pastry-fantasy in a facile, painterly rendering of a world *perdu*. An 1891 railroad station by Henri-Thomas-Edouard Eustace is so supercolossal in scale that it had to be framed on the museum wall, or it could not have been brought into the building. Tony Garnier's Central State Bank of 1899 symbolizes and synthesizes what had by then become known, internationally, as the Beaux Arts way of building: the axiomatic French classical manner for the imposing freestanding public monument composed in a calculated, progressive hierarchy of functions, movement and spaces — composition, *marche* and *parti*.

A single gallery is devoted to two of the most important, realized structures of leading Beaux Arts architects — Henri Labrouste's Bibliothèque Sainte-Geneviève of 1845-50 and Charles Garnier's Paris Opera of 1861-74, each a textbook study of successful 19th-century design. Modernists have been able to admire the library for its handsome and progressive metal framing; the Opera, in spite of the brilliant social and ceremonial planning that it displays, has baffled them with its sensuous decorative excess. Two other galleries contain photographs of executed Beaux Arts buildings in France and the United States. And as a complement to the exhibition, the Architectural League has prepared a guide to Beaux Arts buildings in New York, available at the museum.

In the final analysis, however, the chief purpose of this show is to serve as the big gun of the reexamination of the modern movement that is currently under way in episodic fits and starts. The aim obviously goes far beyond historical or aesthetic exposition. Its calculated objective is to provoke a far-reaching critique of all contemporary architecture. There has already been much criticism and debate about this subject of course, but most of it tends to be either smugly academic or chicly exotic and arcane in its cultural and historical references. The architect-debaters themselves are given to such gestures as adding naughty paste-on moldings to their safely modernist facades. Most of this has been a tempest in an eyedropper, based on self-indulgent *épater la bourgeoisie* aesthetics. The one real contribution has been the heretically perceptive work of Robert and Denise Scott Brown Venturi, with its emphasis on the aspects of complexity and contradiction in architecture, and of inclusivity rather than exclusivity in the environment.

But as important as such a contribution may be, it is still a fragmentary response to a large philosophical problem. In addition to polemical discussion, there is a burgeoning interest in the phenomena of the near past and the modern movement's near-misses. Books are proliferating on Art Moderne and Deco and the Skyscraper Style and such early figures as George Howe, who, with William Lescaze, designed the seminal Philadelphia Savings Fund Society Building. There is bound to be a resurgence of critical analysis of work by almost forgotten or downgraded names, among them Ely Jacques Kahn, Barry Byrne and Irving Pond. The transitional buildings of Bertram Goodhue and James Gamble Rogers, who have always made the modernists profoundly uneasy, are in for inevitable reevaluation.

The focus will shift, not always clearly. It is also likely that this aesthetic revival will further obscure the essential contributions of men like Clarence Stein to social planning. The cardinal virtues of the modern movement — clarity, simplicity and logic, qualities extremely rare in art and life — are going to be compromised and downgraded. They are fragile, easily compromised values at best, the first casualties of confusion, pretension and perverted creativity. These rational responses are the essence of good and great architecture of all periods and styles, as necessary to the Beaux Arts as to the Bauhaus. Bad architecture is by nature unclear and irrational (not to be confused with the delights of complexity and contradiction). But elaborate bad architecture, the worst kind of all, is what the wrong kind of theory can produce.

Not the least of the probing will be institutional — the role of the Museum of Modern Art then and now. Indeed the relation of the Beaux Arts administration in Paris to state and economic power could usefully be examined and compared to the situation in architectural patronage today. There will be a lot of belated bandwagon jumping. But we have reached a point in history where a kind of flawed perspective is beginning to emerge. And the mirror of hindsight combines revelation and narcissism to a seductive degree.

One lesson always looming implicitly in the Beaux Arts exhibition is that less has indeed become less. Its primary protest is against the relentless stripping down that has characterized the modernist aesthetic. By demonstrating what the modern movement denied, it forces the thinking viewer to reconsider what Drexler calls the "platitudes of functionalism," or the modern doctrine of functionalism as a "euphemism for utility." It is also a euphemism for economy and a rationalization for cheapness when building costs are rising relentlessly — a factor Drexler might consider more seriously. (The nonthinking viewer, as always, will like being told what to think by the Museum of Modern Art. But that brings up another subject — whether trends are found or made by our powerful institutions.)

Drexler's point is that utility, or the narrow adherence to use and functional structure as the primary source of the building art, has had an unexpected and undesired result: the impoverishment of architectural design. So many of the expressive and stylistic possibilities of art have been rejected by the modernist practitioner either as superfluous hedonism or as a dangerous kind of playfulness that is not essential to survival — a rationale and rejection that are the routine, predictable, joyless accompaniment of all revolutionary doctrine. Not just decoration but sensuosity and symbolism are casualties. In architecture the suppressed (and unsuppressable) instinct for pleasure and experiment has reemerged as a distorted kind of "play" with form — the stretching and torturing of structure into perverse works of object-sculpture with equally perverse structural and functional rationales — the Venturis' "ducks." Today's architect has built himself into a corner.

At the same time that the museum is pointing out these failures, it is perpetuating one of the most serious fallacies of the modern movement — the exclusive ideal of the isolated monumental building carried over from the Beaux Arts by the modernists, a concept that proved impervious to revolution or modification. This institution, dedicated to the life and art of our time, is insisting that nothing of importance has changed except style — that only the monument is still architecture. And it is saying this in the face of a radical change in environmental perceptions that has profoundly altered the art of architecture in our day.

Still, the examination of the Beaux Arts has an almost eerie relevance right now. By the end of the 19th century the work of the Academy reached the point where it was increasingly dedicated to forced and fantastic formal invention, while fundamentally adhering to the monumental conventions of the Beaux Arts style. Modern architecture has reached that same point (it is also today's Academy) of strained invention within what appear increasingly to be the crippling restrictions of functionalism. The problem here is not with functionalism per se, but the doctrinaire and almost mindless paralysis to which it has been reduced. Today there is also the jarring effect of such architecture on the receiving environment to be considered as well as its place in the history of cities, which are the remarkable survivors of continuing, temporal catastrophes. The barriers to dealing understandingly with the academic past are still great, however; in painting there is the overload of unacceptable sentiment and emphasis on surface, and in architecture the hurdle of a puritan ethic of structure and design.

These questions of art and function, meaning and invention, of creativity and sterility, of commission and omission, are being asked in all of the arts today. But the situation is perhaps unique in architecture. If what is being debated, to a large extent, are the limitations of reduction, or the validity of minimalism, it is above all architecture that has made the philosophy and practice of reduction into a moral imperative rather than an aesthetic exploration. Modern architecture since the Bauhaus has based its claims not just on purity of form but on purity of art and soul and societal mission. Only now are we seeing the death of the architect as a self-conceived superman, or kind of god, in a world that scarcely wants him.

Perhaps he was more of a god when he built palaces and pantheons, but both princely and social roles have turned out to be exercises in futility. The end came to the Beaux Arts in small things: the design of an elevator, an electric chandelier, a utility pole. They had to be conceived of as a sedan chair, an electrified candelabrum, a torchère or baldachino with wires. The intrinsic failure was the inability to visualize the needs of a newly industrialized society, to come to terms with the kind of construction it would require. This the Beaux Arts never even grasped. It could not recognize the real substance and challenges of the 20th century. Modernism is clearly entering another age of problematic transition. Are the answers eluding us now?

Through the Artist's Eye

IT WAS POSSIBLE, LAST YEAR, to see *two* Woolworth Buildings in Lower Manhattan. The original is in its accustomed place on Broadway at the foot of City Hall Park, having survived, since 1913 the praise of the distinguished critic Montgomery Schuyler (who hailed it on completion as a shapely, satisfactory and eye-filling work of art), the scorn of the modernists (who managed to dismiss its 52 Flemish Gothic stories as a deceitful and ludicrous sham) and an impassioned reappreciation by architects and scholars today.

The second Woolworth building was part of "Ruckus Manhattan," a wry sculptural re-creation — if that word can serve a marvelous melange of art, wit, social satire and succinct architectural observation — of the life and landmarks of Lower Manhattan. The reality and its reinterpretation were within walking distance of each other.

"Ruckus Manhattan" is a 6,400-square-foot exhibition by Red Grooms, created with his wife, Mimi Gross Grooms, and 21 helpers (elves?) called the Ruckus Construction Company. This walk-through show of small-scale buildings and full-scale figures was six months in the making in the unoccupied ground-floor space of I. M. Pei's handsome new skyscraper at Pine and Water streets, courtesy of Orient Overseas Associates and Creative Time, an arts organization dedicated to bringing the creative process to the public. It was cosponsored by the Marlborough Gallery and supported by grants from the New York State Council on the Arts, the National Endowment for the Arts and numerous individuals and businesses.

The real Woolworth Building is an unparalleled combination of romantic conceit (would you believe Gothic ogival lambrequins, or choir stall canopies, for cornices?) and soaring structural drama. In 1913 the skyscraper was a relatively new achievement, and the steel-framed tower clad in the exquisitely crafted detail of delicate, creamy-white terra cotta was, briefly, the tallest building in the world. It is still one of the most beautiful and impressive buildings of modern times. Art is alive and well in the Woolworth Building from the brilliant, vaulted mosaics of the richly decorated lobby to the Gothic fancy of the crown at the top. Myth and magic are once again in good architectural repute.

Schuyler, whose judgment was close to impeccable, called the eclectic design a light and suitable way of expressing the thin-walled, powerful metal skeleton that made such height possible, and he praised the building's exotic verticality as a miraculous and appropriate blend of aesthetics and technology. Cass Gilbert's masterpiece still "looms in the gray of dawn or haze of twilight, its white spectrality shining over city and river . . . an ornament to the city and a vindication of our

What Montgomery Schuyler called the Woolworth Building's "white spectrality" has been renewed by a cleaning of the terra cotta facade. Myth and magic are as much a part of this skyscraper as its structural steel. (Irving Underhill, Museum of the City of New York)

artistic sensibility," as Schuyler wrote 62 years ago.

The Woolworth tower of "Ruckus Manhattan" bends forward jauntily. Held firmly in the protective embrace of a dragon, the building rises with a cheerful and total disregard for gravity and the plumb line. The dragon's rainbow wings rise and fall gently; its mouth opens and shuts with mock menace. Its painted scales are made of nickels and dimes. A doll-size Frank Woolworth gazes out of his tower, and in one of those loony shifts of scale that are a Grooms trademark, a revolving door allows one to enter a small, womblike model of the lobby. Every distorted detail is perfect.

And the building is alive. It glitters and gleams, spoofs and celebrates; it seems inadequate to call it caricature or satire. To this viewer, it is inspired comment. The entire project is carried out with an eye so skilled and sure that it grasps the most salient features of every structure and turns them into a succinct statement on the human and urban condition.

It was a particular delight to have the real buildings just beyond the exhibition space's glass walls. The twin towers of the World Trade Center rise a blandly undistinguished 110 stories. The Grooms Trade Center towers are 30 feet high and a cockeyed triumph, a lighthearted critique of the skyscraper ego. One shaft narrows in fake perspective with a canvas cloud pinned to its top, and the other widens in reverse perspective, with an easy disrespect for architectural overreaching — a perfect so-what response to their size.

After all the words that I wasted in print to suggest that the buildings' weak pin-stripe design is an inadequate expression of some of the world's most massive construction (the Woolworth Building, with all of its delicate romanticism, never made that misjudgment of basic architectonic relationships), the Ruckus artists have achieved the ultimate putdown. They have simply turned the ribbon-thin mullions into looped and tangled spaghetti.

A few blocks away is One Wall Street, the Irving Trust Company headquarters, an Art Deco masterpiece of 1932 by Voorhees, Gmelin and Walker. The Grooms One Wall Street does a stylish backbend and flies a banner "In Irving We Trust." And around a corner from a Stock Exchange replica with a splendidly disheveled see-through colonnaded facade, a ticker-tape parade plunges down Broadway next to a bone-filled crypt in the Trinity Church graveyard. Figures of loungers on the Federal Hall steps sit beneath the aloof, modeled feet of a George Washington who turns into a painted horizontal flat abruptly at the knees. A crooked West Side Highway, obviously in terminal disrepair, sports bubble-domed cars, a ship in full sail and a Hertz truck. The Statue of Liberty, endlessly intoning Emma Lazarus's doleful doggerel, wears red platform shoes. Beneath it all, sewer alligators embrace.

Throughout the work, the monumental and the human factors coexist in a marriage of screwball scale and evocative detail, using techniques from full sculpture to the comic strip. But the real technique is visual irony. Both people and buildings are lovingly observed — from the cultural microcosm of the New York newsstand (full size) to a fine jumble of old brick buildings (miniaturized) adjoining the Woolworth Building in a nice demonstration of how the gorgeous and the mundane lie down together in city streets.

Like a tipsy matron with a tiara, a small building with a crowning acanthus cornice makes it clear that a shabby old structure has been robbed of its pretensions to dignity. In the same way, the costumes of bravura and outrage of the human inhabitants — in contrast to the building-costumes of institutional solemnity — are presented knowingly as body speech in the New York idiom.

Someone else will have to deal with this work in the proper art-critical context of the Pop art tradition or satirical realism, or whatever framework is appropriate. For me, it is a cultural-aesthetic-architectural document that deserves its own permanent room at the Museum of the City of New York. Because it *is* New York. And it is nonpareil architectural criticism.

In Lower Manhattan, the somber classical facades jostle the cheap plastic luncheonettes in recognizable street scenes that join magnificence and triviality. Life imitates art.

Reflections on the Near Past

IMMORTALITY IS CONFERRED in devious and unexpected ways. If you're an architect, there's always hope. The latest switch in architectural immortality has come with the remake of *King Kong*. The producers have been running a full-page ad announcing that their first full-page ad was so popular — with 25,000 requests for full-color reprints — that they are working around the clock to fill orders. The ad shows King Kong breaking up airplanes with his right hand and clutching whoever plays Fay Wray in his left hand, standing astride — and this is the point — not the Empire State Building, as in the original film, but the World Trade Center towers.

The Empire State Building, of course, is a star in its own right, with an enduring romantic charisma. Somehow it implies every cherished legend of New York glamour, from the glittering speakeasy era to the suave luxe of the 1970s. It is genuinely immortal. By contrast, and as a symbol of the city, the World Trade Center towers are consummately uninspiring. (They still sell more Empire State Buildings in the 5 and 10.) And whether the producers of the film are aware of it or not, the change they have made is fraught with cultural and aesthetic implications.

Today's tall buildings are not stars. They are impersonally impressive at best, giant nonentities at worst. Another movie, *The Towering Inferno,* for example, was not about a building you could recognize or cherish. This was simply a large object to which catastrophe happened.

I could offer an intellectually seductive explanation of the change, with dithyrambs about the antihero and the antisymbol and how our vision of men and monuments has been altered. This is a populist age in the arts, led, of course, by the elite, and we are tearing down symbols (symbolically) and elevating the ordinary with determined reversals of good and bad and beautiful and ugly. It is a vision that can be hopelessly counterproductive, or it can provide some rich dividends in much more complex and sophisticated ways of seeing life and the world. Antiart is true to our times.

But the real reason for the change in the tall building is far more down to earth. It is just as rooted in culture and history, but it is less an act of philosophy than an expression of profitable pragmatism. It is a truism that today's tall building is strictly the product of economic calculations, tempered by codes and the law. Those boxy flattops that have replaced slender spires to jar the skyline and the viewer (architects and city fathers would be surprised at the amount of public concern over a city's skyline) represent the best buy in structural space.

Corporate growth and computerizing are also prime contributing factors. Today's huge corporations require huge floor areas in stacks; no builder is going to offer them a tapered tower. And no one could care less about a skyscraper version of the Mausoleum at Halicarnassus — a favorite conceit of the 1920s. Status is conferred by sheer size and the comparative quality and solidity of materials and fittings. The business of America may be business, as Coolidge said, but it has also become its art.

This phenomenon has been reinforced uncannily by the modernist architectural aesthetic. The 20th-century architectural revolution claimed the higher beauty of utility over ornament; it endorsed the look of the machine product as an artistic end. It enshrined the functional aesthetic. But it is an awfully short and dangerous step from the kind of expert and delicate adjustments that turn utility into art, and from the recognition of those adjustments to the most ordinary solution, or the least design for the money.

This deterioration is sanctioned, in a sense, by the modernist "less is more" philosophy. At its finest, less *is* more, and the finest is limited to a few men, such as

A landmark that is less well understood by the public is the Seagram Building. "Less is more" is
meticulously calibrated for a refinement of proportion and elegance of detail not found in "glass box"
knock-offs. (Philip Johnson Collection)

Mies van der Rohe. Mies's work is magnificent, with a stripped, subtle, hard-edged and demanding beauty that is going to symbolize the 20th century for the rest of time. It is also poorly understood and badly knocked off. Even so, the glass box vernacular that grew out of his style is some of the best "background" architecture in history.

But this is an arcane and specialized aesthetic — it was undoubtedly easier for the popes to buy the overt grandeur of Borromini. Business clients rarely understand or

The most recent King Kong found infinitely superior footing on the flat-topped twin towers of the World Trade Center, but the Empire State Building still wins the public's architectural Oscars. (New York Convention and Visitors Bureau)

want it. They are pursuing sleek space-profit formulas and effective technological solutions that no longer aspire to the kind of moving artistic greatness in the timeless and spiritual sense that architecture, and particularly the big building, has always held a primary concern. (Try standing in front of a Hawksmoor building in London without this visceral hit.) Objectively, the skyscraper's immense, efficient and impersonal blandness is a perfectly accurate picture of much of the architectural art of our age.

So dull, so prosaic, in fact, are most of today's ambitious big buildings that New Yorkers now value, for their quite accidental aesthetics, the staggered shapes of the setback buildings required by law until the early 1960s. The zoning code was changed then to encourage straight-sided towers, something architects had pushed for in the name of both architectural and civic art. Now the "wedding cakes" add the interest of eccentric form, at least, to the speculative norm. Their outlines also define a style and a time and a place, a combination of which art and culture are made.

This ambivalent view of today's construction art is not written in rage or resignation; it is not a cry for impossible change. The needs and responses of big building design today, if not immutable, are certainly justifiable in realistic terms. History is not a process to be short-circuited by dissenters. And there will never be any more great buildings than there are great architects.

Art, however, remains a life instinct from Lascaux to Ronchamps, and it is always going to produce civilization's touchstones. The skyscraper is the miracle and monument of the 20th century. Its progress, curiously, has linked development and decline. Watching the emergence of the tall building in New York in 1913, the critic Montgomery Schuyler could still write that "hardly any American owner is quite so boeotian as not to show 'a decent respect for the opinion of mankind' in the appearance of his skyscrapers. . . . It is a public malefaction to protrude a shapeless bulk 'above the purple crowd of humbler roofs.'"

Montgomery Schuyler, where are you now?

Rediscovering Chicago Architecture

AN EXHIBITION CALLED "CHICAGO ARCHITECTS" (Cooper Union, 1976) is full of uncelebrated, quirky, sometimes dramatic and generally unknown buildings. There is only one example of a famous Chicago School "skyscraper" — D. H. Burnham and Company's curtain-walled Reliance Building designed by Charles Atwood in 1894-95 — and it is paired with the same architect's totally traditional Beaux Arts Hall of Fine Arts for the Columbian Exposition of 1893. Modern critics have lauded the former and ignored the latter.

This is, in fact, the point of the show. The two pictures are a deliberately loaded juxtaposition. The catalog states immediately that "the organizers of this exhibit of Chicago architecture wish to pay tribute to all those architects who were passed over by the first generation of historians of modern architecture." And the subject matter consists of the work "left out" of orthodox accounts of the Chicago School and its role in the modern movement.

What we are dealing with, then, is revisionist history. As such, the show is both an iconographic feast and an exercise in provocative scholarship. And it is important at a time when serious revisionism is on the rise in assessments of the modern movement and official theory and history are being attacked on all sides.

The aim of the sponsoring Chicago architects — Laurence Booth, Stuart E.

The Frank Fisher Apartments, designed by Andrew N. Rebori in 1938, a small, streamlined gem, is one of Chicago's lesser known stars. The styles of the recent past are increasingly admired by those who record and practice architecture. (Hedrich-Blessing)

Cohen, Stanley Tigerman and Benjamin Weese — reinforced by Stuart Cohen's knowledgeable catalog, is to explode and expand the doctrinaire view of the Chicago contribution. That view, canonized by Sigfried Giedion, divides Chicago architecture into two schizophrenic parts: the small-scale, personal, domestic developments of Frank Lloyd Wright and the Prairie School, and the technological development of the structural frame and the tall building, known as the Chicago skyscraper. The palm of modernism was then supposed to be handed to Europe in the early years of the 20th century for the International Style, while Chicago languished and waited until the 1930s for Mies van der Rohe to revive its progressive structural tradition.

All that happened, if not exactly as recorded. No one disputes or denies Chicago's skyscraper contribution; the confirmed achievement and monuments of modern architecture are not being rejected or downgraded. But a lot of other things apparently happened as well — particularly in those supposed doldrum years — that have either gone unrecorded or have been consciously suppressed because they did not fit into accepted theories or timetables.

"Chicago Architects" combines rediscovery and reevaluation with irony and a bit of hubris. It is also quite polemical. There is the sound of an axe grinding quietly. But the material contains genuine implications for a broader, more objective understanding of modern architectural history than the hygienically edited standard texts provide of what went on here and abroad. In fact, history and architecture may never be quite the same as this and similar rediscoveries unfold. We are finding a pluralism of ideals and styles that makes 20th-century architecture far more intricate and dramatic than doctrinaire modernism has allowed, as well as perceiving an American contribution and continuity that may prove to be increasingly significant.

"Chicago Architects" was organized as a response to a larger show of more traditional skyscraper-engineering emphasis, "One Hundred Years of Chicago Architecture," at the Chicago Institute of Contemporary Art. Most of the work in this "countershow" does not begin from engineering considerations. Cohen, in his text, characterizes it as romantic rather than pragmatic in approach. The buildings are almost all intimate structures closely related to personal experience — houses, schools and churches, rather than commercial construction, in a galaxy of styles.

Cohen also points out that it is quite logical for society to want styles for its churches, museums, libraries and civic buildings different from the style produced commercially by engineering and economic expediency, no matter how elegant that expression may become. This actual variety is a more accurate reflection of American culture than those isolated examples where a structural rationale has been promoted by modernist doctrine as the only "appropriate" solution.

But even the structural rationale can be romantic. George Fred Keck's remarkable "Crystal House" — all glass with delicate metal trusses — built for the Chicago World's Fair in 1934 and Buckminster Fuller's original (Chicago-born) Dymaxion House of 1927 were both perfectly capable of being produced. They were simply romantic-technological visions whose time had not come. Immediate offshoots appeared in Bertrand Goldberg's mast-hung gas station and ice cream stand — precursors of Marina City's round-towered, world-of-tomorrow look.

There are clearly traced lines presented here of International Style and Art Deco in Chicago in the 1920s and 1930s, from Keck, Holabird and Root, Paul Schweikher, Barry Byrne and the Bowman brothers. (I found many of these in the research files of the Museum of Modern Art in New York in the 1940s, and they are probably still there.) There are fascinating aberrations, such as the 1930s work of Andrew N. Rebori, which suggests both the Russian Constructivism of Constantin Melnikoff and the Parisian chic of Art Moderne. Early Shingle Style Frank Lloyd Wright houses are selected as forerunners of the angular mannerisms of Harry Weese and Walter Netsch.

Specifically, what is dealt with here is ideology, as much as history. There is an increasingly recognized, profound ideological split between the structural-functional aesthetic of the orthodox modernists and the "formal, spatial, and consciously symbolic issues" that preoccupy a considerable group of young architects now. This is fueling a revival of eclecticism, not as conventional, academic borrowing, but as a means of image making — and all is grist for the mill. This urge for style and symbolism has been minimally addressed by the historians of the modern movement.

That is why this kind of history so intrigues the present generation of practitioners; it is with a special eye that the past is being reexamined and, for better or worse, used in their own work. Today's eclecticism is a creative, cannibalistic combination of erudite nostalgia and extremely sophisticated aesthetics. It needs revisionist history to feed on. The results are acutely artful exercises in cultural memory and personal value projection — very arch and intriguing — but these are not simple or innocent times.

Nor is this a simple or innocent show; it contains much to debate. Image makers are not going to supplant problem solvers, and technology can be as elegant as symbols. Right now, history is being revised as a polemic for style, which is where we came in. But in this case the near past is being raided rather than discarded. In the process, a great deal is being learned, much of value is being restored to the record, and a sound and necessary input is being gained. The rewriting of history is part of the continuing historical process.

Mies: Lessons from the Master

GENIUS IS SELDOM ACKNOWLEDGED by its own generation; we wait for the authentication of Charlton Heston playing Michelangelo as superman in supercolor.

But we have had our supermen: Frank Lloyd Wright playing himself, and Le Corbusier playing Scrooge while producing timeless spatial and sculptural delights, and Mies van der Rohe. This is the triumvirate that so decisively affected the course of architecture in the revolutionary years of the 20th century, evolving the look, structure and function of a new kind of man-made world in natural and inevitable synthesis with society's other radical changes.

Mies was a massive, craggy man, given to few public pronouncements, whose person and work shared a tacit monumentality.

The Miesian aesthetic — strict, strong and subtle — is a correct, ordered and logical architectural solution for our day. That it is not the only solution goes without saying; but each artist must have his personal vision which he carries as close as possible to its ultimate perfection. Mies's vision rested on the acceptance of modern technology as it stunningly appeared in his youth.

Trained as a stonemason, bricklayer and delineator of plaster ornament, he saw steel and glass as the fabric of a new world of shimmering skyscrapers and floating pavilions of stringently rational and elegant simplicity. He produced work of a purity and power as great as anything the art of building has ever known.

But technology is not art, and form only follows function as a starting point, or life and art would be much simpler than they are. The key to the art of architecture is the conviction and sensitivity with which technology and function are interpreted aesthetically, in solutions of practical social purpose.

Mies's structure, often the hard, straight-lined strength of the steel frame, is reflected in exterior metal detailing of painstaking refinement that speaks directly and logically of his way of building. These details are often as expressive as Sullivan's foliate ornament was of its underlying structure, and it is the quality and effectiveness of this expressive balance that marks the good, or great, building.

The proportions of a Mies design are so sensitively adjusted, his understanding of the richness of marble, the brilliance of glass and the substantiality of bronze so sensuously sure, his feelings for the materials of our time so overwhelmingly rich and yet so far from vulgar, that no one has matched the precise and timeless beauty of his buildings. The Seagram Building, for example, is dignified, sumptuous, severe, sophisticated, cool, consummately elegant architecture — architecture for the 20th century and for the ages.

The Miesian example is a lesson of principle. But in too many cases the Miesian

Mies van der Rohe turned the 20th-century engineering and structural revolution into a new architectural aesthetic; he raised the elements of building to a kind of minimalist poetry: the Federal Court and Office Building in Chicago. (Bill Engdahl, Hedrich-Blessing)

principle has been ignored and the Miesian example simply "knocked off" in the cheapest Seventh Avenue terms.

Without fine materials and meticulous details, Mies's diamond-sharp doctrine of "less is more" becomes a most ordinary formula. Raised above the shoddy and speculative, however, it is a competent and appropriate formula and it is here that Mies's signal importance, as the source of a genuine popular style, has been so much misunderstood.

The "glass box" is the most maligned building idea of our time. It is also one of the best. Whatever its deficiencies, and there are many, due to the complex factors of architects who are less than perfectionists and businessmen who are less than philanthropists or sociologists, it is the genuine vernacular of the mid-20th century. It derives legitimately from Mies's masterful and meaningful innovations, and it serves legitimately the needs of a commercial society that builds on an industrial scale. It does this with sheer and brilliant modern magic and with as much validity and suitability as the last great vernacular style, the Georgian.

Mies stood for discipline, and this is becoming a lost architectural virtue. He stood for logic, which is now a contortionist's trick. He stood for style, in its highest and most valid meaning of the expression of standards and techniques of a particular historical time.

He came to work in Chicago in 1938. Except for a brief stopover at Harvard after leaving Germany, Chicago is the city that he made his own. He built there a significant handful of handsome apartment houses, the start of a campus for the Illinois Institute of Technology, an impressive federal court and office building that is one of the city's showpieces.

Two more buildings are in construction in the Federal Center, the first structure for the huge Illinois Central air rights tract is in work, as well as what may be the most important skyscraper in the country — an immense 50-story IBM building on the river, adjacent to those other show-stopping structures, Bertrand Goldberg's circular Marina City towers.

There are at least half a dozen very large, new, excellent buildings in Chicago influenced and executed by a second generation trained by Mies until the late 1950s, during the period when he headed the IIT School of Architecture. The outstanding example is the monumentally successful Civic Center with its Picasso-adorned plaza, its dramatic 87-foot spans faced with rusting steel designed by a combination of talents from three local offices: C. F. Murphy, Skidmore, Owings and Merrill, and Loebl, Schlossman and Bennett. The most radical designs of the Chicago branch of the top big business firm of Skidmore, Owings and Merrill, long firmly rooted in the Miesian aesthetic, are here. The 100-story, tapered, diagonally trussed John Hancock Building is a distinctive, looming obelisk against Chicago's windy skies. Architecturally, Mies's Chicago is not the Second City anymore.

Thirty years after Mies's arrival in Chicago the world has caught up with him, but it still does not understand his work. His art is subtle, structural, professional. His remarkable refinements escape the casual observer. His buildings do not provide the cheap, easy effects of fake elegance with which the public gulls itself as a substitute for the real thing.

The world knows now, as the profession knew even 40 years ago, that this quiet man of serenity and strength, whose art distills the deceptively simple essence of complete sensuous sophistication, was one of the great men and great artists of our age.

Even without real understanding, it brought to him in his 80s the major commissions that were denied to his talents when he was younger: the Berlin Museum, the IBM Building, a Lloyd's Bank building in London, the multistructure Dominion

Crown Hall, built 1950-56 at IIT in Chicago, housed architecture and planning classrooms in Mies's idealized "universal space." At the time, Mies thought it "the clearest structure we have done, the best to express our philosophy." (Hedrich-Blessing)

Center in Toronto. It is now possible to live in Mies apartment houses in Chicago, Detroit, Newark, Montreal and Baltimore. It is not possible to do so in New York. (It remains a mystery how New York's status-symbol-conscious rich can continue to accept, at the nation's highest prices, residential architectural trash.)

What may well rank Mies as the most important of the form-giving triumvirate in the final analysis is the fact that he did so much more than bring the highest art to architecture. He took the basic tools of the structural revolution that changed the world irrevocably and magnificently in the 20th century — steel and glass — and turned them into a system of structural aesthetics with subtle variations that belie any literal interpretation of his methods. He handled this system with such logic and beauty that he transformed both the building and the vision of our time.

His work is the refinement, over a lifetime, of a revolution. His buildings are not the sketches made on the backs of envelopes on high-flying jet planes between international construction sites that have become part of popular 20th-century hard-sell architectural mythology. The pivotal skyscrapers, houses, museums, schools and office buildings cover over a half century in one of the most important periods of the building art. They are the end product of painstaking study and restudy of a theme that was explosively radical after World War I and has been fully realized today. If city streets are lined with ordinary offspring, this is common to every creative age. They are preferable to the petty, picturesque vanities that pass for innovation.

Can anyone stand unmoved at the top of a steel-framed skyscraper today, looking out across a city's glittering 20th-century towers, glass walls reflecting clouds, sky and structures in a massed, changing pattern of light and color? This architecture is not static, any more than life is static. Can anyone fail to recognize and react to this miracle of our time? Mies is basic to the miracle.

In the natural pendulum swing of revolution and reaction, of stimulus and rejection — and 20 years is just par time for the course — an entire generation of architects has turned its back on Mies. Twenty years have inevitably revealed the deficiencies of the First International Style; the limitations of a rigid functional aesthetic applied to the complexity of later 20th-century architectural needs, from planning to urban sociology, are clear. As always, the pendulum swings too far.

Only in Chicago has the Miesian lesson been properly learned. For Chicago proves that while Mies's personal brand of consummate elegance cannot be copied — the massive, subtle rhythms of the Federal Building are breathtaking — his basic philosophy can and does lead to significant further developments of structure and style.

Two of the most important buildings in modern architectural history are found in most of the basic textbooks on the subject: Mies's prismatic and curved glass skyscraper projects (unbuilt) of 1920-21. On the Chicago horizon now there is a curved glass building, Lake Point Tower, by second-generation architects Schipporeit and Heinrich. It is, almost, the dream realized. It is still considerably less than the dream. Mies's dream of perfection is elusive and vulnerable and, except for fellow professionals, too rarely recognized by his contemporaries. History will see him as one of that small body of men after whom the world is never the same again.

The Future Grows Old

THE NEAR-LEGENDARY, radical modern house that Walter Gropius built for himself in Lincoln, Mass., in 1937 — the revolutionary architectural shot heard across the country — is being acquired by the Society for the Preservation of New England Antiquities. The architect's widow, Ise Gropius, is giving it complete with original Bauhaus art and furnishings, views of hills and apple orchards, and an incredible complement of birds.

It is an occasion for pleasure and a few gentle reflections. There is, first, the lovely, subtle paradox of the Gropius House, that clarion call to the future, as an authenticated antiquity. How inexorably time turns the avant-garde into history! And how much delicate irony can be obtained from the fact that this house marked the conscious rejection of history in terms of emulation of past styles (indigenous tradition was the superbly rationalized substitute) and the declaration of a new aesthetic and a brave new world. Thirty-eight years later, the revolution has become commonplace, and there is revolution against the revolution. The new aesthetic is the norm, and the brave new world grows old. The landmark takes its place as part of the history that it has spurned, and the movement that rewrote history becomes history. Always, history wins.

Nor are there any clear-cut definitions of art or antiquity. All those made-in-the-Bauhaus furnishings of the 1920s — a rare collection that any first-rate museum would covet jealously — were only 50 years old at the time of Walter Gropius's death and were therefore classified by the IRS, under inheritance tax laws, as "obsolete." When does obsolete become antique? In 100 years, by true-blue, Red Queen, IRS logic. Brought out of Germany in the 1930s, first to England and then to America when Gropius came to Harvard to head the Graduate School of Design, they have already run the gamut from radical to camp to classics of the minor arts.

The art history books will tell you that Gropius's arrival was the signal for change, both through example and architectural education. The school had been languishing in the Beaux Arts stereotype with design exercises for regal casinos and hôtels de ville while the vanguard of modernism was shattering the intellectual barricades in Europe. Gropius's house, designed with Marcel Breuer, who followed the same escape route from Germany, was an instant landmark when it was completed in 1938. And the generations Gropius taught at Harvard from 1937 to 1952 went out to build and teach in turn, transforming the American landscape — to an extraordinary degree — in the image and philosophy of the master. The fact that a revolution won is a revolution lost by the very nature of victory compounds both irony and history.

A trip to the Gropius House today, whether one knew it personally at the time of its greatest impact or as a standby of art history courses, is a sentimental journey. The neat, white structure sits on a hill, in a proper New England landscape of fields and woods — both timeless and a period piece. On a recent visit a reluctant spring had barely greened the grass over the stony earth; an almost invisible cloud of yellow and russet suggested buds on bare branches.

It is hard to remember that the house was built as a daring object lesson in the compatibility of 20th-century technology and art — an ardent polemic as well as a home. To anyone expecting a doctrinaire, Teutonic, textbook exposition of functional purity and rebellious doctrine, it can only be a surprise. This is a conventional house now, familiar, lived in, *gemütlich*. The scale is intimate, the ambience informal. Plants run riot in the light rooms, there is all the impedimenta of accumulated family living, and the birds — the amazing birds — dart, fly and feed beyond the glass window walls that frame huge tree trunks and distant views.

The famous innovations are all standard practice now; you must look closely to see them: the fireplace stripped of traditional mantel trim and frame that became a modern cliché and embattled anachronism (the argument raged for years about the romantic vestigial hearth versus "honest" mechanical heat); the wall of bracket-held bookshelves; pictures not hung, but placed casually on shelves and surfaces; the lightweight, movable, casual furniture with emphasis on function; rooms that flow into each other; and of course, the glass walls with panel heating and exterior overhangs that both let in, and regulate, enormous amounts of seasonal light and sun. It is a handbook of the new rules of 20th-century domestic architecture, grown old gracefully.

The famous Bauhaus furnishings of tubular steel, canvas and wood are comfortably shabby now, and some of the chairs have achieved their original objective of mass production. The tables of curved tubes connected to wood surfaces with carefully visible screws no longer have the conscientiously handcrafted machine look with which they came out of the Bauhaus workshops. To the uninitiated, they would look a little like something put outside a thrift shop as a come-on bargain. To the knowing, they are a delightful historical curiosity: aesthetic morality (the implied honesty of modern materials and machine manufacture) married to an elitist industrial art.

Is it unsuitable to say that the house is charming? The delightful guest bedroom with its toe-to-toe beds in white, black and red, and the small master bedroom with its glass-walled dressing room, liberated forever from "bedroom suites," were

The once-revolutionary Gropius House in Lincoln, Mass., is now a landmark of early modern domestic architecture. Owned by the Society for the Preservation of New England Antiquities, it is open to the public. (Damora, SPNEA)

startlingly different in their day, but are extremely comfortable and inviting now. The downstairs and upstairs porches that united indoor and outdoor living areas with such novelty seem routine. The use of the horizontal wood siding of traditional New England construction in the inside hall is suitable, not startling. And what was most unconventional at the time — the selection of all hardware and built-in accessories from standard catalogs and frequently from industrial sources — gives a distinct nostalgic flavor, although they were among the most radical of the house's modern features.

The building was not only not custom-made, in this sense, but it was constructed rapidly, from spring to fall in 1938. The cost, $18,000, was financed by a Lincoln sponsor, Mrs. James J. Storrow, because the Gropiuses had no funds. They paid rent until they could buy the house from Storrow's estate after her death.

There is a strong scent of Art Deco and Industrial Style in such details as door and cabinet handles and lighting fixtures, including a fine torchère. An angled glass-brick wall, in spite of its pleasant logic as a light conductor and divider, cannot escape the stamp of camp. The famous outdoor industrial steel spiral stair that was almost a symbol of stark new aesthetic drama against the flat white wall plane is now a pure 1930s touch.

Taken in its entirety, the house is as much a period statement as any Bulfinch treasure. It meets the same standards of style, significance and authenticity. The rationale of its acquisition by SPNEA is incontestable.

The Gropius House is, in a sense, a symbol of a simpler and more innocent time; it was a moment when aesthetic rebellion was seen as a social need and as "the puritanical devotion to truth which characterized everything Gropius did," according to G. Holmes Perkins, a former Harvard colleague. Truth was so much more easily perceived then; right was so clearly distinguishable from wrong. The angels were an identifiable band. If the results, with the hindsight of years, seem more complexly shaded, they are no less remarkable. This is indeed the kind of history that changed the world.

Building the Real World

I WISH PEOPLE WOULD STOP ASKING ME what my favorite buildings are. I have favorites, because I believe quite passionately in the elegance and beauty of an appropriate solution to a problem. Quality, while almost a lost art, is never obsolete. The new false gods of cheapness and expendability bring more problems than they solve. Excellence always has, and always will, ennoble man and his surroundings if it is properly combined with a sympathetic involvement with the human condition.

But I am not that wildly attached to my favorite buildings, even though I will champion the new ones or fight for the old ones — to the death, naturally. I do not think it really matters very much what my personal favorites are, except as they illuminate principles of design and execution useful and essential to the collective spirit that we call society. For irreplaceable examples of that spirit I will do real battle. It has been too long ignored, with increasingly disastrous human consequences.

The reason the question turns me off is because it demonstrates such a profound misunderstanding of what architecture in the 1970s is all about. There is a tragic lag from the historical definition of architecture to the definition and comprehension of the art of building today.

The problem is as basic as the definition of the word "architecture." The history of architecture has been taught as a progression of monuments. Thank God for them. Without them, we would have a hard time claiming a civilization. As a consequence, however, most of us think of architecture as a series of isolated great structures, related only by style, country or sequence in time, which are the historian's tools for order and classification. They have little to do with the building of the real world, of which masterpieces are such a small part and "nonarchitecture" is such a large part, for very tangible better or worse. I find myself talking about that world to people who are thinking about monuments, with a disturbing communications gap.

Architecture is the art and science of building the entire man-made environment, in terms of the way it works as much as the way it looks, and like everything else it is in a state of metamorphosis and revolution. I am not suggesting that works of architectural art are obsolete. That would be ludicrous. The point is that we are in the midst of an extremely important shift in the perception and consideration of the critical relationships between a building and its surroundings and the people who use it or are affected by it, with emphasis on effect.

The effect can be salutary or catastrophic; it can even have a chain reaction over a large area. It can help shape or destroy anything from a neighborhood to a society. That makes architecture, correctly understood and practiced, almost frighteningly important. And it is.

The architecture critic is dealing only tangentially with the production of beautiful buildings. What counts overwhelmingly today are the multiple ways any building serves a very complex and sophisticated set of environmental needs. What is it part of? How does it work? How does it relate to what is around it? How does it satisfy the needs of men and society as well as the needs of the client? How does it fit into the larger organism, the community? What does it add to, or subtract from, the quality of life?

In these terms, even a very beautiful building can be very bad architecture. And what Robert Venturi has indelibly dubbed the "dumb and ordinary" building may serve cheerfully and well. It is a matter of measuring by the priorities and values that a critically changing world not only requires, but demands. We have not, until recently, subjected architecture to this yardstick, and that is in some part responsible for our environmental debacle.

The new architecture is a humanistic equation for which creative and qualitative standards are absolutely essential. I part company with those who find it intellectually fashionable to jettison these standards for a kind of cosmic sociology. The results of the lack of qualitative standards are all too clear in the junk around us. Creative poverty has a lot to do with poverty of the spirit, which is a direct byproduct of poverty of the environment. The architect has a lot to answer for.

So has the client, the administrator, the banker, the lawmaker and a host of others. But appalling results are not justified by fingering the faulty machinery that cranks them out. Every one of these sources is being questioned today, along with a lot of other institutions as well.

Our cities are polarized. Architecturally, they consist of formless masses or tremendous statements. We build the impressive, overtly costly behemoths of the affluent commercial society while abandoned housing, without replacement, turns into architectural and sociological disaster by the mile. Building is for the rich. Think about that. In New York, the towers of the mammoth World Trade Center rise aggressively over everything else, gleaming like new-minted money — the architecture of power. Housing is unaffordable. What is built for ordinary people and ordinary purposes, like a place to live or the pursuit of happiness?

Like every profession, architecture is indulging in considerable soul searching and self-flagellation with social issues. It is groping toward a redetermination of purpose and practice in a revolutionary period that has left conventional practice behind because it provides no answers — or the wrong answers — to environmental questions.

Today we expect the architect to deal with these environmental matters. However, we err if we do not still expect him to be an artist. If, in our own time, he has created an inordinate number of "ducks," as the Venturis put it, buildings straining after symbolism when there is nothing to symbolize, it is because he has misjudged or dead-ended his artistic role. This role is, and always has been, to solve a problem — symbolic or functional or both — with brilliance and beauty. And this work has produced the peaks of civilization and subjective experience.

WHERE THE PAST MEETS THE FUTURE

Lively Original Versus Dead Copy

SAN FRANCISCO HAS FINALLY DEMOLISHED what may have been the world's most romantic modern ruin — Bernard Maybeck's crumbling chicken wire, lath and plaster Palace of Fine Arts, a beloved, elegant bit of Corinthian-classic pastry erected for the Panama-Pacific Exposition of 1915. A replica in steel and concrete will replace it.

"Let the thing fall down in peace," said Maybeck before he died in 1957. But its admirers had other ideas. Why not raze the disintegrating old landmark and build a new one just like it?

Alas, we can think of many reasons why not. They have to do with the value of a lively original versus a dead copy, the integrity of a work of art as expressive of its time, the folly of second-hand substitutes for first-rate inventions, the aesthetics and ethics of duplication measured against the creative act.

We can think of only one reason to justify rebuilding the lovely, evanescent structure. It can stand as a $7.7 million monument and symbol of a current attitude toward the architecture of the past so fallacious, so insidious and so dangerous that those of us who have helped nurture the preservation movement in this country can do little more than weep.

Theoretically, this is the moment of triumph. The preservation ball is beginning to roll after a long, uphill fight. New York City has a landmarks law. The federal government has named Brooklyn Heights a registered National Historic Landmark equal to Boston's Beacon Hill. Concern for the national architectural heritage is flowering in the public consciousness and action has started in many communities.

The tragedy is that it seems to be starting off briskly in the wrong direction. The only triumph right now is the archeological fake, or reconstruction. This is a newly built scholarly copy of an old building that does nothing to save anything from the bulldozer.

For every Brooklyn Heights, which preserves a historical continuity of real buildings of the real past, there are numerous projects that will put up brand-new "aged" imitations mixed with a few dislocated victims of throughways or urban renewal for spuriously quaint little groups of instant history in sterile isolation. Across the country the genuine heritage of the 19th century is still being razed to be replaced by elaborately built synthetic 18th-century stage sets more pleasing to 20th-century taste.

This disease, which we have previously called galloping restorationitis, evades the sticky problem of saving the real thing by letting it be bulldozed and putting up a copy at a more convenient time or place. This way, the real estate man can have his cake, and the preservationists can eat it. What they are eating, of course, is crow. The result is a lot of sham history and sham art. And it is receiving massive infusions of some of the country's best philanthropic money.

The unwitting source of the infection has been the suave, scholarly and phenome-

---

Although Maybeck asked that it be allowed to "fall down in peace," San Francisco rebuilt his Palace of Fine Arts. Re-creating the past rather than treasuring its survivals is a skewed preservation priority. (California Historical Society)

nally successful restoration of Colonial Williamsburg. To point this out, as we have learned painfully, is equated with a kind of treason.

Nevertheless, Williamsburg is an extraordinary, conscientious and expensive exercise in historical playacting in which real and imitation museum treasures and modern copies are carelessly confused in everyone's mind. Partly because it is so well done, the end effect has been to devalue authenticity and denigrate the genuine heritage of less picturesque periods to which an era and a people gave real life. This alone is history. The rest is wishful thinking, or in plainer words, corruption of preservation's legitimate aims.

Today a majority of the country's projected preservation proposals are heavily dependent on copies and costumed atmosphere. Ambitious plans start with restoration of existing buildings and then tip the balance to the deliberate manufacture of "authentically reconstructed" landmarks and synthetic style. In New York the outstanding quasi-historical monument is Fraunces Tavern. It is every schoolchild's 18th-century touchstone. Fraunces Tavern is not an 18th-century building at all. This "landmark" was built in 1907 virtually from scratch, starting with a few old timbers. It gives schoolchildren a fair idea of what a Georgian building looked like and it gives local businessmen a fair lunch. But it is not old, it is not authentic and under no circumstances is this kind of thing preservation.

"Preservation," according to the National Trust for Historic Preservation, which has listed official definitions and priorities, is the retention and repair of genuine old buildings that still stand.

"Restoration," given second priority by the Trust, is the more extensive work of putting a deteriorated landmark back in condition.

"Reconstruction," at the bottom of the Trust list, is the erection of a modern copy of a no longer existing structure on the basis of educational value. It is justified only when all else fails.

Preservation is the job of finding ways to keep those original buildings that provide the city's character and continuity and of incorporating them into its living mainstream. This is not easy. It is much simpler to move a few historic castoffs into quarantine, putting the curious little "enclave," or cultural red herring, off limits to the speculative developer while he gets destructive carte blanche in the rest of the city.

There is no cause for optimism in New York. In addition to the economic problem of making the past work in this peculiar city, there is also the chilling certainty that philosophically and nationally we are heading the wrong way.

This Time Everyone Wins

T HIS TALE IS CALLED HOW TO HAVE your cake and eat it, too. It is a classic American urban drama of the bulldozer versus progress in which, for a change, everybody wins. It is the story of the new Albany headquarters for the New York State Bar Association.

The story ended with the unveiling of a project for a building complex that is a sophisticated triumph in that most delicate, complex and poorly understood art of the environment: urban design. It did not start that way. It began with everyone on collision course, or completely normally for any American city.

In April 1968, the New York State Bar Association announced that it had negotiated the purchase of 2, 3 and 4 Elk Street, adjacent to the state capitol and to court

The Albany headquarters of the New York State Bar Association incorporates the past without turning it into a charade: The life of these 19th-century houses was extended by making them part of a new building. (George Cserna)

buildings, and would demolish the houses for its new headquarters, to be designed by New York architect James Stewart Polshek. The lawyers were quite certain that they wanted a fine, new, modern building.

Elk Street, or what remains of its iron-trimmed, four-story brick row houses of the 1830s, is Henry James Albany — evocations of another age when the city combined traditional society and gubernatorial politics in more gracious surroundings and at a more stately pace. The houses face Academy Park and hold a tenuous line for period amenity against institutional encroachment. The street and its houses were designated as landmarks by Albany's Historic Sites Commission created in 1966.

Instant outcry followed the lawyers' announcement. With every "good" intention of making the new structure "blend" with what would be left of a then totally decimated row — other parts have already been violated — the lawyers never knew what really hit them. What hit them immediately was the Albany Historic Sites Commission. This protest was followed by the concern of the Hudson River Valley Commission and a continuous barrage from the local papers, the *Times-Union* and the *Knickerbocker News*.

The Hudson River Valley Commission is a state agency that has the right to hold public hearings and review projects within one to two miles of the river from its source to Lower Manhattan, to determine whether they would have an "adverse effect on the valley's resources." Although its powers and recommendations are only advisory, its functions were invoked.

A hearing was held on April 15, and sentiment for preservation ran strong. The Albany Historic Sites Commission was joined by the New York State Council on the Arts, the Albany County Historical Association, the Center Square Association, the Schenectady Historical Society, the Eastern New York Association of Architects and an assortment of public and private persons from Mayor Erastus Corning to those who felt, not always with as much clarity as conviction, that there was something important on Elk Street that ought not to go.

Without the ultimate cooperation of those whose action is being questioned, this show of sentiment means nothing. The Hudson River Valley Commission held a similar hearing last fall in Troy, N.Y., where feeling ran just as high for keeping a far handsomer street of unified brownstones called Doctors' Row, which the local renewal agency planned to demolish for a dismal new doctors' building. The commission recommended against demolition, and after a brief academic pause for a nonmaterializing sponsor, the city bulldozed, anyway. (The neolithic planning policies and practices of small-city urban renewal in the United States is a sad subject in itself.)

The Albany houses individually are not architectural gems or notable historic monuments. The cry, as is so often the case in American cities, was "They may not be great, but they're the best we've got." The real point was made in hearing testimony by Bernd Foerster, professor of architecture at Troy's Rensselaer Polytechnic Institute, who stated that the significance of Elk Street far exceeds the importance of the separate structures. This was sensed by others who saw the street as the increasingly rare, still-living fabric of another, past lifestyle of the city that it would be infinitely poorer without.

To the trained eye it was a classic case of urban design. The values involved were the qualities of streetscape, through special period scale and character, and the role of the whole row as a "wall" or strengthening space enclosure for the park and as an "anchoring point" for the state capitol complex and Albany's past. What was significant was the cultural, aesthetic, historical and human sum of the parts. These are the concerns of the professional urban designer that add up to felicities of scale, style and ambience, which are a large part of what environment is all about. It is very rarely about monuments or single masterpieces.

To make a long story short, the lawyers got the message. They did more than that; their architect set to work to make a valid use of the old buildings without sacrificing a proper solution of the bar association's modern needs.

The result is a demonstration project of how to use the past without turning it into a charade and how to extend its fabric functionally into the 20th century for the best kind of living environmental continuity. The philosophical and design lesson here is of national importance. So is the lesson for preservation.

There is, too, the inevitable note of irony. After fruitless attempts to find someone who would save its old, outgrown headquarters, the bar association sold its landmark building on Washington Street — built in 1789 and later remodeled — to a real estate developer who has demolished it for a 22-story office building.

The idea of merely retaining the Elk Street facades and destroying everything behind them was rejected immediately as "false-face preservation" by the architect. What Polshek has done is to keep the main part of the houses, to a depth of about 30 feet, and to use those 19th-century front parlors for reception space, a conference room and the president's office.

Behind these handsome rooms there will be a glass-enclosed corridor, facing a multilevel open plaza and the new building, joined to the old ones by another connecting corridor. The landscaped plaza between will provide entrance to both new and old structures.

The new building will be uncompromisingly new. Its deference to the old ones will not be in the kind of copying or "adapting" of style or details that leads to smug architectural pratfalls but in a basic sympathy for scale and compatible contrast. The bulk, for one thing, will be broken into three stepped, skylit structures: one for reception, the second for a 35- to 40-foot-high grand hall for meetings and group functions, the third for offices. The design is a conscious accommodation of the best of both worlds.

There will be approximately 30,000 square feet of space, and the cost will be something over $1 million. The cost is higher than for demolishing and building new, but the bar association could not buy the luster added to its institutional image. About 85 percent of its functions will be in the carefully programmed new space, the rest in the old houses. There is no sacrifice of utility to antiquarianism. And it all works.

It works in a creative, contemporary solution of sensibility and cultural maturity that promises richness, interest and a variety of pleasurable environmental experiences embracing past and present that should be a prime objective of 20th-century urban design. We hope the lawyers live happily ever after.

A Sensitive Succession

I N THE CURIOUS MESS THAT IS Boston's Back Bay around Copley Square — a series of striking new construction projects connected, to use the word loosely, by sloppy disorder that cannot even qualify as messy vitality — there are some outstanding buildings. But the new Boston Public Library by Philip Johnson and John Burgee would be outstanding anywhere. It poses, and solves, a number of functional, structural, environmental and aesthetic problems with mastery, and represents the kind of unity of program and solution that is what the best architecture has always been about.

The building was 10 years in planning and construction, with requirements and budgets turned inside out, and it is fortunate that it took that long. Ten years ago Philip Johnson was not the architect he is today. Other cities have his learning pains; Boston has his best work.

The new central library addition, as it is called, is a $24 million, 10-story structure that provides 170,000 square feet of public space and currently houses more than 600,000 volumes.

The new facilities accommodate 1,200 people at one time, offering prints, films, music and audiovisual aids as well as books, and they have been judged functionally excellent in their initial operation. Since the opening, user figures have risen, at a time when libraries are fighting for attention and survival.

The new structure abuts the original McKim, Mead and White Library of 1895, which is one of Boston's most proper, elegant and cherished landmarks. Although the new wing is larger and in a totally different style, the two buildings relate reasonably well. The addition upstages the old library with its bigger and bolder themes, but it does so with impeccably good architectural manners. It does not diminish the original structure except in scale.

It is also abundantly clear that this is a major, contemporary Philip Johnson work, just as the 19th-century palazzo is distinctly a McKim, Mead and White classical gem. The new wing takes no back seat to its distinguished predecessor. Johnson has had the good taste to indulge in no false modesty.

He has built a complicated structure of outwardly deceptive simplicity. For classical, arcaded refinement, it substitutes the assertive scale of 60-foot bays between massive piers and the bold plasticity of large lunette windows with canted facades and heavy, cornicelike projections above.

Similar materials, cornice heights and arched openings help the new Boston Public Library be a good neighbor to the old building. However, Philip Johnson indulged in no false modesty next to McKim, Mead and White's more refined work. (Atlantic Photo Service)

The delicacy and elegance of the older structure clearly set it apart as a landmark of another age. It conspicuously lacks the brutalism of its successor; the richly textured details have an assured gentility. (SPNEA)

Compatibility with the McKim building was a primary condition of the assignment. Different structural systems almost a century apart dictated changes in span and appearance. But the original roofline was to be held, with maximum space to be provided within those restrictive height limits.

The same Milford granite that served McKim, Mead and White was to be used, and for this the original quarries were reopened. The structures are connected on two levels.

Beyond that, the relationship rests on no superficial decorative recall other than barely suggestive forms and the uniform rooflines; it is based on a very sophisticated visual expression of an unusual structural system that is an essential part of the design and uses of the new building. This is extremely well worked out, technically and aesthetically. The solution is therefore much more than skin deep.

The building has to be read inside out to grasp its skill and understand the full measure of its success. At its heart is a 60-foot-high court that slices through its center. The space is washed in natural light from nine skylights that recall the building's plan of nine equal squares.

The entire structure has only 36 supporting columns. They are placed at the perimeter and in groups of four around the great hall. From these columns, the architects and consulting engineer, William Le Messurier, have hung 16-foot-deep trusses at the seventh floor, from which the third through sixth floors are suspended. Both space and flexibility are gained from this device, which eliminates forests of smaller columns and heavy floor slabs.

A post-tensioned concrete slab forming the second floor gives the same advantages of openness. The first and second floors are thus also column-free working areas. Mezzanine bridges appear to float, supportless, due to a highway type of construction, over the ground level. All of this creates totally flexible, uninterrupted space, more floor area than conventional systems would provide, and incomparable spatial and aesthetic drama. This is an almost grimly handsome building. But its quality is incontrovertible.

Floors that literally measure an acre in size are clear as far as the eye can see, except for equipment and furnishings. Programs have unaccustomed freedom of plan. And there is a complex interplay of the spaces as seen from the great hall that is quietly spectacular.

This focal hall and its ceremonial stair are also faced with Milford granite. There was an unhappy time when budget problems eliminated its use, but it was restored largely through construction efficiencies and economies of the contractor, Vappi and Sons. The Architects Design Group of Cambridge are the local associated architects.

The McKim structure is in the process of being converted for research uses. Its fine, golden marble and Gustavino tile vaulting preserve the quality and technology of another era, although a kind of informational vandalism of signs and showcases has had a disquieting effect. The famous murals are sooty and invisible. The open garden court remains a soothing oasis.

The library's director, Philip J. McNiff, whose concern for computerized catalogs is matched by his ease with the art of architecture, has said, "The lifting of the spirit and the lifting of the mind are related." The best buildings in Boston have a tradition of playing that dual role.

The Creative Continuity of History and Art

PETER COOPER WAS A SELF-MADE MAN with a fortune gained from glue and iron rails, and a passionate attachment to New York. He founded and endowed the Cooper Union for the Advancement of the Arts and Sciences, a tuition-free school open to anyone of "good moral character," and housed it in the Foundation Building constructed at Astor Place in the 1850s. At the time, the building stood for the most advanced 19th-century technology and style, in the structural use of early steel beams and in the Italianate chic of Fred A. Petersen's rather stolidly arcaded facade.

One hundred and fifteen years later the building had experienced a number of changes, including the addition of some extra stories that give a rather awkward proportion to the original scheme, and the gradual transformation of what must have been fairly straightforward interiors into a shabby maze. The cylindrical elevator shaft that Cooper so prophetically included for the future (he was sure that elevators would be round) had been given a rectagular cab, and visitors milled through a boiler room to get to the basement Great Hall, the setting of Lincoln's famous "Right Is Might" speech. The building had been designated a city landmark and listed in the National Register of Historic Places.

The School of Art and Architecture continued to occupy the Foundation Building, although the School of Engineering had gotten a dumb and ordinary (no compliment intended) new building across Seventh Street in the early 1960s.

A decade later, the trustees, with President John F. White, decided to renovate the Foundation Building and commissioned the head of the Architecture School, John Hejduk (a Cooper Union architecture graduate) and Professor Peter Bruder (a Cooper Union engineering graduate) to do the job. The first intention was simply to clean it up and bring it up to code but that involved so much work that logic dictated a more extensive and creative solution. The rehabilitation took two years and the operation was a success.

That success is notable on interlocking philosophical, aesthetic and functional levels — in a way that comments significantly on the values implicit in the act of preservation. Hejduk has done more than present New York with a refurbished landmark and the school with efficient new quarters. He has asked some serious questions about use, history and art, and he has answered them visibly, with logic and style. The Cooper Union renovation is an outstanding example of the real meaning of preservation at a time when the "recycling" of older buildings of

The Cooper Union is a "tough old building" that has developed layers of aesthetic meaning like the rings of a tree. What no longer exists is suggested in spirit by John Hejduk's modern interior remodeling. (Cooper Union; © 1985 Judith Turner)

architectural merit is becoming increasingly common.

These are not simple questions, and Hejduk's thoughtful answers range through an assortment of strengths and subtleties. What he has done, in essence, is to put a new building in the old shell. The programming of that new plan is conceptually and spatially elegant. It is a modern solution that still manages to evoke the past even though literal conservation has been sacrificed in many places. Compliance with current codes has hidden the fine, foliated cast-iron columns in sleek, fireproof plaster, and the original plan is recalled but transformed for contemporary uses. But what no longer exists is still suggested in spirit. Calculated new-old contrasts add an extra dimension to the building appropriately expressive of its 20th-century life.

A good old building should develop layers of aesthetic meaning like the rings of a tree, continually enriched, rather than violated, by contemporary functions. This process does not include the abortive accretions of expediency, but the appropriate revisions of space and use. Pickling à la Williamsburg, or restricting restoration to the limited doctrine of "accurate reconstruction," is actually an evasion of history. (There are some buildings of museum caliber, of course, where only this process will do.) That kind of preservation is a form of mercy killing.

In the new Cooper Union plan, studio spaces and "cells" are virtually where they were in the northern sector; the south end is still used for formal circulation. But there are significant differences. The space has been opened for greater simplicity and a contemporary aesthetic. What was dark is now flooded with light. What was closed and fragmented is now an expanded spatial geometry. Where stairs and walls have been moved, the round elevator shaft stands virtually as abstract sculpture, played against the light-filled drama of the Victorian windows.

The counterpoint of new and old is constant. The first two floors, housing the library and exhibition and administration space, are now treated as an intricate construct of volumes and planes no older than de Stijl and Le Corbusier. A play of partially opened and closed spaces is viewed from above and across through interior windows. Trompe l'oeil vistas appear flat and painterly at first, and then resolve themselves progressively in three dimensions. On the top floor, one wall of the "Peter Cooper suite" is the floor-to-ceiling translucent glass face of the building's old clock, with the 19th-century works poised like freestanding art in front of it.

"It's a tough old building," Hejduk says with obvious affection. "I wanted to keep the feeling, which ran from Palladian to industrial, from bottom to top. It was good, solid stuff." It also has extraordinary scale and an unreproducible generosity of proportions and ceiling heights. This amplitude is emphasized by bright, white loft spaces dimensioned by forests of columns on their original modules.

The structural work, by the Fuller Construction Company, was an engineering spectacular. The south end of the building was gutted, and the exterior walls were temporarily braced from outside. For a while this "cathedral" space "found" inside was astounding. (The cast-iron columns discarded from the reworked south end disconcerted a number of watchful observers unaware of the total scheme.)

On the north end, two floors of bearing walls were removed to accommodate the library. The original framing above these walls was literally jacked up to remove the load while new structural steel was inserted. Then the old cast-iron columns on the upper floors were realigned. The building still rests on the original granite arches and cast-iron columns of the restored and updated Great Hall.

Cooper Union is now the best of both worlds. Its "Renaissance" shell is intact. And the clarity and detail of the consciously sophisticated modernism of the interiors speaks of the creative continuity of history and art. Almost symbolically, Peter Cooper's round elevator shaft is finally fitted with a stainless steel tube. "My joy is boundless," says Hejduk.

A Heightened Sense of Past and Present

THE BANK OF TOKYO HAS A particularly fine location, just above Wall Street, facing Trinity Church and its historic churchyard, which includes among its markers and pleasant greenery a row of cherry trees given by the bank some years ago. The Bank of Tokyo has occupied offices at 100 Broadway as a rental tenant since 1952, first as an agency of the parent bank in Japan, later as the New York State–chartered Bank of Tokyo Trust Company.

At one point in the building boom of the 1960s, the bank arranged to put up its own new building, a bit farther down Broadway, but the plans fell through. When the 100 Broadway lease came due in 1973, the bank decided on a long-term lease based on renovation, with costs to be shared by owner and tenant. The owner improved all basic services, and the bank embarked on total remodeling of the interiors as well as exterior renovation, with its own architects, Kajima International, Inc., under the direction of Nobutaka Ashihara. (Ashihara, who had worked for Kevin Roche John Dinkeloo and Associates, credits Kevin Roche with sympathetic advice about respecting the old building's style and integrity.)

At present, the Bank of Tokyo occupies 13 of the 21 floors, with options for the rest of the space in the next 10 years, and it has tailored all of its floors to its specific needs. As Jiro Ishizaka, general manager of the main office, says, "Where would we get a better address?"

Nor could they easily find a better building. One Hundred Broadway is one of those sleeper landmarks (undesignated) of which New York has so many more than anyone realizes — an outstandingly fine early skyscraper built 1894-96 as the American Surety Building by Bruce Price, one of the better known architects of the time.

Price called his Beaux Arts design a "rusticated pillar," and it followed the popular aesthetic conventions of the day. The new, steel-framed tall building was treated as a classical column on a vastly enlarged scale, its height divided into proportionate approximations of base, shaft and capital. The white marble facade, newly cleaned and extraordinarily rich, features a row of two-story, attached Ionic columns at the base, a shaft of 12 rusticated stories and an increasingly ornate top of seven stories with pilasters, pediments and a coda of cornices. Above each of the ground-floor columns is a full-scale, sculptured classical figure, and two more figures rise above the first of the cornices to embrace a central window with a fine French flourish.

This facade has been beautifully cleaned and restored. The visible changes are new windows and a modernized ground floor. Where the front of the building was originally flush with the backs of the columns, it is now set back a few feet to create an arcade. This passageway is a genuine amenity in Lower Manhattan's congested streets. It also represents a sacrifice of store space for a civilized urban gesture.

The new, set-back front is of clear glass, without mullions, its crystalline modernity a striking contrast to the classical marble columns. The space behind the glass has been completely opened up for a stylishly contemporary banking floor in stark white marble, with accents of black, dark brown and emerald green. This 320-foot-high banking floor is surrounded at its periphery by a mezzanine and second floor, open to view through dark gray glass.

But the most spectacular contrast is where part of the former lobby area has been retained as a kind of central "court," in the all-white open space, marked off only by immense, round, brownish-gray marble Corinthian columns, which rise the full 32-foot height to an intact, elaborately coffered bronze-gold ceiling. Suspended from this ceiling, in a deliberate contrast of style, is the sharp geometry of a large brushed aluminum sculpture in the form of a warped rectangle, hanging point downward, by

The Bank of Tokyo chose to remodel Price's American Surety Building rather than build an anonymous new building. A stunning, sharp-ended Noguchi sculpture suspended from a coffered ceiling was removed later by uneasy bankers. (© 1976 Ezra Stoller, ESTO)

Isamu Noguchi. It is a studied and stunning transition from 19th to 20th century. The total effect is of a dramatically successful counterpoint of new and old.

The separate office entrance, at the south end of the arcade, is a long, narrow space that retains a superbly ornate, black and gold coffered ceiling and upper walls; the lower walls are now faced in more of the pure white marble, with elevator doors of mirror-finished aluminum. Above these plain, polished, light-reflective surfaces are the gilded masks, putti, acanthus motifs, wreaths and arabesques, theatrically illuminated on a dark ground.

Strict preservationists will probably cavil at the loss of all but selected parts of the original ground floor interior and their calculated combination with starkly contrasting surfaces, rather than more faithful restoration. I find the result a model of a sensitive, sophisticated, rational solution for contemporary use and the bank's particular needs, with maximum architectural and cultural impact and a heightened sense of past and present. It works, and so does the building. The floors above are simple and standardized, with lighting designed for energy conservation.

There are a few unfortunate touches and design uncertainties; the newly gilded and incised exterior lettering, for example, is not as good as the former signs, although the building directories inside are elegant graphics. But what counts most is that the Bank of Tokyo has opted for a handsome, recycled structure rather than the standard anonymity of most new buildings. The combination of the tastes, crafts and uses of two different eras has resulted in maximum stylistic drama. The bank has gained a sense of quality and identity. It has made a gesture of art and urbanity that reflects well on both the client and the city.

On a Wing and a Tour de Force

THE LEHMAN WING OF THE METROPOLITAN MUSEUM OF ART, open to the public after a stormy five-year course from concept to reality including a trip through the courts, is now a fait accompli and a tour de force. Fait accompli, because construction is complete, making all of the heated controversy about the Lehman collection's disposition and housing, including pressures for museum decentralization and a lawsuit to prevent expansion in the park, almost — but not quite — academic. Tour de force, because it carries out a highly questionable program with consummate ingenuity, artistry and skill.

What the Met and architects Kevin Roche John Dinkeloo and Associates have produced is a coolly impersonal and quite exquisite small museum dedicated to the myth of the perpetuation of the personal stamp of the donor, through a stipulation of the bequest that seven rooms from Robert Lehman's 54th Street house be re-created as they were in his lifetime, as part of the building and its installation.

If one can, as a start, accept as desirable the reproduction of a 1959 Paris decorator's version of how to turn 1905 rooms designed by the architect of Grant's Tomb into an "appropriate" background for Renaissance art — the rooms laid end to end in the park (buried and blind) instead of top to bottom on a city street — then one will have no ambivalent feelings about the building.

If it seems a little ludicrous or less than ideal for the art — then this handsome building falls down, conceptually, like a pack of elegant cards. But if the premise is accepted, the talented agility with which this curious handicap is metamorphosed into a structure of considerable aesthetic drama can only be admired. It is a neat trick, superbly executed. On these terms, it is a classy job.

Let me make my own feelings clear. I am split right down the middle. I believe that the Met has done the wrong thing impeccably. The architects have designed their way out of the trap set by the terms of the gift — and it is a trap no matter how glossed over by smooth rationalizations — with taste and expertise. The quality of the collection and the pleasant way the building functions for the viewer are, in the end, the all-important factors. It is my personal feeling, however, that the pavilion vastly overcelebrates the collection and the donor. Having said this, let me describe how well a dubious thing can be done.

The Lehman Wing, which cost $7.1 million and is completely paid for by Lehman funds, is set like the jewel of the Met's crown, on the building's main axis at the west, or park side. It is approached through the entrance wall of the original museum building, an 1880 Ruskinian Gothic remnant by Calvert Vaux and Jacob Wrey Mould, preserved by order of the Landmarks Commission.

The addition is a near-square set at 45 degrees to the central structure, topped by a pyramidal glass roof. This roof covers an 82-foot-high open court at the heart of the building, treated like an orangerie, with trees and movable chairs. The lovely moods and mutations of daylight and sunlight, so long banished from so many artificially lit modern structures, are rediscovered and celebrated here.

The walls are of solid masonry construction, of the same buff Indiana limestone quarried for the old Vaux and Mould building. Paralleling the four court walls are wing walls that screen stairs to a lower level, where there are drawing galleries and a library and offices. As these walls rise to upper gallery level, they become open frames, offering views of the painting galleries beyond the court that add elaborate planes to the visual space. These spatial effects are calculated with the greatest care, at once dramatic and subtle, simple and complex.

Surrounding the court are two rings of galleries. The skylight continues, sloping, over the first ring, the natural light reinforced by tubes of artificial light shielded by louvers. The second ring contains the "period" rooms. There are, of course, superb study and storage facilities. The museum's director, Thomas P. F. Hoving, and his architectural administrator, Arthur Rosenblatt, have been model clients.

Ordinarily, I love museum period rooms. I grew up in them, as a solitary city child exploring art and history, and the peculiar timelessness of the soft, gray false light through false windows leading to no real world, sealed in a silent, strange serenity, has always been a magic way of capturing another century or style. For me, they are discovery and nostalgia.

These are not great rooms; they are just elaborate rooms filled with great things. This is a trip to nowhere, unless one is curious about the ideas of *richesse* and suitability with which the collection was housed by its owner — hardly a sufficient reason to go to all this trouble. (But getting the collection was obviously good and sufficient reason.) Balanced against the stairway with no destination and the windows with no views is the advantage of a continuous, horizontal traffic pattern over a tight, vertical town house, now that the collection has "gone public." But even with that change, the museum anticipates "showings" or "ticketings" for the small rooms to accommodate the crowds that have become its way of life.

If crowds permit, there are some fine effects to be enjoyed. The architects have not underplayed their hand. The impact is strongly architectural; the visitor gets the court, not the collection, as his first impression. Although the building is actually not large, the style is monumental. There is a moment of uneasiness, in fact, in the transition from the strength and scale of the court to the much smaller scale of the paintings on the surrounding walls. It succeeds in part because the process is eased by some brilliant, almost sleight-of-hand installation: museum theatrics of placement and lighting knowingly underplayed.

Ingres's striking portrait of the Princesse de Broglie is directly on axis across the building as one enters; an outstanding Balthus nude is luminously focused at the end of a long vista between stair walls; large and stunning tapestries emphasize the faceted gallery space between the period rooms. The small, movable gallery chairs (by Ward Bennett) and the passage of people on two levels and in the court below serve to humanize the monumentality and bring the building to life. The drawing galleries on the court floor level, opening onto that light and leafy oasis, add a sense of intimacy to the pleasure of the contents.

But the best view of all was not created; it was there. Facing that marvelous 1880 wall from the far side of the court, one blesses the resolve of the Landmarks Commission. Vaux and Mould upstage Roche and Dinkeloo. The tactility and proportions, the bold style and texture, the strong coloristic effects of striped buff stone and red brick lunettes in the five pointed "Gothic" arches of boldly contrasting buff and gray blocks, the soft salmon brick, make the new structure seem limited in range and somewhat pallid. Past and present together are a knockout aesthetic. The new building is a cool, beautiful statement; but there is more real sense of architecture in that one old wall.

Outside, Coffey, Levine and Blumberg's landscaping is a curious blend of bucolic illusion and covert security. Tons of earth are piled up against the structure, almost

Where the old Vaux and Mould wall meets the new Roche Dinkeloo wing of the Metropolitan Museum, past and present join for a richly theatrical effect and a rewarding cultural continuity. (Norman McGrath)

covering the galleries and leaving the glass roof exposed, for a steeply inclined hill rising from an elevated walk at the edge of the East Drive. This mound is being gentled with flowering magnolias and a carpet of ivy. Again, neither money nor taste is being spared to make it beautiful, and although there is less usable land for the public (the museum promises more later), it is about as successful a compromise with nonpark use as could be effected. It is not going to make park conservationists happy.

The questions that remain unresolved are large ones about a museum's proper urban and environmental role. The Lehman Wing is the first addition of an estimated $50 million expansion that will increase the museum's collections enormously and enlarge its space by almost a third, upping the present overwhelming 950,000 square feet by another 350,000. The recent gifts of museum-size collections such as the Lehman pictures, the Rockefeller collection of Primitive Art and the Temple of Dendur — construction for all is in progress — become a kind of museum overkill or engorgement with no viewer able to see or absorb more than a small fraction of the whole.

The Met is a champion acquirer; for a while the Cooper-Hewitt decorative arts also seemed slated for absorption. Instead, the city has gained the Carnegie House for a Cooper-Hewitt Museum where the fine, small-scale possessions will not have to compete with overwhelming grandeur. Some years ago there were plans to annex the Whitney Museum; in its own distinctive building now, it provides another kind of museum-going experience.

Infinite possibilities exist for museum-size collections to provide a diversity of resources and pleasures to other neighborhoods. The small museum is a nucleus of development, a generator and reinforcer of values, an incentive to community activity, a diversifier of function, an unparalleled social and urban asset. There are threatened landmarks, such as the Villard Houses in midtown and the Custom House downtown, crying for this role.

The Metropolitan has chosen to interpret decentralization as the provision of aid and loans to community facilities. That misses the point. The museum as neighborhood anchor goes beyond such generous gestures. It is a city-strengthening physical resource; it can stabilize, enrich and renew to tremendous urban advantage.

That is why this superbuilding venture for more and more supercollections in the mother lode in the park disheartens the thoughtful urban critic. There is no doubt that the city's loss is the Metropolitan's gain. But if the critic counts among his finest memories the unique impact and joys of the encompassable small museum, associated with special parts of cities, often with its own style, subject, beauties and eccentricities, the reaction to the Met's program is depression and alarm. Numbness and numbers are no substitute for the intimate aesthetic experience. And the Lehman Wing, for all of its splendor, is a suave and seductive exercise in some of the less admirable aspects of the world of art and museology.

Capital Failures

THEY ARE RUINING WASHINGTON. "They" are not just the speculators with the Ivory soap structures lining rebuilt streets (many of the buildings look as if they'd lather); "they" are the usual assortment of bureaucracies, banks, government offices and institutional headquarters.

Washingtonians know it. Residents have been complaining for years about the creeping characterlessness that has been eroding this city of wide skies and particular architectural charms. The curious thing is that so many of the crimes are committed in the name of suitability, symbolism, progressive development and other assorted and misleading rot and nonsense. The result is always the same: one more block of exactly the same thing that adds up to even more nothing at all. The effects, urbanistically, are easily analyzed: attrition of interest, elimination of variety, including detail, period, image and use, reduction to the redundancy of one deadly dull style and scale.

The only variations are whether windows are boxed in or out, or which particular cookie mold has been used to form the facade. What has almost disappeared is the real Washington, a city of streets with their own local look, a combination of Federal houses restored or reused as bars, shops and restaurants, with the odd old theater or bank or office building that bespeaks the 19th-century capital, and that add up to the kind of amenity and ambience that are also architectural and social history. It has been a distinct, evocative and recognizable Washington. There is less and less of it all the time.

The problem may be that Washington, the seat of history, fails to understand what history really is. At any rate, it misses the point of urban history abysmally. It is not so much the George-Washington-slept-here syndrome as the classic monument fix.

The 18th-century house that was the Washington headquarters of the American Institute of Architects was dealt a body blow by the heavy horizontality of the new building behind it — a curious lesson from a design group. (© 1973 Ezra Stoller, ESTO)

By focusing on those classic monuments, observers, or nonobservers, miss the essential infill, the background buildings that provide the flavor and framework that set the stage for the monuments. Without these contrasts, monuments become an unreal and colossal bore, whether they are genuine national shrines or institutional, cultural or pseudocommercial blockbusters. Washington's "development" is so wrong-headed that it wrings the heart.

One is subject less to heartache than to serious disappointment, however, when faced with another new building in Washington that had an extremely sensitive historical and environmental problem: the new headquarters for the American Institute of Architects at 18th Street and New York Avenue. The new building has been constructed just behind the Octagon, William Thornton's 1799-1802 landmark house that the Institute owns, treasures and used as headquarters, with additions, until it outgrew it.

It isn't that the new structure is not a reasonably good building. If the AIA was looking for symbols, or standards, however, it has come up only with what might be described as high-level average. It seems to function and it would be adequate enough almost any place but here. It is far from a great building, and the Institute probably couldn't swallow a masterpiece anyway, being a corporate entity. Institutional clients are happiest with conventional competence; they are uneasy with brilliance.

But this is not the point. The point is that the AIA set itself the conscious and sensitive task of designing and erecting a building to go with the Octagon. It was to be an object lesson in the blending of new and old in the particular way that Washington needs so desperately and muffs so consistently. After all, who but the architects could, and should, set an example?

It was also to be an object lesson in how to go about it. The AIA held a national competition. The solution it came up with, by the firm of Mitchell-Giurgola, promised to be exceptional. Then a lot of traumatic things happened.

There seems to be little question that some of the leadership and membership was uncomfortable with the quite unconventional Mitchell-Giurgola design, which was an outstandingly creative answer to the difficult problem of blending scale and style. It dealt in sophisticated subtleties, using what was at that time, but has ceased to be, an offbeat vocabulary, clothed modestly in compatible brick.

Complications immediately ensued. The program and the site were enlarged so that the building had to be redesigned and rescaled. This version was submitted to the Fine Arts Commission. The review process became horrendously involved in personalities and serious questions of how far an advisory body should go in "dictating" design specifics.

Ultimately, everyone fell on their faces. The Fine Arts Commission rejected the design, and the AIA accepted the rejection. They did so on the grounds that the Institute felt bound to uphold the principle of design review as "the best known means of maintaining order in the face of all the pressures leading to chaos."

The AIA's reaction was either chicken or preposterous. Whatever the design's shortcomings may have been, and whatever the commission's reservations may have been, the scheme was conscientious, concerned and able, not a speculator's destructive, free-wheeling horror. In retrospect, the Fine Arts Commission seems to have been guilty of an overbearing misinterpretation of its role for an extraordinary and dubious imposition of its own taste. On these grounds, the AIA should, and could, have stood firm, without compromising its belief in the review board function. It could, in fact, have helped to clarify that function constructively and appropriately, and aided in the proper definition of review board responsibilities. It is understandable that at this point Mitchell-Giurgola resigned.

The AIA then started over. The Architects Collaborative of Cambridge, Mass., provided another design. This one the Fine Arts Commission approved as suitable, a completely mysterious inconsistency of reasoning. Because it does not work at all in terms of the "appropriateness" that was supposed to be the criterion — as a structure that would respect and enrich the style and substance of a historic property.

Its insistent, dominating horizontal bands of precast concrete destroy rather than preserve scale. The design is brutally insensitive to Thornton's far more delicate detail. The Octagon has lost presence; it now looks like a toy. The Octagon garden, while almost the same size as before in square feet, is unbelievably diminished by too much paving and too few trees and the heavy-handed, looming presence behind it.

But what is more subtly bad is that the new building fails conspicuously to promote a balance between past and present, whatever its declared intentions. Degrees of design quality become moot. It moves the "other Washington," the wrong kind of Washington, right up to the Octagon's back door instead of cherishing and extending the Octagon's ambience. How fine an architectural act that would have been. One remembers the old brick stables that served as a library and the handsome, neighboring red brick Lemon Building, and wonders how, and where, their obvious lessons of sympathetic materials and urban relationships were lost.

Monumental Questions

I N THE SPRING OF 1967, at New York's cozy Museum of Contemporary Crafts, a tiny, tidy selection of models, photographs and sculpture called "Monuments, Tombstones and Trophies," set neatly among primly potted chrysanthemums, dealt with a huge, unsettling theme: the validity of memorial construction for our time.

It did not, ostensibly, start out to do this. The overt purpose of the exhibition was to explore the broad potential of 20th-century commemorative art, from conventional memorialization to social protest. It was meant to demonstrate new forms, materials and meanings for an old, almost timeless use of art and architecture. But the question of why it seems to be so difficult today to produce a convincing or moving monument pertinent to our times seethed quietly beneath the surface of the show.

The examples, by artists, architects and engineers, ranged widely. There were photographs of Eero Saarinen's famous parabolic arch in St. Louis with the improbably Pop name of the Jefferson National Expansion Memorial. There were the even more improbably Pop baked potatoes and giant ice cream sticks proposed for public streets and squares by Claes Oldenburg, who also contributed the idea of a huge, monolithic cube as a memorial plug for the intersection of Broadway and Chambers Street. The monumental traffic backup would be as impressive as the monument itself, and one assumes that it was an implied part of the design. The subject was literally run into the ground in Michael Steiner's buried drainpipe, into which the viewer would peer for his symbolic kicks.

The show had moon monuments, portable monuments, temporary monuments and disposable monuments — a deliberate contradiction in terms. It included memorials and tombstones that did their level Pop best to put down society and its more tiresome conventions, an effort yielding diminishing returns as the once-shocking vocabulary of aesthetic protest takes on an almost old-shoe acceptability.

Shock is like dope; you have to keep increasing the jolt. The "trophies" ran the full familiar gamut of aesthetic black humor from the satiric visual non sequitur to generously applied genitalia. Most were one-line, one-time sight gags.

But all served to focus on an inescapable, nagging, unasked and unanswered question — the legitimacy or visibility of monuments in today's culture and society. It is a sticky question, as almost a decade of unsuccessful effort on the part of the Franklin Delano Roosevelt Memorial Commission, for example, clearly demonstrates.

In that case, the basic issue was never faced. Matters of size and style, traditional representation versus abstract forms, were all superficial considerations. They were aesthetic red herrings obscuring the pertinent problem of whether a traditional memorial stressing traditional values can be produced convincingly and responded to sincerely by our age. Even the best intentions of the best artists and architects seem consistently to fall flat, or at most to achieve a bland or lukewarm artistic or associative success. With few exceptions, the memorial vacuum is filled only with the most redundant and weary clichés.

No false heroics or rhetorical bombast mark Maya Lin's somber Vietnam Memorial in Washington, D.C.; it is a moving tribute to the grim losses of war. Suspicious of its abstract forms, veterans insisted on the addition of a heroic statue. (Bill Clark, National Park Service)

The fact is that the emotional, intellectual and spiritual climate of the 20th century has changed so much in response to a radically changing world that the familiar memorial is an anachronism. Mere structural mass does not impress when a miraculous technology has made superhuman scale the everyday norm. Simple nobility verging on pomposity or sentimentality reflects nothing of the strange and shifting values of these peculiarly transient revolutionary, violent and questioning times. This is an age of moral uncertainty, of strange twists of behavior and judgment, of hope, cynicism and despair, of horrible destructive potential and new cosmic frontiers. The old yardsticks for men or monuments simply do not apply.

When art does not reflect or contain the thought and standards of its own age, when it is not infused with the meaning or values of its time, it has no meaning or value at all. That is the dilemma of the conventional memorial built today. It offers false reassurance to the unsophisticated that the old values still exist, but the more aware are unmoved and unconvinced and even a little ashamed of its sham heroics. It seems spurious and oversimplified; at best, hollow; at worst, a mockery.

It is not surprising that the only modern monuments of any measurable impact are those dedicated to a particularly grim form of modern death. They are the memorials to 20th-century group massacre that eschew most traditional figurative symbolism, such as the hovering slab of the Fosse Ardeatine in Rome.

This does not mean that there are no longer men or ideas worth honoring. There are heroes, even when the antihero is acknowledged and in vogue. There is beauty, even when the tastemakers look on it suspiciously as a deceptive instrument of sensuous depravity used to gull the unwary or the undiscriminating. But there are no longer the cultural absolutes, the emotional innocence, the intellectual faith and naiveté that legitimize the kind of monument that correctly expressed that faith and naiveté in an earlier time. Thoughtful men are no less concerned with society; it is just that their faith and feelings are infinitely more vulnerable and complex.

The great memorial era really ended with the Victorian Age. Sentiment and the search for sublimity, intensification of feeling, were all 19th-century goals. It was the style to take one's Sunday stroll in a well-landscaped cemetery, with suitably dramatized intimations of mortality. And of immortality, as well. Emotions were large, elementary and exaggerated. Standards were literary and moralistic, and so was the full spectrum of the arts. Nobility rode high and noble heroes charged unremittingly across public spaces.

Today the 19th-century hero charges through a traffic jam or guards a slum, which says far more about the unheroic standards of our age. Aesthetic puffery has little place in a time of tough questions and answers and terrible uncertainties. Man was never more mortal or his world more insecure. His values were never more in flux. The exhibition offers no better comment on today's human condition than Carl André's pile of sand, meant to sink invisibly into the surface of the grave.

Of Symbolism and Flying Saucers

HOW DO YOU FINISH AN ANACHRONISM? How do you complete a cathedral begun too late, beset by conflicts in symbolism, construction, art and costs, overshadowed by skyscrapers, clinging to obsolete crafts, mismeasured for glory and miscalculated for meaning in the modern world?

The Cathedral of St. John the Divine, on Morningside Heights, was conceived in 1891 as the world's largest and latest of the great medieval line that ran from Arles to

St. John the Divine is a paradigm of the cosmic uncertainties of our time. Declared an unfinished symbol of human priorities in the 1970s, construction has now begun again. The National Cathedral in Washington also proceeds at a Gothic pace. (© 1980 Philip Trager)

Amiens. There was only one thing wrong. It was not the product of a cathedral-building age. The medieval cathedral was a superb structure, the creative flowering of a special confluence of forces at a particular moment in time. Its synthesis of technology, necessity, timeliness and expression is the basic formula of all great architectural art.

Out of context, the formula is not reproducible. The same moment and the same results never come twice. Archeological copying will not make it so. This is an ineluctable reality of art and life. Until it is understood, we will continue to have the pious reproductions, the dead reconstructions, the vacuum-packed imitations and the false, nostalgic standards that, at best, evoke only the second-hand suggestion of the artistic glories of some other age, or at worst, throttle creativity and subvert values in our own.

When the design for St. John the Divine was projected, the church spire was already losing out to the commercial tower — a kind of symbolism, if one wished to look for it, that the cathedral was no longer the physical capstone of the city or of society and could no longer offer the comforting assurances of an older, more familiar symbolism merely by increasing the size of its traditional forms. The medieval cathedral already belonged to history.

And so the cathedral sits unfinished, not through the inexorable process of the evolutionary architectural change of the Middle Ages, but through conflicts over aims, objectives, symbolism and commitment of church funds in the 20th century.

The misconceptions of its builders are reflected accurately in the vicissitudes of its construction. When a church evolved from Romanesque to Gothic from the 11th to the 13th centuries, art and history, not a board of trustees, made the decision. When St. John the Divine was redesigned from Romanesque to Gothic, Ralph Adams Cram, the Gothic revivalist who replaced the original firm of Heins and La Farge in 1911, opted for the change, and it really didn't matter.

It was not important because neither style grew out of the conditions of the time. Neither was a creative act. The game was archeological and the choice was arbitrary. The basis was personal taste. Art is never taste. It is the synthesis and catalyst of the complex factors of any cultural era, modified, if you will, by taste, but taste alone is cold, thin stuff, tenuously related to a genuine aesthetic product.

What all this leads up to is the simple fact that it doesn't really matter how the cathedral is finished now — a subject that has been the cause of some little rarefied furor. It is merely, again, a matter of taste. The forms and meanings of the building are so totally removed from the social, spiritual and aesthetic mainstream of the 20th century that the result, whatever the decision, will inevitably be cold, thin stuff.

A careful and conscientious effort has been made by the firm of Adams and Woodbridge to solve the problems that exist. The cost of the central tower planned for the crossing and of the completion of the west towers would be prohibitive today, even if stonemasons were available for the work, which they are not. The "temporary" Guastavino dome, guaranteed for 10 years and going for half a century — a testament to that fascinating and now equally historic form of tile construction — is to be replaced.

The architects have been forced, ironically enough, by that same evolutionary process of art and history that the cathedral ignored, to go to modern concrete construction in the name of cost and practicality. They are providing elevators in the piers that will support the beams for a "modern Gothic" glass and concrete lantern to substitute for the unbuildable crossing tower, because labor to change an electric light bulb, for example, is too costly today to permit the bulb changer the inefficiency of toiling up stone steps. Count the anachronisms, architectural and otherwise, in that sentence. You can only finish a superanachronism like St. John the Divine with more of the same, and there is not much to be said in praise or blame.

Which brings us to the final ecclesiastical architectural question of why religious building today is in such a curiously depressing and distressing state. Few religious institutions now fall into the trap of mock-medieval. They seem to be going for mock-modern instead. Almost all have adopted modern design as a kind of trademark of the contemporaneity of their outlook and needs.

And that is precisely the trouble. They distort today's architecture into a trademark, or gimmick, and not much else. Never has so much progressive technology ended up as so many visual tricks. Never has so much experimental structure been so decoratively misused. Never has the doctrine of free aesthetic expression been so abused or engineering advances so superficially vulgarized for effect. There are exceptions, of course, but they are aggressively outnumbered by churches poised like moon rockets, synagogues of country-club luxe in jazzy concrete shells and far-out flying saucer chapels.

Perhaps it is still just a matter of taste. Or of a lot of bad architects. But more likely it has to do with the unresolved relationships of spiritual needs and physical symbolism in the 20th century, for which no number of flashy cantilevers or catenary curves provides convincing answers. If St. John the Divine sought safe, standardized symbolism, the modern church pins its faith too often on specious novelty. The matter comes back once more to the validity of solutions that are a legitimate and natural expression of an age, as opposed to those that are wilfully or arbitrarily conceived. It is an area of pitfalls and complex philosophical possibilities. But it comes full circle to art and history again.

AFTERWORD

Still Kicking

LET ME SAY THAT THE SATISFACTIONS of the urban critic's job are few, but they are monumental. If some of these essays seem mellower, if the tone seems a little less desperate, if the thread is no longer a sustained wail, it is not because there are any fewer battles to be fought; it is because they are taking place on different ground. The situation has changed. The campaigns are now being waged with the backing of an unprecedented public commitment and a vastly increased public knowledge. It is proving difficult for even an unenlightened political leadership to retreat on the environment.

What has happened is that there is a far more sophisticated sense of architecture and a deeper response to the built world today than ever before in history. And this comprehension is developing an almost universal constituency. The voice-in-the-wilderness role has passed. In these years, a kind of wisdom has emerged. People have learned to see and feel the city; they are consciously involved in the technology and aesthetics and human effects of its buildings, spaces and styles. These considerations have become — true test of relevance — political issues.

We have been through the total rejection of the freestanding monument as irrelevant to society; we have survived the pendulum swing to advocacy architecture which set social needs as the sole criterion of practice. The truth is somewhere between art for art's sake and art for society's sake; but art is the eternal constant. We are finally beginning to understand its true role.

We know now that the art of architecture is extremely sensitive, sophisticated and complex; that it is the art of solitude and of the total city; of aesthetic absolutes and urban synthesis; that both body and soul must be satisfied. We are only beginning to understand why, and how. But we are setting higher standards for the form and quality of cities and the kind of life that they produce. The challenge, even without an uncooperative economy, is staggering.

This is actually a period of transition between knowledge and practice, comprehension and effect, and these writings reflect that state of the world and the art. It would have been tempting to weight the score with small triumphs — there is really a rather remarkable list — but that would be misleading in the face of the dimensions of the problems that remain. We are dealing with a large victory of attitude and perception laced with a lot of small defeats.

On the plus side, there has been a near-total reversal of attitudes toward the past. Preservation, the woolly, sentimental cause of those little old ladies in tennis shoes, is now endorsed by astute developers everywhere in an avalanche of imaginative recycling of old structures of diversity and dignity. This is being done with taste, wit, educated judgment and a firm grasp of such esoterica as historical and cultural relevance and urban variety and enrichment. [Tax credits have helped.] It isn't just a movement; it's a mild stampede. I've thrown my tennis shoes away.

Neighborhood conservation has become a priority in cities everywhere, based on

---

One of New York's long-running battles has been over St. Bartholomew's controversial plan for an office tower on its valuable Park Avenue garden site. The spirit of man and the spirit of the city are not separate things. (© 1981 Walter Smalling, Jr.)

a growing recognition of the values of community and its roots in the history and amenity of the physical setting. In a complex and still-evolving national about-face, bulldozer speculation has been slowed less by recession than by the concept of neighborhood, an idea and reality evolving through the innovative use of a variety of legal, government and architectural tools that never existed before.

The level of architectural design has risen significantly across the country (although I will be the first to admit that you won't find a masterpiece on every corner), along with the frequency of professional response to the human and urban condition. To take the most unpromising indicator, one need only look at that traditional slough of mediocrity, public and institutional construction. There is, of course, no moratorium yet on instantly disintegrating courthouses and county seats and expressions of fallible vanity, and Washington remains a disaster area. But Boston's handsome Government Center, or the recent buildings of New York's Civic Center, with far-above average structures and open-space treatment, are clear demonstrations that the standard of official construction has been raised light years beyond that of a generation ago, when the norm was unadulterated hack.

One finds that the infrastructure of the city is also responding to design. New Yorkers have quietly celebrated a small explosion of plazas, passageways, greenery and places to sit (we need much, much more). Carefully reworked zoning regulations have transformed sterile spaces into increasingly pleasant and knowing demonstrations of urban design expertise. Other cities have successful pedestrian malls and revitalized Main Streets. There are brilliant exercises in design and urbanism in such places as Atlanta and Minneapolis. For every inevitable atrocity in America's largely rebuilt cities, there is at least one distinguished performance or redemptive architectural act that was inconceivable a few years ago. And in the best commercial work, professionalism has quietly married art.

Any country that can build like this, and that has developed the sensitivities to past and present and a wise, sympathetic awareness of identity and place, can't be all bad. But the paradoxes are baffling and tragic. We can do some things almost too well, and other, essential things, not at all.

We can create masterworks of technology, but we cannot house our poor or keep open our schools and libraries, or make simple commitments to basic human needs, just as we are beginning to understand what those needs are. We have made no impression on the city's worst pathology, the ghetto slum. Still, we are developing a kind of social, cultural and aesthetic consciousness unparalleled in history, based on a growing knowledge of the nature, effects and components of the built world. At the same time we have a government renouncing that vision and retrenching on those values at the moment of their most spectacular flowering, and an economy that cannot support them at all. And there is never any moratorium on the four urban horsemen: expediency, obstructionism, stupidity and greed.

This is an extremely troubling and uncertain time, but I would not swap it for any other. It is a source of extraordinary gratification that I have seen the environmental and architectural climate change substantially, and the level of public concern and comprehension rise meteorically, even though there has been no discernible progress toward a dubious Utopia. In fact, this selection of essays starts with a few classic kicks. They are aimed at those monumental structures of high visibility and high aspirations that should represent the American architectural genius at its best and have failed to do so. Our most conspicuous disasters are in the two essential areas of cultural symbolism and the provision of housing. But there are many successes and pleasures to celebrate as well, in new and old buildings and in a burgeoning sensibility to the built environment. I measure success by the street corner. My obsessions are now shared and my coconspirators are everywhere. Assuming survival, the battle for the future is well joined. I'll still be kicking buildings for a while.

SOURCES

Most of the essays in this book were published originally in the *New York Times*. The following list indicates the original publication dates in the *Times* as well as other publication sources.

Preface
"Huxtable Was Here" *(Will They Ever Finish Bruckner Boulevard?* 1970)

How to Kill a City
Death by Development (February 12, 1968)
The Architectural Follies (February 14, 1965)
Singing the Downtown Blues (April 16, 1967)
Side Street Sabotage (December 15, 1968)
"Senza Rispetto" *(Kicked a Building Lately?* 1976)
Bad News About Times Square (February 9, 1974)
New York: Dead or Alive? (April 6, 1975)
Covent Garden: Omens of Absurdity (November 8, 1968; June 4, 1971;
      January 12, 1975)
Skyscraper Asparagus (November 16, 1968)
London's Second Blitz (June 27, 1971)

Preservation or Perversion?
The Impoverished Society (May 5, 1963)
The Art of Expediency (May 26, 1968)
A Vision of Rome Dies (July 14, 1966)
Grand Central Tower Grotesquerie (June 20, 1968)
Perspective on the City: Three Buildings (November 6, 1975)
Where Did We Go Wrong? (July 14, 1968)
Goodbye History, Hello Hamburger (March 21, 1971)
Only the Phony Is Real (May 13, 1973)
Kicking a Landmark (September 29, 1968; January 5, 1975; June 22, 1975;
      September 21, 1975)
Putting the Breaks on "Progress" (November 19, 1968)

The Fall and Rise of Public Buildings
Whatever Happened to the Majesty of the Law? (July 22, 1966)
An Exercise in Cultural Shock (October 4, 1973)
Can Anyone Use a Nice Anglo-Italianate Symbol of Graft? (July 7, 1974)
Anatomy of a Failure (March 17, 1968)
Anatomy of a Success (October 30, 1967)
Culture Is as Culture Does (June 21, 1968)
Coming of Architectural Age (May 4, 1968)
Victoriana Lives (January 28, 1972)
The Bizarre and the Beautiful (May 9, 1976)

Urban Scenes and Schemes

Manchester, N.H.: Lessons in Urbicide (December 22, 1968)
Syracuse, N.Y.: Ugly Cities and How They Grow (March 15, 1964)
St. Louis, Mo.: Success and Blues (February 4, 1968)
Saratoga, N.Y.: Losing Race (March 10, 1968)
New York: Sometimes We Do It Right (March 31, 1968)
Lower Manhattan: Where Ghosts Can Be at Home (April 7, 1968)
The Blooming of Downtown Brooklyn (March 30, 1975)
Salem, Mass.: Renewing It Right (September 7, 1975)
New Orleans: The Old American City (April 21, 1974)
Marblehead, Mass.: Spirit of '76 (September 16, 1973)

Old Friends and Delights

Jefferson's Virginia (March 9, 1975)
Art and Nostalgia and the Great World's Fairs (October 28, 1973)
The Skyscraper Style (November 17, 1974)
Beaux Arts Buildings I Have Known (November 9, 1974)
A Hard Act to Follow (January 24, 1971)
Friends in Public Places (September 15, 1974)

The Near Past

Rediscovering the Beaux Arts (*The New York Review*, November 27, 1975)
Reflections on the Near Past (February 1, 1976)
Through the Artist's Eye (December 21, 1975)
Rediscovering Chicago Architecture (March 14, 1976)
Mies: Lessons from the Master (February 6, 1966; April 28, 1968)
Building the Real World (April 11, 1971)
The Future Grows Old (May 18, 1975)

Where the Past Meets the Future

Lively Original Versus Dead Copy (May 9, 1965)
This Time Everyone Wins (July 21, 1968)
A Sensitive Succession (September 24, 1973)
The Creative Continuity of History and Art (December 8, 1974)
A Heightened Sense of Past and Present (December 28, 1975)
On a Wing and a Tour de Force (May 25, 1975)
Capital Failures (March 17, 1974)
Monumental Questions (March 26, 1967)
Of Symbolism and Flying Saucers (December 4, 1966)

Afterword

Still Kicking (*Kicked a Building Lately?* 1976)

INDEX

Buildings and sites are listed under city names; page numbers in italics refer to photographs or captions.

OTHER BOOKS FROM THE PRESERVATION PRESS

ALL ABOUT OLD BUILDINGS: THE WHOLE PRESERVATION CATALOG. Diane Maddex, Editor. This fact-filled, catalog-style book offers a lively, readable mixture of photographs, drawings, resource listings, case histories, excerpts and quotations. It provides a wealth of information organized into 15 major subject areas. 436 pages, illustrated, bibliographies, index. $39.95 clothbound, $24.95 paperbound.

WHAT STYLE IS IT? A GUIDE TO AMERICAN ARCHITECTURE. John Poppeliers, S. Allen Chambers, Jr., and Nancy B. Schwartz, Historic American Buildings Survey. Building Watchers Series. One of the most popular, concise books on American architectural styles, this portable guidebook is designed for easy identification of 22 styles of buildings at home or on the road. 112 pages, illustrated, glossary, bibliography. $7.95 paperbound.

MASTER BUILDERS: A GUIDE TO FAMOUS AMERICAN ARCHITECTS. Diane Maddex, Editor. Introduction by Roger K. Lewis. Building Watchers Series. Forty major architects who have left indelible marks on American architecture — from Bulfinch to Venturi — are profiled in this concise introduction. 204 pages, illustrated, bibliography, appendix, index. $9.95 paperbound.

BUILT IN THE U.S.A.: AMERICAN BUILDINGS FROM AIRPORTS TO ZOOS. Diane Maddex, Editor. Building Watchers Series. A guidebook-size history of 42 American building types, the book presents essays by noted authorities explaining the forms as a response to the functions. 192 pages, illustrated, bibliography, appendixes. $9.95 paperbound.

OLD AND NEW ARCHITECTURE: DESIGN RELATIONSHIP. National Trust for Historic Preservation. In this provocative book, 20 well-known architects and preservationists tell how old and new buildings can coexist — giving their own solutions, explaining why others fail and suggesting how design review should work. 280 pages, illustrated, bibliography, index. $29.95 clothbound, $18.95 paperbound.

ARCHABET: AN ARCHITECTURAL ALPHABET. Photographs by Balthazar Korab. Here is a new way of looking at architecture — through the eyes and imagination of an award-winning photographer in search of an alphabet in, on and around buildings. Juxtaposes dramatic photographs with quotations by architectural observers from Goethe to Wright. 64 pages, illustrated. $14.95 clothbound.

AMERICA'S COUNTRY SCHOOLS. Andrew Gulliford. The first book to examine the country school as a distinctive building type, it captures the historical and architectural legacy of country schools (from dugouts and soddies to frame buildings and octagons) and provides ideas for preserving them. 296 pages, illustrated, appendixes, index. $18.95 paperbound.

AMERICA'S CITY HALLS. William L. Lebovich, Historic American Buildings Survey. Two centuries of municipal architecture are captured in this book featuring 500 photographs of 114 city halls in 40 states. 224 pages, illustrated, bibliography, appendix, indexes. $18.95 paperbound.

WITH HERITAGE SO RICH. New introduction by Charles B. Hosmer, Jr. This classic preservation book shows why America's architectural heritage should be preserved and helped spur passage of the National Historic Preservation Act of 1966. 232 pages, illustrated, appendixes. $18.95 paperbound.

AMERICA'S FORGOTTEN ARCHITECTURE. National Trust for Historic Preservation, Tony P. Wrenn and Elizabeth D. Mulloy. A lavish overview of preservation, the book surveys in 475 photographs what is worth saving and how to do it. 312 pages, illustrated, bibliography, appendixes. $14.95 paperbound.

HOUSES BY MAIL: A GUIDE TO HOUSES FROM SEARS, ROEBUCK AND COMPANY. Katherine Cole Stevenson and H. Ward Jandl. A unique guide to nearly 450 precut house models sold by Sears 1908-40, from bungalows to colonials. An introduction traces the program's history and captures the pride and memories of Sears house owners. 375 pages, illustrated, bibliography, index. $24.95 paperbound.

RESPECTFUL REHABILITATION: ANSWERS TO YOUR QUESTIONS ABOUT OLD BUILDINGS. Technical Preservation Services, U.S. Department of the Interior. This primer answers 150 questions most frequently asked about rehabilitating old houses and other historic buildings. The answers are based on the Secretary of the Interior's Standards for Rehabilitation, which are reprinted in full. 192 pages, illustrated, bibliography, glossary, appendixes. $9.95 paperbound.

To order Preservation Press books, send the total of the book prices (less 10 percent discount for National Trust members), plus $3 postage and handling, to: Preservation Shop, 1600 H Street, N.W., Washington, D.C. 20006. Residents of California, Massachusetts, New York and South Carolina, please add applicable sales tax. Make checks payable to the National Trust or provide credit card number and signature.